Highland Journey

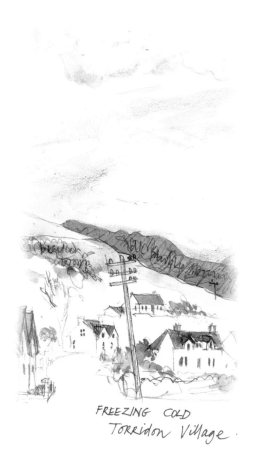

FREEZING COLD
Torridon Village.

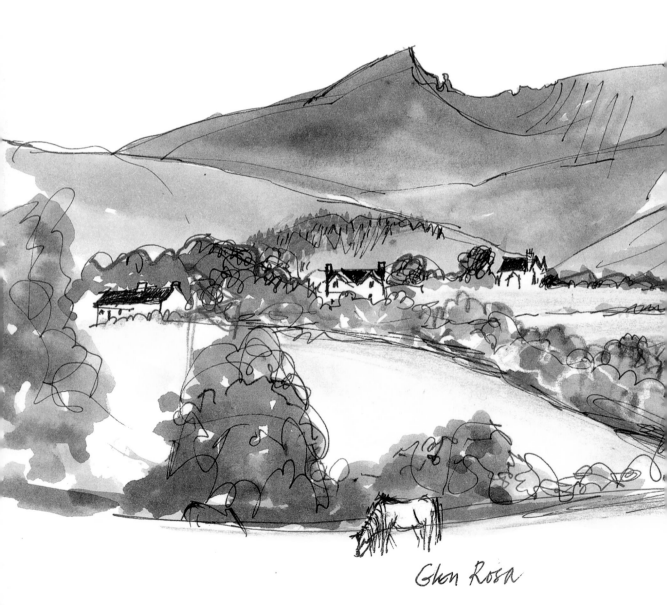

Glen Rosa

Highland Journey

A SKETCHING TOUR OF SCOTLAND RETRACING THE FOOTSTEPS OF VICTORIAN ARTIST JOHN T. REID

Mairi Hedderwick

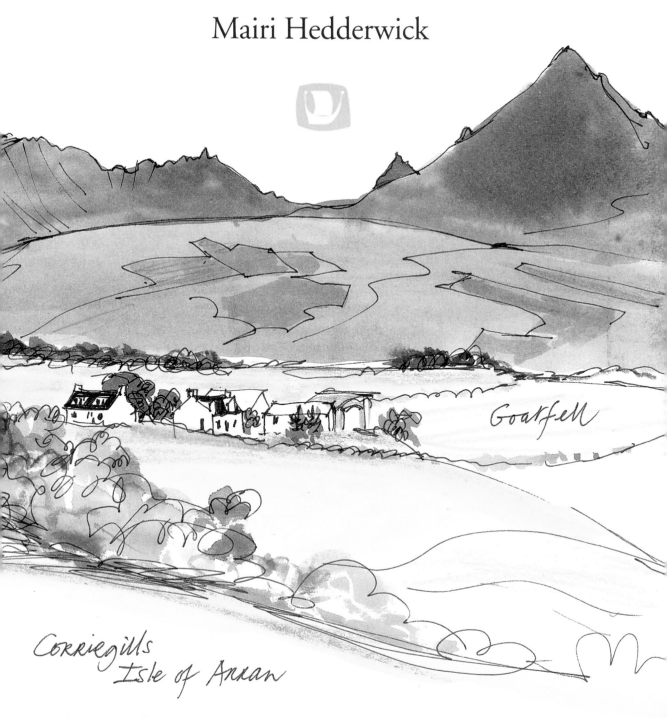

Goatfell

Corriegills
Isle of Arran

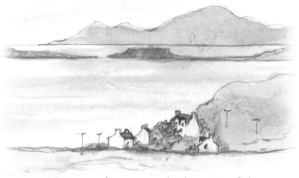

Waternish . Isle of Skye

This edition published in 2009 by
Birlinn Limited
West Newington House
10 Newington Road
Edinburgh
EH9 1QS
www.birlinn.co.uk

First published in Great Britain in 1992 by
Canongate Press plc, Edinburgh

ISBN 978 1 84158 793 6

British Library Cataloguing-in-Publication Data.
A catalogue record for this book is available from the British Library.

Designed by Mark Blackadder
Printed and bound by Bell & Bain Ltd, Glasgow

Contents

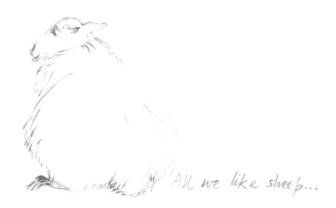

All we like sheep...

Introduction VII

Introduction to the Birlinn Edition XIII

Ramble One 1
Leith • Bo'ness • Stirling • Doune • Callander • The Trossachs • Loch Lomond • Tarbet • Arrochar

Ramble Two 58
Glasgow • The Clyde • Arran • Bute • Ardrishaig • Crinan Canal • Oban • Staffa • Iona • Mull • Coll • Tiree

Ramble Three 99
Oban • Ballachulish • Glencoe • Fort William • Caledonian Canal • Invergarry • Fort Augustus • Loch Ness • Inverness

Ramble Four 123
Skye • Portree • Sligachan • Coruisk • Staffin

Ramble Five 133
Dingwall • Kinlochewe • Torridon • Gairloch • Dundonnell • Ullapool

Ramble Six 145
Isle of Lewis • Stornoway • Gress • Garrynahine • Barvas • Ness • Butt of Lewis

Ramble Seven 160
Isle of Lewis • Wick (via Dingwall) • Thurso

Ramble Eight 169
Aberdeen • Bridge of Don • Ballater • Balmoral • Braemar • Devil's Elbow • Spittal of Glenshee

ART RAMBLES

IN THE

HIGHLANDS and ISLANDS

OF

SCOTLAND

By JOHN T. REID

AUTHOR OF "ART RAMBLES IN SHETLAND"

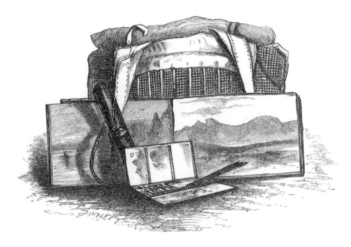

WITH

156 Sketches

TAKEN FROM NATURE AND DRAWN ON WOOD BY THE AUTHOR

ENGRAVED BY DALZIEL BROTHERS

LONDON AND NEW YORK

GEORGE ROUTLEDGE AND SONS

1878

Introduction

I first came across John T. Reid's *Art Rambles in the Highlands and Islands* in a cottage on the Isle of Skye in the autumn of '89. The maroon and gold-embossed front cover of the book did not have a back and the linen thread stitching frayed through the flapping spine. The daughter of my hosts, the MacLachlans, had found the copy in a secondhand bookshop in Greenwich and sent the birthday gift back to one of the areas that had inspired John T. Reid's sketching tours of 1876.

I had arrived in Skye for a gentle weekend somewhat listless and bored with life, nothing exciting on the horizon. As I thumbed through the creamy gold-edged pages I was immediately attracted to the many engravings that depicted the landscape and landmarks of the north and west of Scotland of over a hundred years ago. Dusty, distant, dramatic in some cases, yet still familiar.

It was then that I got the idea to retrace JTR's footsteps, find the exact spot from which he sketched and redraw the same scene 114 years later.

Not only would I recreate his images, I would travel exactly as he had with

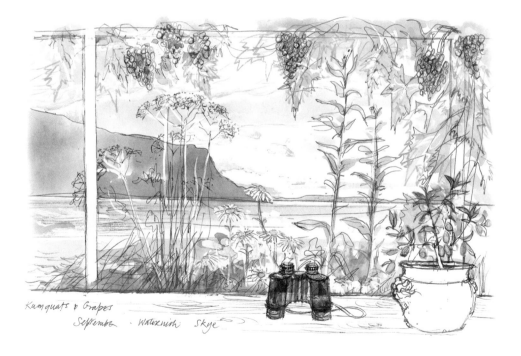

Kumquats & Grapes
September · Waternish Skye

JTR a knapsack well charged with stores for the soul, the mind, the brush, and the body, and carrying with me a large sketching umbrella, a camp stool, a waterproof case to hold a folio for drawings, fourteen inches by ten in size, and a small courier bag for the colour box, a brush case, and a water flask.

I might even wear Victorian dress? I would sell up my house in Inverness and base myself in Edinburgh from whence JTR embarked on his Rambles. With a trusty 'Goliath' (the name he gave his umbrella) and a faded cotton knapsack, thus I, too, would wander the hills and glens with my new-found companion, Brother Brush – his name for fellow artists met along the way.

All these thoughts only took seconds to formulate. I would write to John, as I was already intimately addressing him, long comparative letters from our concurring time-warp landscape. He might even become my lover, spiritually speaking that is …

Between the idea/And the reality/Between the motion/And the act/Falls the Shadow.
T. S. Eliot

It took four months to retrace JTR's footsteps in fortnightly forays with gaps for recovery in between. 'Goliath' was reduced to one of those collapsible circumcised little nylon jobs, the fading cotton knapsack replaced with a stout modern waterproof backpack and, prudently, the Victorian Ladies' Rambling Outfit left in the theatrical costumier's wardrobe. I did not take a camp stool.

I did sell up the house and lodged with friends in Edinburgh in between Rambles. I did not write letters to 'John', except one. Much as he would have loved my pastoral poesy (nobody else would) and church attendances en route, the step-we-gaily day-long marches of prodigious mileage, he would not have been able to make head nor tail,

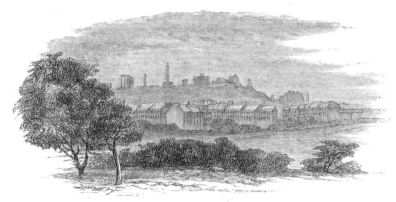

CALTON HILL FROM ROSEBANK.

VIII

however, of the Keycard funding of the journeys, the televisions at the foot of 'hostelry' beds, the tarmacked roads, conveyor belts of exhausting fumes and staggering slipstream let alone the very necessary roll-on deodorants.

This instead is the story of the shadow of JTR that followed me as I followed him; sometimes faint, other times sharp. Above all strongest in the wild places where not much has changed over all these years.

The end of the nineteenth century was a period of great beautifying and improvement in Edinburgh. JTR was in his early thirties in 1876. He was living with his mother at 21 Broughton Place, a fashionable area of town then as now. Times were settled. As a boy, JTR would have been brought up on a diet of Imperial Confidence and Mints on a Sunday. The waxed linen map on the wall of his classroom on Mondays flushed with pink. Britain was the greatest power in the world.

Sons – and daughters – of Empire travelled far and wide with impunity. Thomas Cook, from humble beginnings in 1841 had, by 1860 with his son, expanded into America and the Middle East offering holidays to a very refined clientele. Books were published by many of these privileged travellers on their return and the first mass 'armchair traveller' audience was born.

JTR, in common with Thomas Cook and many others of his class, was a strong believer in the Temperance Movement. In fact Thomas Cook's business was founded originally to wean the working classes away from the Demon Drink by organising railway excursions. The missionary zeal comes through in JTR's writing but, thankfully, the main theme of the book is that of the travelling artist.

Not everyone wanted to find out about foreign parts: Queen Victoria had had her first extended stay at Balmoral by 1843. That fashionable event and her enthusiasm for the poetry of the Trossachs' original tourist officer, Sir Walter Scott, spawned the first generation of holiday house owners in the Highlands and Islands. All this mobility was possible because of the rapidly expanding railways, northwards and westwards. In July 1874, two years before JTR set off on his Rambles, the Sutherland and Caithness railway was opened, taking the line all the way to Thurso. There was no holding back of the 'tartan tours' of Mr Cook, especially in the Central Belt. Just as with present-day bus parties, the popular beauty spots crawled with 'excursionists'.

Queen Victoria not only set the fashion for Highland Residencies. She also captured the romance on paper. Every Victorian worth his or her aesthetic salt could turn off a neat watercolour or two before tea. Whilst doing research for this book I was ever hopeful of coming across an original John T. Reid watercolour. 'Victorian water-colourists? Two a penny,' yawned one, unnecessarily bored, I thought, antiquarian dealer.

Painting was for pleasure for a good number of the middle and upper classes. Public exhibitions – even in Thurso – encouraged more and more people to experiment with brush and paint. Painters' camps sprang up all over Scotland. At Cambuskenneth near

Stirling there was an artists' colony where shaggy Highland cattle, the first to be brought to the Lowlands for purely decorative purposes, could be sketched from the safety of a shed on wheels which could be towed to any visual angle of choice.

Famous artists like McCulloch, MacQuirter and Landseer were known as Scottish Romantic painters. Their subject matter the wilderness of the Highlands and Islands unsullied by advancing industrialisation.

City life in 1876 was dirty, smelly, noisy. Industrial and domestic pollution far worse than it is today. The wide open spaces were becoming accessible to the general public and no longer feared as in the days of wolves and bears, but embraced for health-giving 'air baths' and, most important of all, spiritual cleansing. Religion and Nature became synonymous.

Let JTR introduce our shared experience:

JTR The author has hope that he who reads this volume will have a share of the pleasure which fell to his own lot while he visited the scenes he has endeavoured to describe and illustrate. He desires that his pictorial pages may aid those whose time is spent in earnest labour, amid the disturbing influences of city life, to live over again the health-giving days spent in our mountain land, and is wishful that his Rambles may prove an agreeable book companion to all who makes its acquaintance.

He has not entered the fields of archæology, history, or science. As author and artist he has enrolled himself a graduate in Dame Nature's school.

John T. Reid
21 Broughton Place, Edinburgh
August, 1877

Just change the sex, Brother Brush, and we are on our way …

Mairi Crawford Hedderwick
Crossapol, Isle of Coll
March 1991

NB: The illustrations for *Art Rambles in the Highlands and Islands* were reproduced by the wood engraving process. By the mid-nineteenth century the burgeoning of the illustrated pictorial rejected the more traditional metal plate method as the wood block could be fitted into the text as though it were another piece of type.

JTR would return from each Ramble with his folio of watercolours and then proceed to draw the image on the wood blocks supplied by the engraver. Not all artists did this, some preferring to leave the whole transfer process to the engraver. The image was recreated on the block as it has been in the original, colour translated to tone and texture. Degrees of hatching from fine to solid shapes stood proud, areas to be left white cut away.

JTR had previously published by subscription a similar illustrated travel book on the Shetland Isles in 1869. The quality of the engravings in that book is very inferior to the Highlands and Islands version. The engravings for the second book were done by the most talented craftsmen of the day – the Dalziel brothers based in London who engraved for Millais, Rossetti and, most famous of all, Tenniel for *Alice in Wonderland*.

Until I see an original John T. Reid watercolour I will never know the quality of the man's work. Engravers, especially those of the calibre of the Dalziel brothers, often greatly enhanced the sometimes amateur efforts of their 'artist' clientele.

Thanks to modern technology my original watercolours are reproduced directly from the sketchbooks by sleight of a camera's impartial eye.

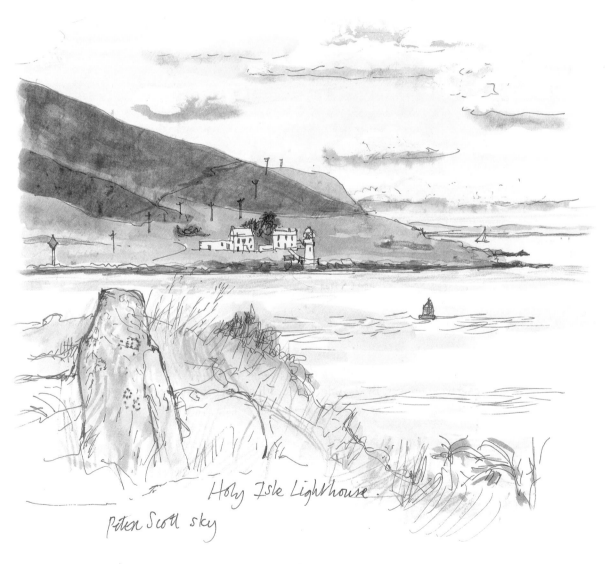

Holy Isle Lighthouse.

Peter Scott sky

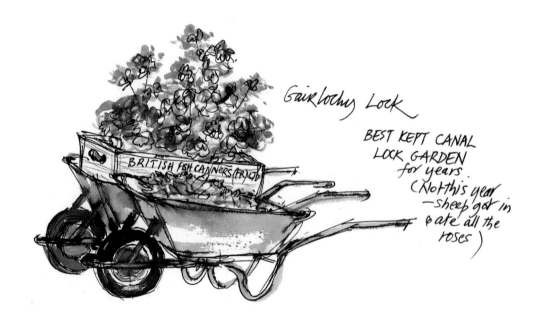

Gairlochy Lock

BEST KEPT CANAL
LOCK GARDEN
for years.
(Not this year
— sheep got in
& ate all the
roses)

BRITISH FISH CANNERS (FR) LTD

Introduction to the Birlinn Edition

The opportunity of having our Sketching Tour reprinted is thanks to Birlinn, who believed in my and JTR's sometimes strained, but always faithful, relationship as we time-travelled through the landscape and seascape of the Highlands and Islands of Scotland.

I have tinkered little with the text, his and mine, save when I thought the two of us meandered to excess. I do not apologize for the vagaries of style of my sketches, conditioned by weather, temperature, time, situation and mood. The formal engravings of JTR's sketches conveniently hide the possible angst of his originals.

I still have not found a JTR original watercolour or sketch.

Nineteen years from now there might well be more marked changes to the views that JTR recorded in 1876 and I in 1991. I'll leave that journey to another Brother or Sister Brush.

Mairi Crawford Hedderwick
An Lanntair
Isle of Coll
March 2009

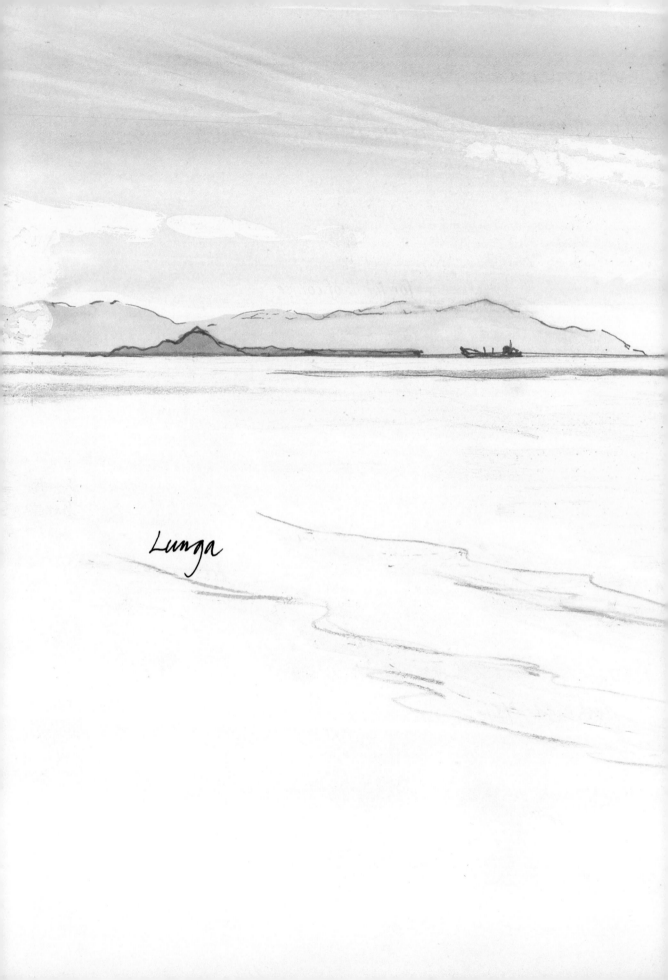

Lunga

for John, of course

utchman's Cap   Staffa   Iona

Treshnish Isles   En route Tiree
                         'Lord of the Isles'

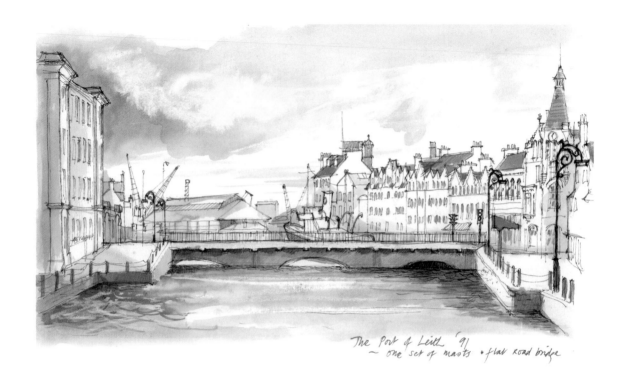

The Port of Leith '91
— one set of masts + flat road bridge

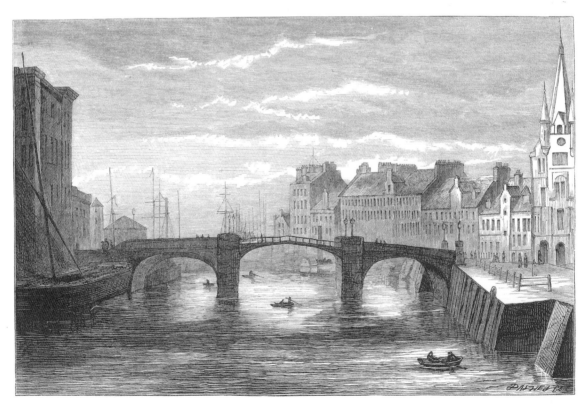

THE PORT OF LEITH.

Ramble One

Saturday, July 14 – Friday, July 27

LEITH · BO'NESS · STIRLING · DOUNE · CALLANDER ·
THE TROSSACHS · LOCH LOMOND · TARBET · ARROCHAR

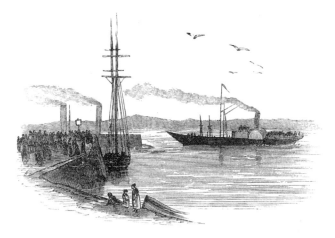

EXCURSIONISTS RETURNING.

JTR On the morning of Saturday, the 15th day of July, 1876, I drove to the West Pier of Leith, hoping to find the Stirling steamboat there … The morning was fine, and all persons and places wore a glad aspect: sunshine lit up the cloudlets, shimmered on the wavelets, sparkled on the windows of the house-lined shore, and transformed even the 'reek' of our famed 'Auld Reekie' into a feature of beauty. Haze veiled the extreme distance, Granton basked in warm sunlight, and the fishing village of Newhaven, with its pier, its boats, and its rocks, was pleasant to look upon, while the seaward and the sunward view was all aglow with exquisitely delicate passages of colour and tracings of form, revealing in dreamy mystery the shores of Fife and the island of Inchkeith.

There's something safe and reassuring about walking in someone else's footsteps. One is a follower absolved of decision making. The mind can wander as the feet plod along the previously designated route. Like hitching on …

Unfortunately the first Ramble from Edinburgh to Stirling, the Trossachs and Loch Lomond just couldn't be hitched on to as easily as some of the others. No passenger boats ply up to Stirling these days.

1

Despite the expansion of the railways in the 1870s, the fastest method of travel from Edinburgh via the Port of Leith was still by boat – even to London, let alone Stirling. A hundred registered boats traded regularly up and down the Forth to Stirling. There were two passenger boats a day, timetables variable because of the tide. JTR missed one of them but, non-plussed, sketched Newhaven from the West Pier, Leith, as he awaited the arrival of the paddle steamer *Loch Mar* to take him up the Firth of Forth.

There are no excursionists waiting at the West Pier nowadays. The rotting stumps and gaping planking are barricaded off and I had to get permission from the Forth Ports Authority to find the spot of 'our' first sketch together. Infill has created miles of reclaimed land that stretches to Newhaven, hidden, from that angle, behind the colossal Rank Hovis Caledonia grain mills.

All was very silent and deserted save screaming terns above and the clank of steel piping being unloaded from a Japanese container ship. Acres of these large pipes, as far as the eye could see – for our oil industry. A few glum seagulls sat hunched on the edge of the rotting decaying old pier waiting for the pleasure boats that will never come.

I was determined to get a boat of some kind or other. After several phonecalls and brazen bargeing-in to boat clubs and boatyards on both sides of the Forth I managed to procure one – or rather, two. Not an easy task as the upper Firth and River Forth are no longer dredged and a boat with a keel for the upper reaches was out of the question.

A pair of silk-cravated sea dogs at the Royal Forth Yacht Club could tell me about the time they got all the way to Stirling by yacht. Oh yes. Celebrations at the Stirling Rowing Clubhouse hazed their return memory. Something about getting snagged on dumped cars in the mud at Cambuskenneth ford. Never do it again. Sorry. Mind you it was a great night. No, they didn't know of anyone else.

I could tell they didn't believe I would be able to do it.

Captain Landels of the Forth Ports Authority finally steered me in the right direction. The Leask brothers who had a converted fishing boat would give me a lift to Port Edgar where I had already liaised with Ollie, the manager of Lothian Region's Sailing School. Their inflatable flat-bottomed rescue launch would take me on up to Stirling. Ollie had not raised a smarmy eye when I had sidled up to him the previous week in the centre's tearoom, my resolve beginning to weaken. No, he had never done it before but he was game.

And so it was on the afternoon of Saturday 14th July 1990 I was standing at Newhaven harbour with a rucksack containing a fortnight's professional and personal paraphernalia, awaiting the arrival of the *Cailleach*.

'The Start' was beginning at last.

The *Cailleach* is a Miller Fifer built for private use in 1962 but modelled on traditional lines. Chunky but elegant at fifteen knots in a brisk Force 4 wind she chopped her way up the Forth. A gentle blue came through high, light clouds; a heavy heat, thankfully, left behind on land.

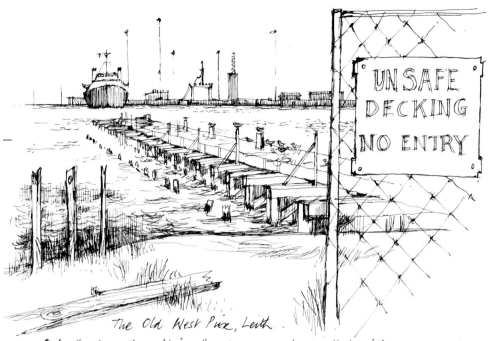

The Old West Pier, Leith.
Only the seagulls waiting for passenger boats that will never come.

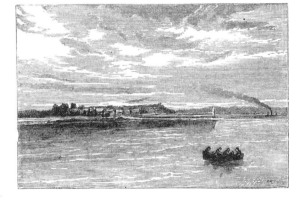

NEWHAVEN.

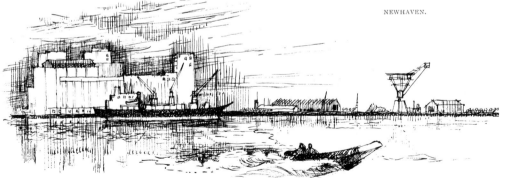

From the disused WEST PIER, LEITH. Newhaven hidden behind Caledonian
Mills a Japanese container ship HYUNDAI off loading steel pipes for British
oil industry. Two men cream round a round in an inflatable dinghy.
A security guard comes up in a van. Have I had permission to sketch?

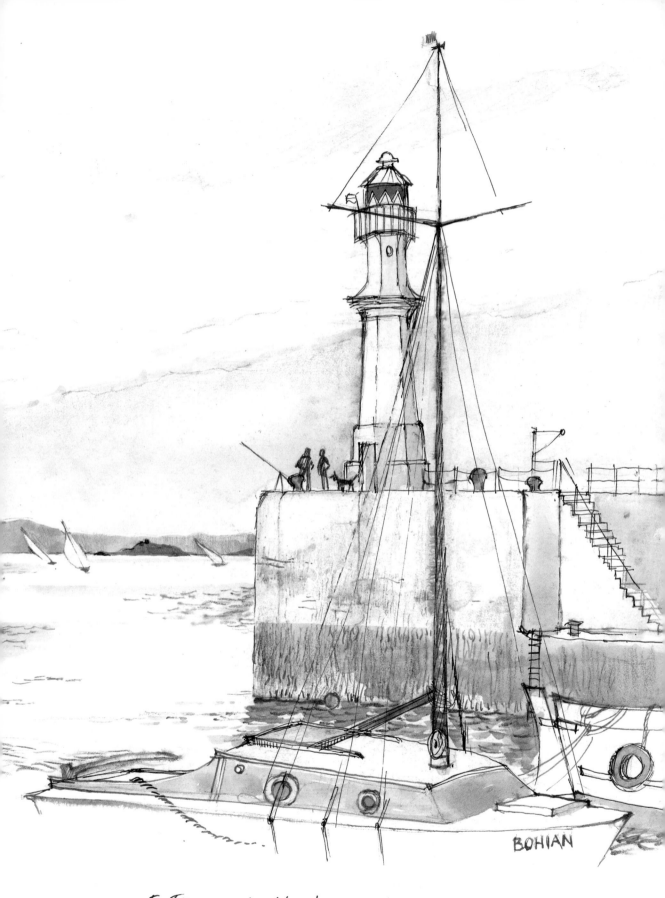

Entrance to Newhaven Harbour
— waiting for the 'Cailleach' to come round the corner

BOHIAN

JTR The 'Lord Mar' paddled her way westward right merrily, leaving in her wake a trail of cream-toned foam, while to the right and left of us we had a variety of coast views and bits of seascape, enlivened with busy shipping. Newhaven again attracted the eye ... I scanned anew our old crouching lion (Arthur's Seat), and the Calton Hill ...

Granton passed, we had a peep at Cramond, a humble seaboard village, divided from the richly wooded grounds of Dalmeny by the Almond, a stream whose course abounds in features of a picturesque character: steep banks, a rocky bed, rich tracery of woods and weeds, old mills, weather-tinted bridges of antique build, rustic cottages, and still, still pools.

The Forth Bridge Railway Company was set up in 1873 but it took a further five years before Parliament gave permission for construction to begin, so JTR did not have the midget-making experience of sailing under one of the Seven Wonders of the World. The slimmer road bridge alongside is enhanced by the more solid beauty and soaring traceries of the rail bridge. Going underneath the two bridges was like being part of an ever-changing computer graphic image. The pattern of curves, grids and axes intersecting, separating, reforming as we passed below.

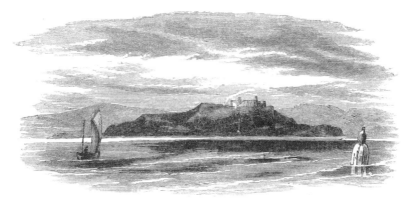

INCHKEITH.

What a revelation this Firth of Forth. On either side landmarks of old and new. To the south the turquoise blue gradations of Granton gasometers and stobs of Silverknowes skyscrapers leading on to the white desirable residences of Cramond. Those mills are now three-floored mansions with penthouse lofts. The woods of Dalmeny still hide the Big House and go right down to the yellow-pink sandy shore. On the other side to the north, Inchcolm Abbey, like Iona, is a visual shock in the landscape. Its ancientness contrasted with the Braefoot liquid gas terminal further up the coast where great pipes claw over the hillside to the cracker plant at Mossmorran.

Port Edgar came too soon. The *Cailleach* tried not to be too snooty about the black rubber coracle waiting for the second leg of the journey. Ollie scudded up the south coast of the Forth doing the exact same knots as the *Cailleach*, which seemed positively geriatric by comparison.

Blackness Castle passed by, its black stone prow jutting into the water. Like the First World War gun emplacements and watch towers on Inchgarvie island made to look like a moored battleship in the middle of the Forth, deception was intended. The fifteenth-century castle was built to look like a boat by an admiral who suffered from chronic sea sickness, ironically.

On towards Bo'ness the late afternoon sun was blindingly gold.

JTR Bo'ness looked so invitingly old-fashioned, that I was drawn to it, and jumped into the shore-bound boat in company with a grey-clad baker returning from a pie-selling expedition with a pie-box of prodigious size. One of our boatmen was 'jolly fou', and turned a ridiculous backward somersault as he was preparing to handle an oar. The square, amply turretted, and many quaint-windowed town house, with its exalted clock-tower, kept guard over the harbour, whose stony arms sheltered a number of ships of various nationalities. Railway goods trucks lined the piers; many canvas-covered stalls, for the sale of sweeties, gingerbread, fruit and toys; a height-and-weight stand, a strength-testing apparatus, a shooting range, and like attractions gave a fair-day look to the town: little children wandered from stall to stall, all eyes and ears, but trade was very flat. It was the last of the annual three days of holiday, and in the morning excursion boats sailed with the majority of the Borrowstownessians to Leith, that they might spend the day feeding the Edinburgh lions.

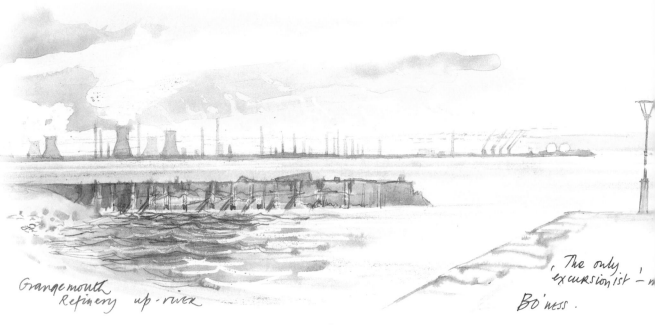

Grangemouth Refinery up-river

'The only excursionist' – m Bo'ness.

I was glad to see a house of ancient build, with lettered on its upper flat – TEMPERANCE HOTEL. The accommodation was limited, but as I was the only patron that day, it proved sufficient …

Ollie had so entered into the spirit of my re-enactment that he happily dropped me off at the old dock at Bo'ness promising to return for me on the late evening of the next day when the tide would be at full flood for the journey up to Stirling.

Borrowstounness – Bo'ness – was once one of the most ancient seaports of Scotland. Now I could almost smell the desolation of the place. Mounds of silted mud like giant silk quilts clogged up the entrance to the dock. The old pier crumbled into the thick grey water. A row of antique railway engines and carriages were lined along by the far dock wall, the rolling stock and home of the Bo'ness and Kinneil Railway and The Scottish Railway Preservation Society. There was no one about.

Bo'ness was silent, recovering from its annual Fair. Immense effort and expense goes into decorating houses, choosing the Fair Queen, her Fairies and Flowergirls. Bands and floats parade through the town. The original Fair in 1779 began as 'a drunken orgy' among the coalminers of the district celebrating their release from bondage as decreed by Act of Parliament.

A palpable stupor hung over the town this late Saturday afternoon in 1990. Or was it just the sullen heavy heat of the day brewing up some storm for the morrow? Whatever, Bo'ness was dead, comatose. And not a sweetie stall in sight. Two carryooteries the only visible source of victuals.

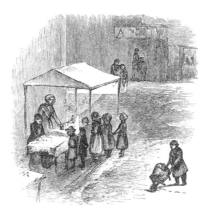

SWEETIE STALL.

The Temperance Hotel no longer existed. The Station Hotel with badly hung curtains and thirties facade had been built on the site. Faithful to the cause I asked for a room. The accommodation was more than limited; torn locks on doors and no sheets. I too was the only patron that day but did not stay. A big old B&B house high upon the hill, which had cost £710 to build in 1887, proved more than sufficient.

Sunday morning dawned bright. People pottered about gardens and parked cars. California-dressed young lazed and looked at each other from the enclaves of park benches.

JTR And so smiled the day when, after a refreshing sleep, I arose and looked out on the town that yesterday held holiday. A Sabbath stillness and a Sabbath sun alike attuned my heart to praise the Giver of countless blessings. My landlord told me he was in the habit of walking to Linlithgow to worship – a distance of fully four miles – and had done so with those members of his family able for this exercise for about twenty years. He was an elder of a Congregational church there…. The sun's rays were meltingly strong, and I was grateful to have a share of my friend's umbrella (Goliath might have made an unseemly sensation, had I taken *him* out for a Sabbath airing) to ward them off. We [walked] slowly, and now and again we halted to drink in a breath of fresh air, and to admire as much of the shores of Forth and its calm waters as the misty veil chose to reveal: the nearer land was beauteously decked with the fresh tints of fields fast ripening, and the varied emerald tones of the green or root crops; the grasses by the roadside and the wayside wild flowers were in their midsummer glory.

There was an interval after the service and before the second sermon, and in the vestry we had a repast of wine biscuits, clear spring-water, and the sweetest of new milk.

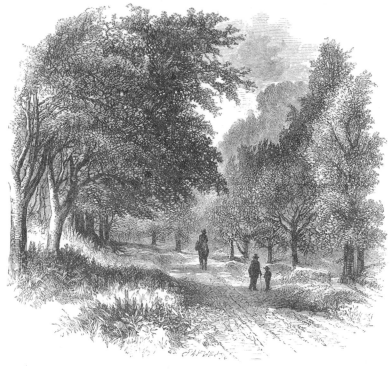

ROAD SCENE.

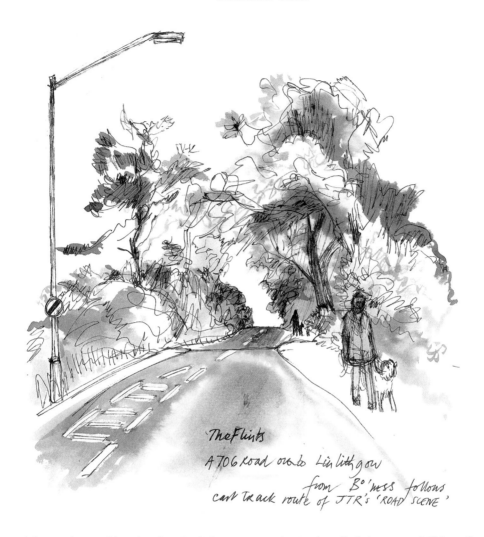

The Flints

A 706 road over to Linlithgow

from Bo'ness follows

cart track route of JTR's 'ROAD SCENE'

The track over 'the Flints' to Linlithgow is now boringly called the A706. Still heavily arboured at the brow of the hill, I tried to work out which trees could have cast their young stripling shadows over JTR's path. It was my first backpack trudge along a busy road. Many, many were to be endured over the months ahead. And this was a minor road.

The aggressive noise and speed of cars, lorries and vans jarred into my reflective mood. Mad fleeing skunks, their fumes gagged my nostrils. Yet the grasses, nettles and beech hedge leaves at the side of the road were brightly green. Bramble flowers snowy white. Their survival gave me heart. I would not buy a dust mask at the next available DIY. JTR was worried about the impression 'Goliath' gave, after all.

Just before the Linlithgow boundary the A706 goes over the broad swathe of the M9. A regular user of that motorway, I looked down on myself bulleting a plastic and metal capsule at speeds well over the maximum and thanked the powers-that-be that cyclists and walkers are not allowed on motorways. The road over from Bo'ness was a country lane by comparison.

Like many old Scottish towns the suburbs of Linlithgow are quiet reserves of large and silent houses. Flowers, some real, some embalmed in plastic, but all set in rigid vases at windows. Not a movement behind straight curtains. In high-ceilinged back rooms there is surely life.

St John's Evangelical Church is right in the town and on the apex of the entrance gable is still the plaque – CONGREGATIONAL CHURCH 1840. The first hymn was in full vocal sway as I slipped in. A young and very handsome preacher from Chicago, Illinois, dripped humid sweat as he preached the sermon. His theme was the 'love letter' of Genesis, God's word, illustrated with a passionate intimacy. He and his fiancée had lived four hundred miles apart during their engagement. Letters were read and re-read. Meanings searched and found between the lines. 'And always the joy of reading again and again at the end of each letter the words "I LOVE YOU!" ' Pretty teenage girls at my side giggled with the thrill of transference.

Somewhere below in the bowels of the church thumps indicated a very active Sunday School session.

At the end of the service tea, coffee, juice and biscuits were served as we sat in maroon velour padded chairs easily nudged round to form spontaneous groups. 'We got rid of the pews. Too formal,' a chummy elder told me.

John, you would have liked the Brethren very much. They wished me well on my travels and apologised for the lack of clear spring water.

A wander through a very quiet High Street took me to Linlithgow Palace and Loch where Sunday families strolled with dogs and picnic bags. Men mucked about in boats. Joe, a member of the voluntary committee that services the boats for fishing on the Loch, was typical of that special breed of urban male recognised by hats with clusters of fishing flies and corpulent red and black wool check shirts, who observe nature and take great meaning from it.

'The two resident pairs of swans keep to their own side of the Loch. Been here for years and God help either crossing the dividing line mid loch.' Unusually, this year had seen six nesting pairs and many more visiting swans. 'The visitors get shunted back and fore across the Loch between both territories all day long.' And as if to prove the point forty young birds, their beaks not yet bright orange, paddle-thrashed past in terror, the resident cob of this side of the Loch in malevolent pursuit. Later he swaggered up the bank with a stiff taffeta-like swish to join his quite unimpressed family busily preening themselves.

JTR My friend took me for a short stroll by the ruins of Linlithgow Palace, and as we sat on the grass, having lungs and mind alike refreshed and renewed, we looked over the far-stretching

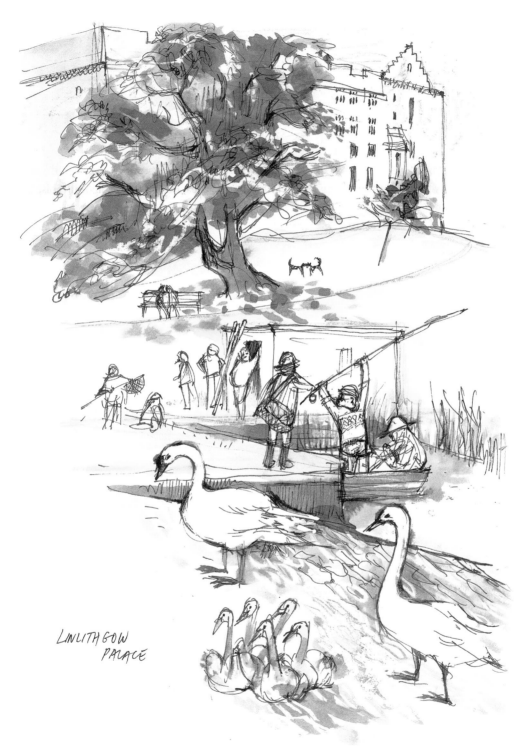

LINLITHGOW
PALACE

Stiff taffeta sound of cob walking by

landscape of hill and mead and wood, and down upon the rippling ever-changeful lake. Willows that bent their pliant boughs over the water, spoke to us of sad scenes enacted in more troubled times, and swans glided to and fro with royal dignity and elegance of motion. I am told two rival families of them have sway on the lake, each holding tenaciously to and fighting desperately for his fishing-ground and seat of empire. Woe to the poor swan who, unprotected by his fellows, is unguarded enough to cross the border!

On the walk back over 'the Flints' to Bo'ness it started to rain. Slow at first, then torrential. That silly umbrella was invaluable, as was the Mary Quant primary-coloured plastic cape bought on a whim. As I sat on a bollard by the old pier waiting for Ollie to turn up I could feel all eyes on my clownish back. The brolly was blue. What a colourful figurehead we must have cut out there in the leaden blur. The other side of the Firth was formless. Would Ollie come?

The billowing bosoms of silted mud slurped as their cleavages filled up with the grey gruel of the incoming tide. Timing was getting critical to catch and go with the high tide up river to Stirling.

In the thick still opaqueness I heard the powerful throb of the rescue launch's engine long before it nosed its way precariously around the half submerged metal stanchions near the dock wall. A young New Zealand woman instructor from the sailing school and a local lad had come for the historic journey, too. Ollie placed the rucksack under a tarpaulin, those first precious sketches, my worry, his primal concern my putting on a life jacket. I sat on the rounded rubber gunwale, not dissimilar to, but firmer than the bosoms of mud below. We faced westwards leaning into the angle and thrust of the

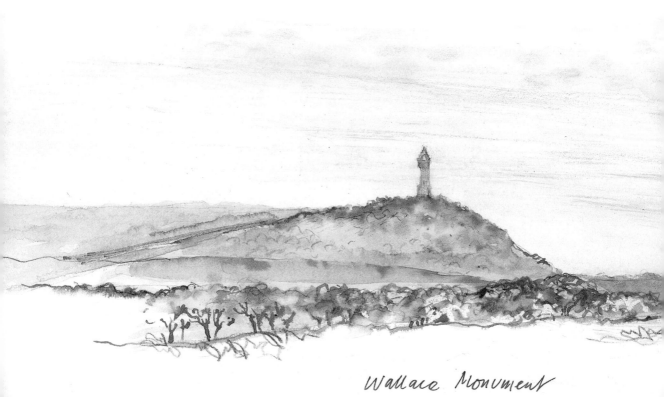

Wallace Monument

launch as it revved out into the misty Firth, rain streaming down our faces and oilskins and into our boots. What a change from the light bright blue of the previous day's sail.

There was no point in crying over spilt skies. The more I tried to make out the landmarks of Longannet and Kincardine power stations, their pylons and giant scallops of cables disappearing into the dim, the more the ghostly shapes seemed to loom out of a *déja vu* in reverse.

Could JTR have mused on the developments that were to come after him as he steampaddled up the Firth on the *Loch Mar* and noted 'the stalks and above ground works connected with the mines' on either shore? Did he see them as visual pollution? Certainly there was an awareness by some of general pollution. And well there might be with houses, offices and factories, in fact every place with a chimney, belching out bronchial poison and nil visibility for weeks on end especially in the winter months. Is it any wonder that sparkling streams and waterfalls were a favourite subject for all the Brother Brushes?

Kincardine Bridge is welded shut now. Originally a section of the middle pier swivelled at right angles to the bridge to allow masted boats to go up river. Another reason why the *Cailleach* had to drop out. The rubber dinghy passed the *Fiona*, a forlorn deserted lugger. It had a *Marie Celeste* quality about it with unattended dinghy and uptilted outboard engine alongside. Black crows hopped heavily out of the hold and flapped into the grey voile of the sky. A net hung down from a boom at right angles to the bow. Salmon fishers? But where were they? The same silent phenomenon at Alloa; three old fishing boats like decayed stage props, again with bow booms and tatty nets hanging down into the rain-pocked flood tide, thick and oily.

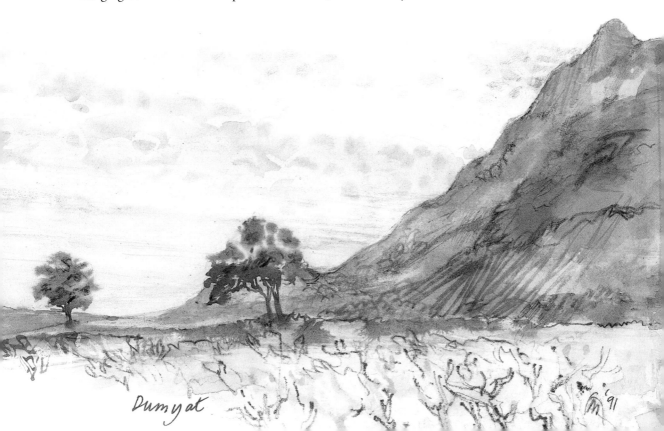

Dumyat

At Alloa the river is still broad. The haze of perpendicular rain was monsoon like. We could be in China or Africa. The Yangtse or the Congo. A surfacing crocodile would be quite acceptable. Visually that is.

Past Alloa and the tall shadow of its brewery, the turns in the river became more obvious and frequent. An island with a lone shepherd's house goes by. The railway bridge nearby caused a lot of feeling with boat operators in Victorian times. The rail bridge is no more, only the stone piers with iron criss-cross stays marking the spot of angry confrontations.

The river started to really meander – that lovely word, first learned at school in geography. Forever poetic not scientific. The Wallace Monument was a far pale pencil smudge. Visibility very poor. We were all cold and damp by now. But the journey went on. Slower as the river became more intimate; reeds at the edge almost within touching distance. Waterfowl. A heron stalkily still. Dank lank growth and then the smells of intensive farming. Chicken and pig sheds stretched for fields on one side. Heavy free-range cows on the other side grazed precariously near to the water; clogging bogging silt even up here.

At times the town of Stirling and landfall were so near then depressingly far as we followed yet another sinuous convolution of the narrowing river. We had always to be on the lookout for floating objects or embedded submerged debris that could puncture the dinghy. The water did not look very inviting. A log slowly passed by at Cambuskenneth Ford going downstream. The tide was on the turn. Imperceptibly, the grisaille effect of the riverscape darkened a tone. A landing spot had to be found soon.

We had been two hours on the journey and Ollie and crew had to get back down river before that tide dropped and darkness fell. We were all very cold by now and tense as we scanned the curves of the bank that brought the town close. Another loop took us away through silent marsh. Nearer again we saw the old rotting steamboat jetty that had served the salt works half hidden by dark overhanging trees. Too dangerous for landing. And then the Stirling Rowing Club stage came into sight, unbelievably devoid of spectators. We really did deserve a welcoming party and three very large hot toddies at least to mark our tremendous achievement. A few boozy faces looked out of the Clubhouse window at our drookit arrival but soon turned back to their beer.

How proud we were none the less. I suggested a dram somewhere more convivial but the tide was not co-operative. I waved and waved until Ollie and crew disappeared back round the first of those infuriating bends in the river. They had another two hours before home and warmth.

And I had to find mine.

JTR With Monday morning I resumed care of my knapsack and had quite a race to catch the boat that left the pier-head for the steamer. On board the 'Lord Mar' again, we were soon cutting our way westward and Stirling-ward, where there lay, still under the mist-clouds, the lovely Vale of Forth and the mountains that enshrine it.

We passed on our right Culross – of old a place of monastic power, but also famed for 'girdles.' Its people long enjoyed the exclusive right of making iron girdles for firing scones and oaten cakes in the days when home-baked bread was the food of the country. On the left we saw Grangemouth – a port busy with the transhipment of goods from sailing and steamships to the transport barges of the Forth and Clyde Canal. After leaving Kincardine on the north shore, we were soon alongside of Alloa landing-stage or wharf, the Alloa of yarn and ale repute. Would that the ale was as tame as the yarn, as full of comfort and as free from vice; that it carried fewer of the heartaches, headaches, empty stomachs, and other sadder ills in its wake! Much of the yarn makes snug homes, laughing wives, and rosy bairns – much of the ale leaves 'Drunkards' wains,' a dark present and a still darker future.

At Alloa we changed many of our passengers and much of our cargo. The sail up the river brought to the eye new landscape objects: outspreading trees, tall reeds, and rank weeds; fields, haystacks, and farm homesteads. Every winding of Forth opened out new combinations of river-course, and tree, and wooded hill. We had many fine peeps of Abbey Craig and Stirling Castle, and a few minutes before landing, we sailed close to the ruins of the ancient abbey of Cambuskenneth, founded by David I in 1147.

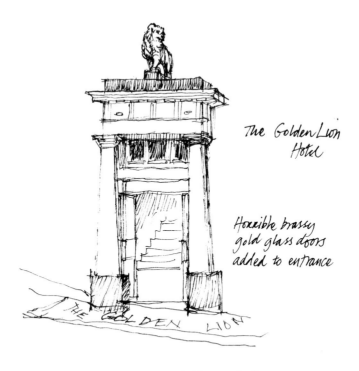

The Golden Lion
Hotel

Horrible brassy
gold glass doors
added to entrance

'Stirling – the Heart of Scotland.' My arrival, like a wriggling spermatozoa, made me think more of a womb. And warmth. I walked for a dreary hour finding only two B&B signs in the main part of town. Both full. Did the others – there must have been others –

do it unofficially, unmarked? Hotels were also full. It was the weekend of the STUC's 'A Day for Scotland', Tartan Festival and Big Rock Bands Concert, everyone said. But this was late Sunday night. Was it the dripping rucksack that turned me away?

The large rotund landlord of the second B&B relented when I turned up sodden on his doorstep once again. It was ten o'clock. All right, he had other property. If I didn't mind staying in 'the lads' flat' across in the High Street? A man with a heart – and a womb. I'd have to come over for breakfast at six-thirty a.m. before he served his residents.

Two slightly but politely amazed workmen watching football on the tele showed me their mate's empty bedroom. After a bath and a meal in the Indian restaurant down below (not another eating place open except the Chinese – what would Scotland do without them?) I collapsed into Hughie's bed wondering if travel and accommodation were simpler a hundred-odd years ago and would I be able to keep pace with Brother Brush and his Rambles.

I bet he stayed in the Golden Lion unbooked, Goliath and all …

The early rise suited me fine. The day was brilliant with sun. The grey mists of the previous day had evaporated in the night, as had my reservations. All was fresh and new. I made my way to Raploch for the sketch of Stirling Castle.

JTR At the brae-foot was the little village of Raploch, which boasted an inn, but, like too many of our wayside inns, its whole trade was in the sale of drinks; and the writer, though a *bonâ fide* traveller, could not persuade the hostess even to make a cup of tea. But a humble cottage having in the window a few groceries, and a ticket with 'Gingerbeer Sold' on it, proved a place of refreshment; and while the cheerful housewife made ready a meal, I got a spot from which to sketch 'Stirling Castle from the Raploch.' In the cottage, with little Teenie, a dear wee lassie, looking hard at me, who fain would speak and come to me, but was too bashful, as most of the Scotch bairns are, and the good-wife busy with her seam, the cup of tea, home-baked bread, and country cheese, all nicely set out, proved a pleasing repast. She would not be persuaded to take more than sixpence as payment.

There is no moor at Raploch now. There is the sprawl of a fifties housing estate instead. A young woman with a child in a pushchair indicated a shortcut by IRA graffitied pebbledash sheds to where 'the view' might be. On the way a man walking a low-slung labrador around the inside perimeter fence of a football pitch, shoved it into the tall weeds if it looked as though it was preparing to defecate.

Clunking thuds came from a seemingly windowless Community Centre indicating bowls being played – or karate? Masculine shouts of approval.

And in between houses, with boarded-up windows and tin-strewn unkempt gardens where thick crops of willow herb flowered in profusion, were manicured patches of

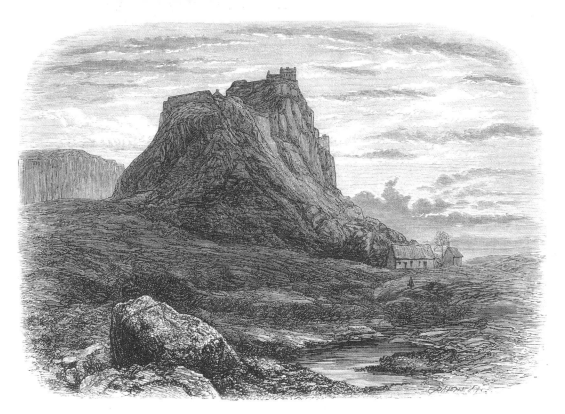

STIRLING CASTLE, FROM RAPLOCH.

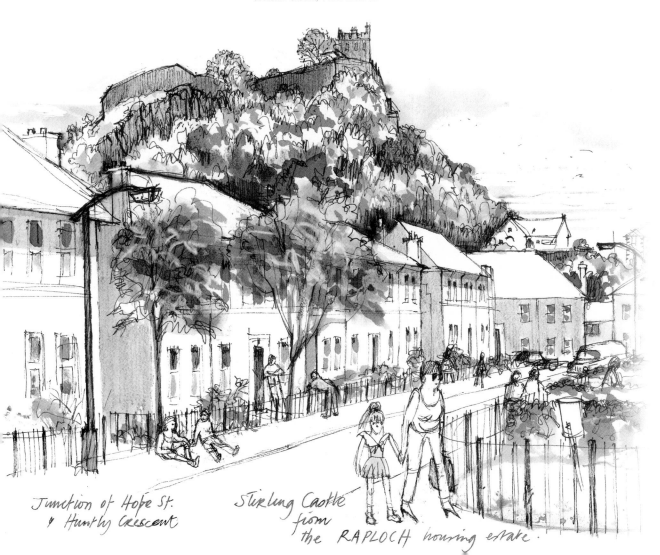

Junction of Hope St.
& Huntly Crescent

Stirling Castle
from
the RAPLOCH housing estate.

horticultural pride crowned with satellite dishes. A free-roaming long-haired Alsatian and a thin gaunt greyhound went about their business. Music from wide open windows breathed out into the thick heat; the persistent beat and repetitive five-note melody was overlaid with designer-heavy breathing and climactic sighs.

The castle, with white hot sun behind it, reared dark behind the sea of shimmering roofs. I had found the spot. People, mostly mums and children, would stop to see what I was doing. Nobody was at all impressed that their houses stood where once there had been a wild open moor. 'Aye, that's the Castle, all right, tho'.'

Raploch was very much in the local news, 1990. In amongst the reports on 'A Day for Scotland', the *Stirling Observer* carried a piece on the children of Raploch Primary School having filled more than ten large boxes with aid for Romanian orphans. 'One little boy brought in half a dozen sticking plasters and told his teacher, "That's for the wee bairns in Romania".'

In the *Stirling Journal and Advertiser* of July 14 1876, after the advertisements for Dissolved Peruvian Guano and Coal at 7/6d a ton, a despatch from New York on the US Government's concentration of 'chastisement' of the Indians after the massacre of

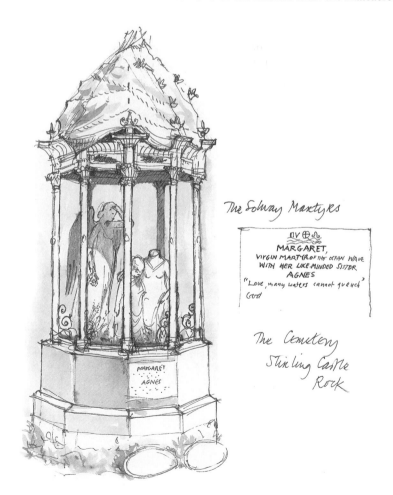

The Solway Martyrs

IHV ⊕ XC.
MARGARET,
VIRGIN MARTYR OF THE OCEAN WAVE
WITH HER LIKE-MINDED SISTER
AGNES
"Love, many waters cannot quench"
God

The Cemetery
Stirling Castle
Rock

General Custer and his troops, and the Agricultural Report for Stirlingshire ('crops had responded at once in the great heat'), there were several items on the 'War in the East'. Turkey had invaded Selvia (Serbia). Familiar patterns. However, 'the news from the seat of war is, as usual, conflicting – both sides claiming the advantage'. Telegrams from Belgrade were quite 'unintelligible'. One wonders if our instant TV coverage of crises and wars is any more intelligible.

One thing is for sure, that little boy's sticking plasters are and will always be needed.

There is a high airy graveyard on the top of the Castle rock. Not a place of gloom but rather the atmosphere of a public park this blistering hot day. Tourists, and organised parties of young people of all nationalities, sauntered or sat under the trees on the grassy edge of cliffs that looked out over the hazed Carse of Stirling.

'Somebody must've nicked the copper off it,' said one young bare torso-ed lad to his mate as they went by a tall seedy gazebo-like monument, its dome wrapped around with faded tarpaulin. 'Great score, graveyards, y'know.' Behind recent already yellowing perspex panels were an Angel of Death and two female figures, one headless, enacting in white marble a *tableau mort* so beloved of Victorians.

JTR After a climb up the sloping tree-shaded side of the castle hill, the cemetery was reached, and prominent among memorials of the dead were statues of John Knox, Alexander Henderson, and Andrew Melville, the Reformers, and of the martyr, James Renwick; also a very lovely piece of sculpture in marble in memory of the 'Virgin Martyrs,' one of whom departed to be with Jesus, as the tide of Solway sped her heavenward flight. The statue is in memory of Margaret Wilson: it shows herself, a maiden of eighteen years, and her little sister, thirteen years of age (and alike condemned, but whose life was purchased by the father, for one hundred pounds sterling, his all), reading the Word of God. A little lamb is lying at their feet, and an angel with a flower in hand bends over them as if just about to deliver a message. These girls were guilty of going to hear the Word of God preached; and the aged woman, Margaret Maclauchlin – martyred along with Margaret Wilson – had been caught in the act of worshipping God with her family.

Their punishment, to be more graphic, was to be tied to a stake stuck far out in the low-tide sands of the Solway Firth. Death was by drowning as the slow incoming tide crept over their heads.

Margaret Wilson's marble head was knocked off by a workman ten years ago whilst painting the inside of the monument. It lies in the graveyard shed. The same workman painted over the plaques below, obliterating the legend. No one can remember what they said. Now we are told that 'Heather Ls James and James Ls Heather 4 EVER.'

Mr Drummond (of the famous seeds) had before he died in 1868 commissioned this and the other statues as memorials to the Reformers, including his own most ugly and out of character Pyramid. He would have trusted that their upkeep be as sacrosanct as their memory. Both have sadly deteriorated in this age of more earthly pleasures and pursuits – even in graveyards. The 'Virgin Martyrs' had in fact had a glass roof. It must have been very lovely.

For the Victorians life was ugly and sinful but death could be beautiful – especially sooner rather than later.

JTR I opened my note-book and pointed to a jotting I had taken of a tombstone, with the following inscription:

1809
ALEX^R•E•MEFFEN,
CHIEF CONSTABLE, STIRLINGSHIRE

OUR • LIFE • IS • BUT • A • WINTER • DAY •
SOME • ONLY • BREAKFAST • AND • AWAY •
OTHERS • TO • DINNER • STAY •
AND • ARE • FULL • FED:
THE • OLDEST • MAN • BUT • SUPS:
AND • GOES • TO • BED:
LARGE • IS • HIS • DEPT:
THAT • LINGERS • OUT • THE • DAY •
HE • THAT • GOES • SOONEST
HAS • THE • LEAST • TO • PAY:

He [Old Andrew the keeper of the grounds] was very wroth.

'Meffen? No! Miller's the name. The stane was selt by 'e Kirk Session. Meffen bocht it, scrappet oot Miller, and putt his ain name on.'

And from the testimony of the stone itself, it was evident a part of it had been lowered to get rid of some previous cuttings.

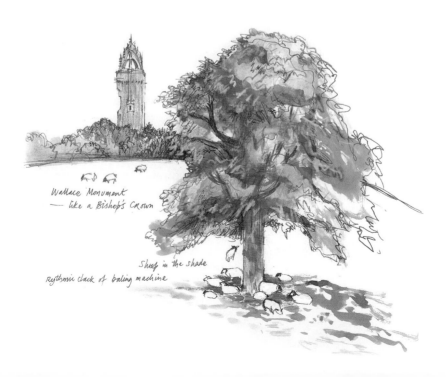

Wallace Monument
— like a Bishop's Crown

Sheep in the shade
Rythmic clack of baling machine

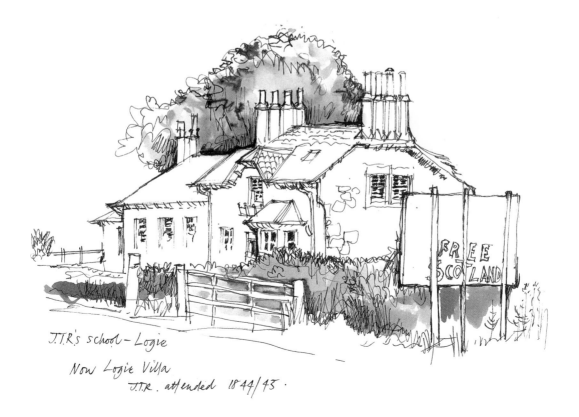

The 'Sea' of the Carse
Early morning mist islanding
Stirling Castle; River Forth showing thro'

Looking down from Wallace Monument

Old Andrew's present-day counterpart added his own cynical comment, 'He obviously fancied the inscription but was too mean to get his own stone made.' Ah, but there could be more to it than that. Who was Miller to Meffen? An early Victorian mystery still to be unravelled? As far as Miller is concerned there can be no R.I.P. surely?

A few years ago Central Police Department mended and cleaned up the stone. Do they know that they are accessories to perpetuating a dastardly act?

The walk from the Castle and town to Causeway Head and the Wallace monument was alongside the main road – at rush hour. Not pleasant, though I had got into the rhythm and mindset of the backpacker's cypherlike existence when walking for long spells, especially in urban areas. Safe enough, physically, when there was a pavement, but the aural and nasal assault was something I never got used to. I have never hated cars and their owners so much. My attitude to the use and abuse of the combustion engine has been changed for life.

It was good to get above it all at the monument to Wallace on Abbey Craig, despite the sweltering climb. The haze over the Carse had become a silvery white sea of mist, islanding the Castle, the cemetery and top of the town. A wispy gap showed one of the 'strangely tortuous windings of the Forth'. Up above we tourists baked.

J.T.R's school – Logie
Now Logie Villa
J.T.R. attended 1844/45.

A cool tree-tunnelled path on the edge of the cliffs took me down through the woods and roe deer trails to a baled field at the back of the Craig to the grounds of Stirling University, once Airthrey Estate. The main road east to Alloa from Causeway Head hummed with that evil traffic but I was in a little world only a few hundred yards away celebrating a rural inscape with a sandwich and a juicy peach. A little clear burn sheltered by a hawthorn hedge had pale flowering waterplants hidden cool at the edge of dark pools. High above were the skylarks.

I rested the rucksack on a bale of sweet hay that would find its way come autumn to starker Highlands and Islands terrain. Crab apple trees already had one side of their fruit pink, yet still there were some flowers on the elders.

JTR spent parts of his childhood in this area. Possibly this field? I communed hard.

JTR Looking towards Dumyat, under the shadow of that outpost of the Ochil range, is the charming estate of Airthrey, its semicircular castle, finely arranged woods, and its winding lake, which when the ice bears has been the scene of well-fought curling matches and pleasant skating rounds. Glad days for the Loggie schoolboy when he is told 'Airthrey Pond is bearing; the grounds are open, a match is to be played;' and 'Boys, you can go and spend the day on the ice!' The sliding and snowballing is all the sweeter that he is invited to a share of the reeking hot potatoes and beef served to the gentry on the ice to keep hunger away.

I was sent to Loggie School with the young villagers, and soon made good progress in the art of smoking *backy* out of a *cutty pipe*. Every Sabbath morning found me lying on the top of Abbey Craig, gazing admiringly seaward, towards Stirling, or away to the mountain and lake land of the west. I loved alike the grey and the sunny morn. Would that from those dreamy days of boyhood I had increasingly paid court to our native landscape, and sought to have my soul drink deeper of its heaven-born charms!

The next day found me and a nostalgically fortified adult JTR on our way to Callander.

I managed to avoid Bridge of Allan High Street by keeping up in the posh part of town following the line of the old road from Logie Kirk. Great mansions with pink knicker-bocker curtains had coy names like Logie Lea and Airthrey Croft. The houses looked empty but not like the Linlithgow ones. No cold owners huddled in the back rooms with cloth dachshund-shaped draught excluders here. One house had knickerless windows. Slow shapes moved behind the curtains. A Nursing Home.

After Bridge of Allan there was no way of avoiding the main road. It was JTR's route – which ultimately would join with the motorway. I took a minor road to the left going under the M9, heading in the direction of Doune. It wound round the high ivy walls of Keir House. A wind had started to come across the Carse, cool and refreshing.

And then I made the mistake of trying a shortcut across stubble fields so beloved of wood pigeons. The underfoot textures were a delight after the tarmac trudge. Dutifully I kept to the edge of the first field until reaching a broad water-filled ditch that was impossible to cross and necessitated a forty-five-degrees turn for what seemed miles. And then another ditch … another forty-five-degrees turn, and trek. Fields in Stirlingshire are very square and very big. The uneven terrain no longer charmed. The weight of the rucksack kept digging me in soft parts and any quick compensating move put me off balance. I must have looked like a drunken Commando. Guns fired from behind in the woods of Keir House. Pigeons clappered overhead. I could be a dying Commando if I wasn't careful.

The last turn, of course, had got me back to the road that I had been so glad to leave half an hour earlier. Furious at the time wasted – this was my first really serious walk with the full pack (ten miles) – I vowed never to leave the road again. The love/hate relationship with Mr MacAdam was finally established.

JTR Near to Doune, not far from a fine avenue of beech-trees, among the roadside grasses, lay a family group, the father black with soot, the mother and three very young children huddled close beside her: these were sleeping; three other children were wide awake, and came to ask a penny from me to buy some bread. I pointed to two large white scones lying on the ground.

'We darna touch them till faither waakens,' I was told; and so they gained their point. He was a travelling sweep, and most likely had done a good morning's work at one of the farms near by. A quarter of an hour after, as I looked out of the parlour of an inn, I saw my young friends mixing an effervescing drink, and dividing to each a share at the public well, and got the accompanying jotting of them while the youngest hopeful was with all his little strength trying to work the pump-handle.

JTR would have loved adding this sketch with that of 'Teenie from Raploch' to his 'folio' and I can just hear his Anglicised voice (he greatly believed in the Union of the Crowns)

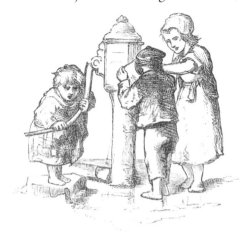

SWEEP'S WAINS.

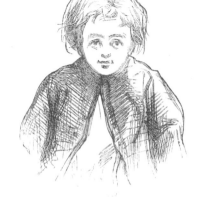

TEENIE.

23

attempting the local dialect as he retold the tale at one of his mother's soirées at Broughton Place on return from his Rambles, bathed and clothed in clean linen.

Victorian artists, *de facto* upper class, had a compulsion to capture the lower classes *in situ*, especially children – innocents soon to be corrupted by the foul ways of the world. Caught on the canvas their grubby innocence was at least immortalised. Like voyeurs, they saw their subjects not as people but as models for self-gratification. The fishing port of Newhaven offered

JTR glimpses of the home-life of that hardy race; the place and the people as an unworked quarry of subjects for the Brush, guided by an appreciating eye and a poetic soul from which only a few surface chippings and one or two larger lumps have as yet been taken.

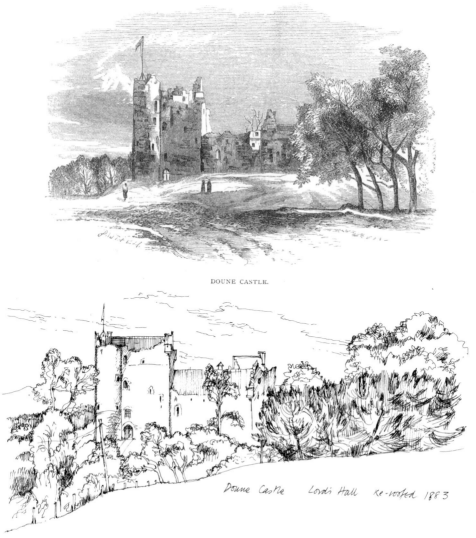

DOUNE CASTLE.

Doune Castle   Lord's Hall   Re-roofed 1883

A bit like us with our Pentaxes in Patagonia.

Would JTR and his Brethren Brush dare sketch their own class as patronisingly? JTR felt strongly about

JTR the poor-tax [which] has had a most baneful influence in sucking out of many in our country the independence of nature we are wont to esteem our birthright, and shutting the hearts of givers into the cold hard groove of a miserable statute allowance.

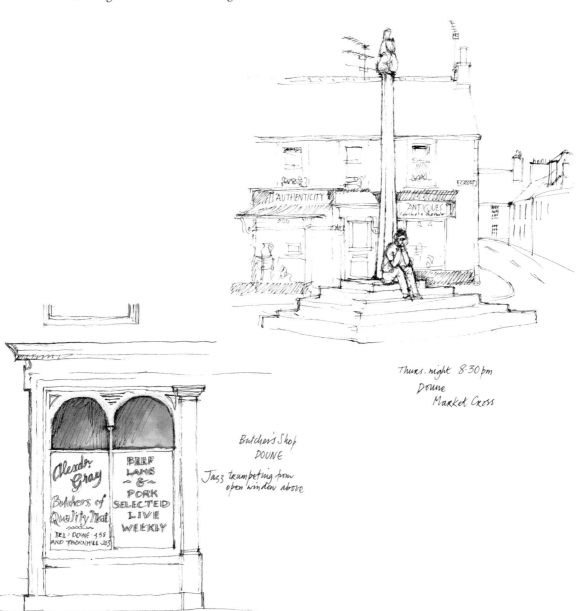

Thurs. night 8.30 pm
Doune
Market Cross

Butcher's Shop
DOUNE

Jazz trumpeting from
open window above

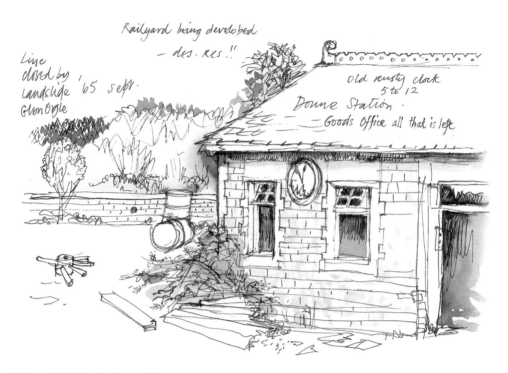

The rapid urbanisation of the Central Lowlands by 1800 caused the old informal ways, referred to by JTR, of poor relief to break down. Poor relief soon became a major political issue, Scotland maintaining that the 'I kent his faither' as opposed to a more centralised system was preferable. But it wasn't as simple as that. There was a new kind of poor. The acute depression of 1843 caused able-bodied unemployed men as well as widows, orphans and the chronically ill or handicapped to need support. With the shifting nature of fast-moving industrial development the problem was much more complicated. England believed in giving minimal provision to this new class of poor – but constitutionally.

If JTR had bought the *Stirling Journal and Advertiser* whilst in Stirling that week he would have seen the section 'Imperial Parliament' which included this report: 'The Duke of Richmond and Gordon, in moving the second reading of the Poor Law Amendment Bill, explained that amongst its main objects were the better arrangement of the divisions of parishes and the conferring of settlement after three years residence, together with provisions for disqualifying paupers from voting at elections, and facilitating the employment of pauper boys in the navy.'

Great sketching material there.

Though JTR had 'reason for thankfulness that as God made our island one home, we are likewise one people, with our hearts and our honour alike one', he was an incurable Scottish Romantic. His defence of 'the independence of nature we are wont to esteem our nature' unfortunately clouded his understanding of a basic human principle.

No person should be dependent on the whim of Victorian-style philanthropy.

I was not liking where JTR was leading me. I much preferred him out on the open road, with or without Mr McAdam.

The only distress I could see in Doune was fourteen-year-old Emma, sitting disconsolate at the foot of the Market Cross with 'nothing to do'. It was just after eight o'clock. The thick heat of the day's ending soaked up the agonised falsetto yowls of an amateur folk singer from an upstairs open window, interwoven with the last shreeps of the swallows.

JTR caught the first train to Callander after being 'sufficiently tired to enjoy a rest'. I was knackered and there is no railway line to Callander from Doune nowadays anyway. That rucksack was just too heavy. I spent the evening, before falling between nylon sheets, parcelling up items to be posted back to Edinburgh. The other 'stylish' anorak for a start. One was enough. Despite its green wellie image it was paper thin but waterproof. The Sony Walkman went too, along with its two sets of extra batteries and Bach's Double Violin Concerto amongst other tapes. No more protection in plasterboard walled B&Bs. How would I survive? The watercolour box! I was desperate to lighten the load. From then on the sketches were overlaid with a colour note shorthand. I was more confident of my photographic memory than my stamina. And a Collins Pocket Dictionary, for heaven's sake! What on earth had I brought that for?

That left me with the clothes I stood up in, a change of knickers and socks and a pair of light sandals, Laura Ashley flowery pants and dangly earrings for 'evening wear', besides the maps, The Book (his), various personal and hillwalking requisites and the little rucksack. I got more and more adept as the Rambles became more far-flung at offloading the big rucksack on postbuses, school cars and lorries. The two of us never once not meeting up with the other at the end of the day.

In the morning after going to the Post Office I found the ruined buildings and yards of the station now with planning permission for 'desirable residences'. 'Beeching cuts,' said a local, adding 'I think'. It was surprising how many people 'couldn't just remember' when the railway closed.

There was time for a browse in the library before the bus to Callander. (No, I was not going to walk. He didn't.)

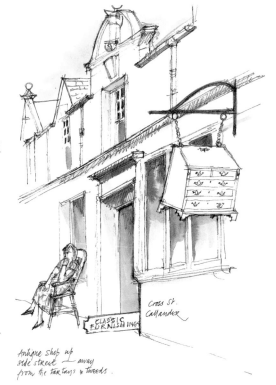

Cross St.
Callander

CLASSIC
FURNISHINGS

Antique shop up
side street ← away
from the Tartans & Tweeds.

Despite the severe library lady eyeing the definitely lighter rucksack, I was allowed to look through local history books. I liked the story of the small boy who ran to his mother when the first train steamed past Callander crying, 'Mither! The Smiddy's awa wi a row o' hooses ahint it!' I remembered noticing the date above the tumbling down railway refreshment room – 1876.

On the bus to Callander there was a young girl thrilled to be going to rehearse in the choir accompanying a popular Scots singer beloved of middle-aged ladies – and young girls, it seemed. It was Callander's Festival week.

JTR At Callander there is accommodation for the many: there are the famed 'Dreadnought' and 'McGregor's' Hotels, and almost every house in the village has apartments for lodgers. After a tea-dinner I left the village, and took a path that would have led me to Bracklinn Falls had I not become so enamoured of and absorbed with bits of hill-side under the mellowing twilight, that I had wandered very far up the path by the mountain-side, into the glen, before I remembered to look for the little side-path that leads into the hollow where that famed fall has its rocky bower. There were few to disturb the seclusion of this glen – only a shepherd lad and his collie, a matron and her two children, and a middle-aged couple who trod the ground as if each step were sacred to them: mayhap in childhood they had wandered over these same braes together, pulling the heather-bell and chasing the butterflies.

And written the lyrics for the singer's songs …

Callander is the first tartan labelled honeypot on the way to the Trossachs. Nothing, from climbing gear and factory woollens to abalone shells in The Shell Centre and white heather in the grocer's, is shy of selling itself. If the pavement were narrower they'd all be out into the street. There was only one antique shop and that was up a side street.

The Threshold Tearoom, with 'Roamin' in the Gloamin' musak and the biggest and lightest scones filled with strawberry jam and cream, is a Barbara Cartland confection of pinks – tablecloths, walls, woodwork, plastic flower festoons. And if you look close there are real little pink carnations in vases on the tight-jammed tables. If there was enough room 'the middle-aged couples' would be up dancing. But there is more serious work to be done. 'Another scone, loov, please.'

On the walk up to Bracklinn Falls the accents changed to French and American. No Victorian drama at the Falls this dry early summer. Just dark slimy dripping cliffs and high sweet sick-smelling bracken. Nor any Brother Brushes in sight – they all work at home nowadays from photographs – but I did bump into a Sister Wilderness, an ex-warden from St Kilda now working with the NCC locally, returning from a plant survey. She pointed me in the possible direction of JTR's 'Braes of Doune' sketch. On the breast of the hill above Callander I was still confused.

JTR had in fact misnamed the view: the Braes of Doune are sweeping farmland to the east of Callander. Why did I have a sneaky feeling of one-upmanship when I finally discovered that on the Ordnance Survey map? He had led me a merry dance through waist-high bracken. Was our relationship being tested?

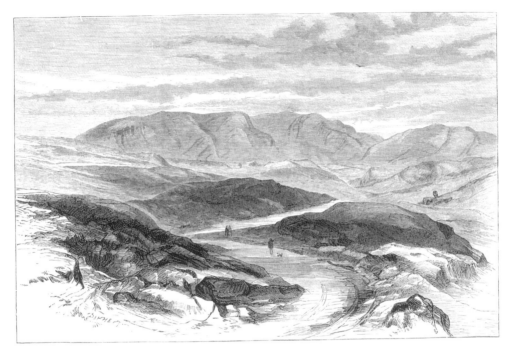

BRAES OF DOUNE.

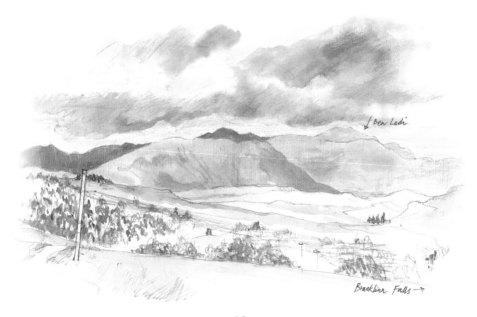

Ben Ledi

Bracklinn Falls →

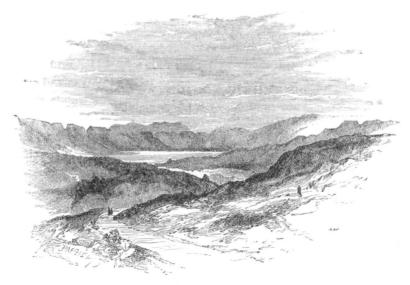

VENACHAR, FROM ABOVE CALLANDER.

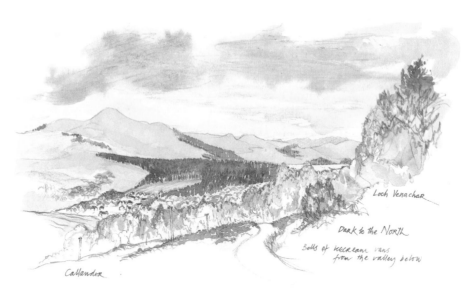

Loch Venachar

Dark to the North

Bells of icecream vans
from the valley below

Callander

'And soon Callander's one street was the path trod, and like tired nature, I too sought rest.' The Dreadnought Hotel still stands, its former coaching days' glory not quite hidden by flush fire doors and racks of PCs and thick gold and silver titled paperbacks. Thistle, clover and rose mouldings adorn the high ceilings. Hazy through the beautiful ochre-stained glass windows by McCulloch and Gow of Glasgow that depict sepia line drawings of Loch Achray and Loch Katrine, are the remains of box hedge lined paths in the garden. Delightfully stylised stone lions guard the side entrance of the hotel. JTR would have entered by the front, the lions on a plinth above his head.

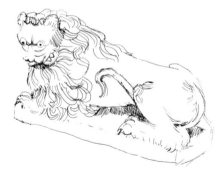

Delightfully stylised lions on ground.
at side entrance to Dreadnought Hotel
used to be on plinth above main door on street)

The lions are at a comfy height now for little ladies' bums as they wait for husbands finishing fags on the pavement before entering the buses that will take them to the 'Trossacks' for the day.

So many of these grand old hotels keep bricks – or rather hand-masoned stones – and mortar together by accommodating five, six coach parties at a time. Meals are on a shift system and the big open hallways with broad oak-panelled staircases are packed with waiting busloads of oldies all determined on having a good time. The noise is not dissimilar to deep litter hens. Sherries and big glasses of beer sustain the evening cackle. But after dinner all is total silence, ears straining for the bingo caller's numbers. The oldies are like a primary school class at test time. Pins could drop.

Travelling with JTR I soon learned to appreciate these initially daunting stopovers. Somehow a room could always be found, it was cheap and old bathrooms at the end of long corridors were always empty. Oldies don't have baths in strange places. There I would soak for hours, reading a book with a gin and tonic on the cast iron bath edge; finally soaking that day's knickers and socks as I sauna-ed in the remaining steam. Maybe fitting in a few languorous stretches of the revitalised limbs. Nobody ever knocked on the door.

A substantial picnic lunch wrapped up in a napkin can be garnered from the next morning's breakfast, as well.

'Kitchen's still the same as in 1876,' said the Liverpool waitress. She thought she had 'coom to the middle of nowhere', having responded to an ad in the *Liverpool Echo*. But the bus parties from the North of England stop her feeling homesick – as she does them. She stood at the door of the dining room wishing them farewell – 'Tarraa', 'Tarraa', 'Tarraa' – after they had stuffed themselves with sausage, bacon, black pudding, tomatoes, mushrooms, fried bread and egg.

At least half of mine, not the egg, was in my napkin already; discreetly stored in my little rucksack under the table in preparation for that day's footstep – or two.

JTR A breath of the morning air, inhaled by a rural leafy road to the east of the village, proved an excellent tonic, and was followed by a leisurely forenoon walk to the Trosachs. I could not leave Callander without stopping by the roadside to sketch in colour the old bridge that crosses the Forth, I saw several brethren of the brush: one had quite a large picture painting in the thoroughfare; it consisted principally of wild flowers …

The glen through which the Lennie and Loch Lubnaig flow merits a visit and may be traversed by rail. The Callander and Loch Katrine tourist coaches passed at full speed, leaving in their rear a cloud of finely powdered dust: this dust rises from the road on very slight provocation, and soon converts him who is dressed in dark cloth into the semblance of a dusty miller. Young men sped their engine-like course, 'doing the Trosachs'. They were too busy to admire the scenery, intent on one object – the accomplishment of a certain mileage within a given time.

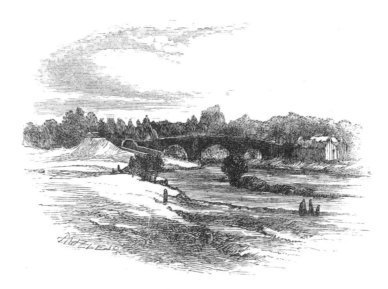

CALLANDER BRIDGE.

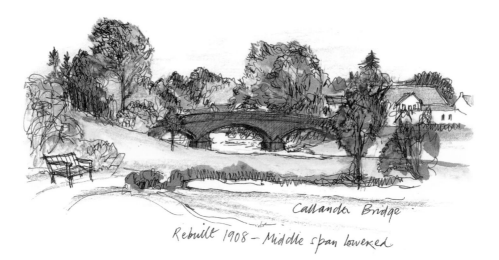

Callander Bridge
Rebuilt 1908 – Middle span lowered

In the interests of accuracy I made for the main road to the Trossachs. To the south of Loch Venachar was a tempting and wooded path all the way to Brig o' Turk. One wood, a local told me, was planted in the battle line patterns of the Battle of Waterloo … But no, I must be faithful to The Route. Even at the risk of life and limb.

I was always taught to walk on the right-hand side of a pavementless road. Some right-hand corners on that road were like a wall of death. It was necessary to zigzag across the road at certain points trying to be as fleet of foot as a heavy rucksack would allow, ears swiveled backwards in apprehension if not in reality like those of the horses that pulled those tourist coaches 'at full speed' over a hundred years ago. Today's coaches go a damned sight faster. How much for my patronising comments on those dotty old oldies. They were now mobile battalions of baddies malevolently ranked behind their bus driver, commanders-in-chief out for the kill.

My vengeful mood inevitably rebounded on old JTR as I kamikazied along. Especially as I discovered on studying the map that the bridge at Callander does not cross the Forth. It is the Teith. Ignoramus! It is very easy for delusions of murder not grandeur to set in if one is a beleaguered road-bound back-packer.

It must also be very easy for travel writers in virgin territory, as JTR undoubtedly was, to pick up local information incorrectly.

But the added sin of committing false fact to the printed page must be every travel writer's nightmare. Unbelievably there is still a kind of reverence for the printed word. 'It was in the papers' being approbation enough for the veracity of anything.

I had reached a lonely house by the lochside near to Brig o' Turk, asking for the site of 'Breadwife's Cottage'. The old retired shepherd was bemused. 'Never heard of it.' His reminiscences of the days of Glenfinglas estate with four shepherds and 'the Boss' belonged to twenty years ago before the glen was flooded as part of the Loch Katrine water supply for the city of Glasgow. The event not only radically changed his life but the landscape that I was about to see. Would JTR be leading me a merry dance again?

Before finding out I had to bed down in Brig o' Turk.

JTR The walk part of the way was by Venachar-side, and shortly thereafter a rustic cottage was in sight: it is the subject of the engraving, the 'Bread-wife's Cottage, Brig o' Turk,' known by this name in the district because the goodwife who lives in it sells bread. Her cottage is a very general place of call for gentlefolks and the common people … Walking tourists have a drink of milk there, and a seat, either out or inside, as they incline. All the countryside seem well acquainted with the shrewd Scotchwoman, who graces her armchair as well as any queen her throne. I was almost forgetting to mention that the cottage and the lady alike can boast a visit on one or more occasions from Royalty, when the Queen spent a season at Invertrosachs Lodge. Artists, too, visit here, and, if civil and she takes to them, they are permitted to sketch the cottage, on condition that herself be not painted …

But it is time I hied me home to my own lodging at Duncraggan Huts …

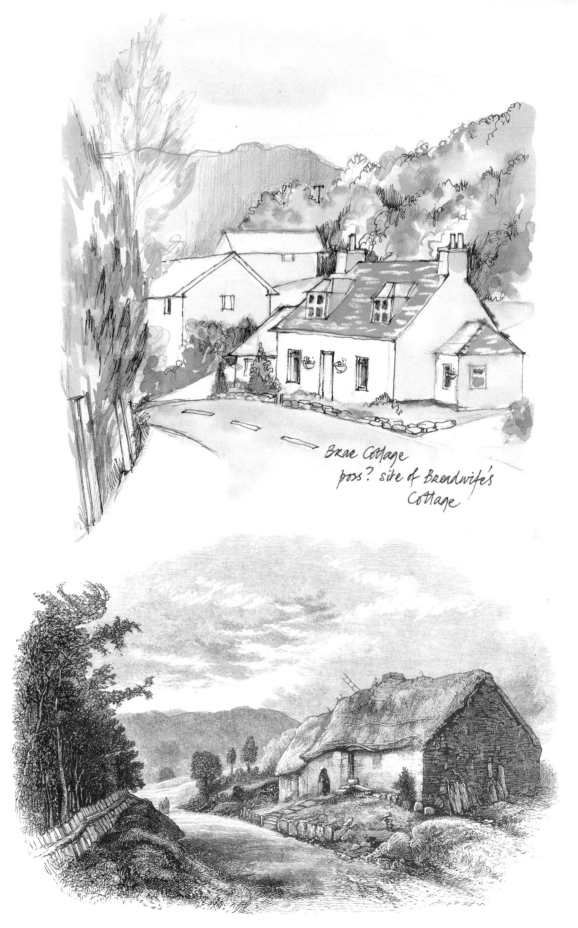

Brae Cottage
poss? site of Breadwife's
Cottage

BREAD-WIFE'S COTTAGE, BRIG O TURK.

Brig o' Turk, and adjoining Duncraggan, is a rebel outpost of certain B&B landladies who decline registering at the Rob Roy tourist centre in Callander. Thank goodness. 'My regulars are coming tomorrow night, dear. But the wee house by the old mill, she might be able to put you up.' Steep staircases and bathrooms that lead off kitchens are not what the tourist office wishes to promote. More fool them. I am all for that evening cup of tea and plateful of devastating carbohydrates in front of the primary coloured nine o'clock news with the previous guests' sheets hanging from the pulley overhead. If registration destroys that genuine sharing of a home with a traveller than I for one will lead a campaign to provide an alternative accommodation register.

The Breadwife's Cottage was difficult to find. Everyone kept mentioning 'Muckle Kate', a giantess of a woman referred to in many local history books; visited by Herself, Queen Victoria, as was the Breadwife, according to JTR. Here I began to wonder at JTR's summations of places visited. He makes no mention of Muckle Kate – or of the famous Brother Brushes that had gone before him. The first cottage that I stayed in was not far along from Yew Cottage where Millais, Ruskin and Ruskin's wife had stayed that wet and cuckolding holiday twenty-three years before JTR's arrival. Not so surprising that JTR did not mention that, given his upright morality. Could I go on travelling with this man and his patronising obsession with the godly, the virtuous and especially the noble, gentle peasant? Even Queen Victoria had a need to sanitise her surroundings. Invertrossachs Lodge was re-named by her to replace the original Drunkie Lodge. Drunkie Loch, for those with a thirst, is up in the forested hills behind, unchanged in name.

'Duncraggan Huts' was a phrase coined by Sir Walter Scott in his Trossachs-based romance *The Lady of the Lake*. It referred to the primitive homesteads of his medieval Brig o' Turk. Victorian artists flocked to the area and lodged, as JTR describes, in just as

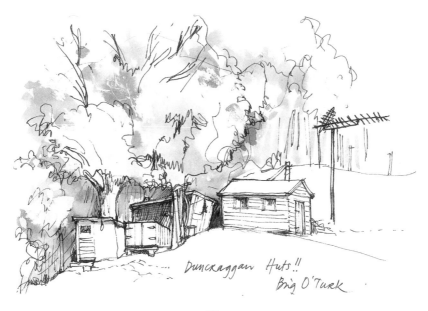

Duncraggan Huts!!
Brig O'Turk

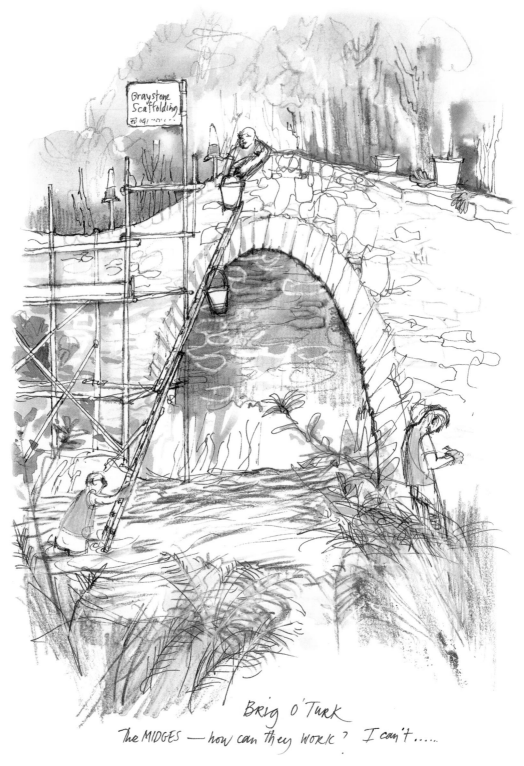

BRIG O'TURK
The MIDGES — how can they work? I can't......

primitive abodes but with much more artistic and anthropological fervour than Scott's huntsmen. The word 'hut' as describing a home somehow always reminds me of Sunday school and those model villages of Africa with real straw roofs and a collecting box inside one of the round papier mache buildings. Did JTR see Duncraggan that way? Was roughing it part of the inspirational experience? Art for Art's sake?

I had a Teasmade and an electric blanket overlaid with linen sheets in my Duncraggan 'Hut'. The stairs were perpendicular; the tiny skylit wood-lined bedroom half the size of the newly extended bathroom with latest shower unit downstairs. I slept like a safe child that night, waking occasionally to blink at the stars through the little cast iron window above my head. What could be more luxurious? And yet I know of at least one Californian lady traveller who would have genuinely deemed such accommodation 'Perrimitive!' Other adventurers, other times. Plus ça change …

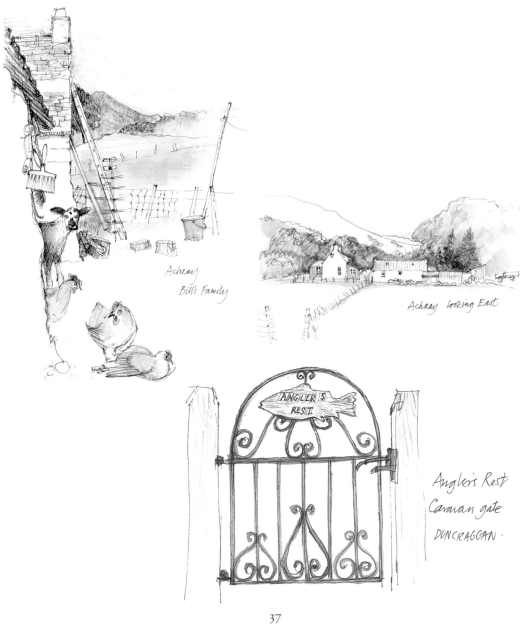

Achray
Bill's Family

Achray looking East

Angler's Rest
Caravan gate
DUNCRAGGAN.

Making for Loch Achray, the next day, I opened a gate for Bill McCabe on his tractor heading to bale hay 'before the weather changed'. The early morning had been grey but by mid-morning sunstroke heat had come through. A seventy-year-old bachelor still working his croft where every homestead in the environs of the Trossachs was either a gallery, a B&B or the country seat of a member of the Scottish Office, he was fierce on the subject of 'the hills'. As a little boy in the twenties, he had gone up the hills with Harry Holmes, a well known Glasgow photographer, for sixpence a day to carry the heavy glass plates.

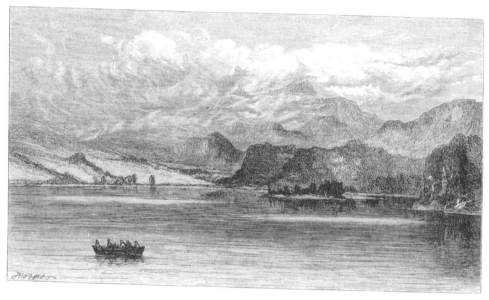

LOCH ACHRAY.

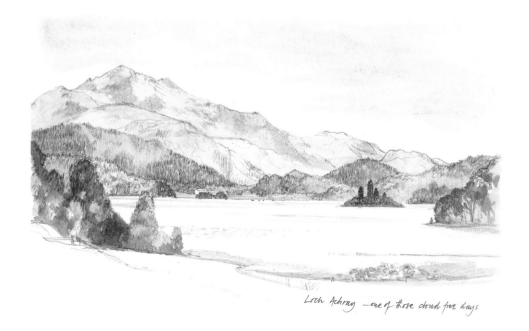

Loch Achray —one of those cloud free days

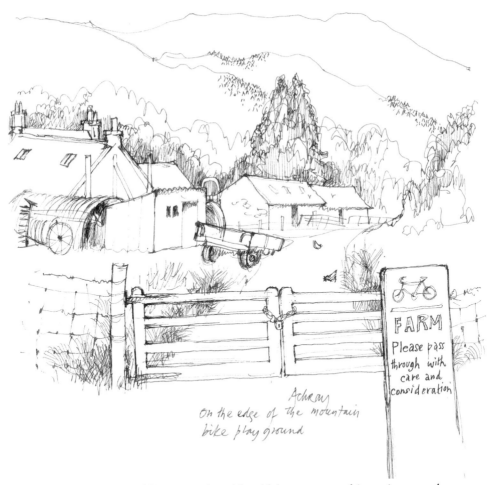

Achray
On the edge of the mountain
bike play ground

I don't think JTR would have employed local labour to carry his equipment; there would have been at least one bucolic, tight-lined drawing of a 'bearer'. But I'm sure other artists of the times would have used the like of young Bill. Brig o' Turk must have been hoaching with Brother Brushes – and a few clandestine Sister Brushes?

'There's too much noise on the hills these days,' said Bill. 'Look up at the Ben [Ledi] and there is always someone on it. Even in winter.'

Despite growing irritations with my mentor, possibly because of growing awareness of being just another member of the visiting hordes, I felt very near to JTR at Brig o' Turk and Duncraggan. Carrying on the Breadwife's tradition is the Brig o' Turk Tearoom. Built of wood in 1923 for the first motorised wave of tourists, 'the nobs', its days are sadly numbered given the sag of its roof and the bouncing of the floor as the local school-aged waiters bring apricot and cinnamon cake to the little tables that have plastic sets of solitaire by the vases of fresh flowers. 'And there is a river running underneath,' said the proprietor.

Customers were most sartorially diverse: the ubiquitous Courtelle and fawn-cardiganed oldies, quartets of Lycra peacock cyclists, sallow French students with well-cut henna-ed hair and a 'Haggis Man' – my son's description, as a little boy, of a tweed jacketed and kilted male of paunch age. Why is it that the outfits of wives of Haggis Men look so anaemic?

39

This hotch potch of travellers all under the same shaky roof, either en route to or returning from the Trossachs, were part of the flowing continuum established by Scott and sustained by JTR and his 'gentility' and now promoted by the Scottish Tourist Board.

Born and brought up on the Clyde I had never visited the Trossachs, avoiding them like the plague on account of their popularity. And here I was, no different from those I took exception to. I was going to have to go with the flow. And to be honest was just as excited now I was nearly there.

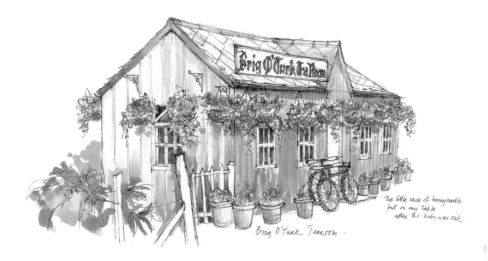

The little vase of honeysuckle put on my table after the baby was sick.

Brig O'Turk Tearoom.

JTR On Tuesday, July 25th, I rose at half-past five – and I am sorry to own this is rather an unusual proceeding on my part – and took a look-out over the landscape as seen from the window of the particular Duncraggan Hut where I was located.

On Tuesday, July 24th 1990, so did I. My rebel landlady had reluctantly agreed to leave out sandwiches on the kitchen table. 'Nothing like a good breakfast to keep you going all day,' she peeved.

I left Brig o' Turk early also because of that 'noise in the hills' and the traffic on the road. I needed to get to Loch Katrine alive. Mist still lay on the low ground. Liquid frost weeped into my boots as I took a short-cut, successfully, through a field. My fingers whitened as I sketched the mist and its magical contouring. Parent oyster catchers woke the village as I dew-dropped my way through their territory.

The bravura of walking on a deserted main road. A wee church came up on the left like a ship floating in the mist. Nature called and country churches often can provide more than spiritual relief. But so often nowadays they are locked – for even the faithful. The key was so artfully hidden I found it easily and after respecting the little church's essence determined to find the 'cludgie'.

My first ecclesiastical Elsan!

I controlled myself and took to the high bracken outside instead. Ghostly horses observed with interest.

The Trossachs Hotel was still abed as I soft-footed past. I recognised the distinctive turrets from Millais' sketchbook. It was a shame they had had such bad weather. For me, 7.15 a.m. by now and a steady warm sun dispelling the ground fog. All silent save the bark of roe deer and the skittering of their hooves over last year's dead leaves in the woods on either side of the road. The rasps of jays or laryngitic cuckoos were soothed by the coo of wood pigeons in the sublime peace before the relentless hum and thrum of cars and coaches to come. A couple of staring forestry vans passed. The human day was starting.

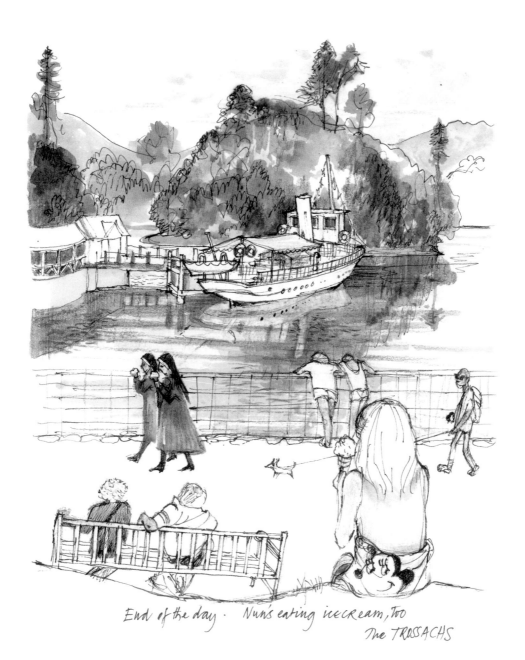

End of the day. Nun's eating icecream, too
The TROSSACHS

JTR Deep-toned velvety lichens mark alike the rocky precipice, the moss-grown boulder, and the birchen stems. Rocks fallen from the heights were deep bedded in the soil; trees slain in the gales lay shrouded in shrouds of more gorgeous tinting than that of mortal man, who is buried deeper; there were dark recesses, where the sun seldom penetrates by a direct ray, and in those shades were posies of tender ferns, verdant tree-sproutings, and pale weak grass; delicate flowerets, rich-toned moss in darkest purple and brown setting; tall rushes growing in stagnant pools of water; heights of rock rising aloft, and tier above tier of trees – mass above mass, leafage, rock, and heather: through such a channel Katrine is reached.

As I walked along the self-same route, twisting and turning through the same dramatic and medieval landscape, I knew I must be getting near to a place of great beauty. Motor car jetsam lined the side of the road: a used disposable nappie, very common – a sure sign, Trossachs car park tickets, snack and crisp papers, cigarette butts. The latter the most indestructible of all.

The car park was fast filling as was the first sailing on Loch Katrine of the elegant *Sir Walter Scott*, built in 1900, the last working screw steamship.

JTR To 'Let Glasgow Flourish,' the silver strand has been wellnigh submerged; only enough of it remains to enable the traveller to discover the place so named. The water-level was raised considerably, and many skeletonized birches stood in weird lonesomeness in the lake, in striking contrast to their gladsome friends, who waved their silvery leaves so sportively above them, rejoicing that the interests of Glasgow have not required their drowning.

Searching for the site of the Silver Strand took me far from the burgeoning crowds.

Glasgow uses more than 240 million gallons of water a day, of which Katrine linked with Glenfinlas supplies 100 million.

Twice the scheme was rejected by Parliament before final approbation in 1855, lead dissolving in the pipes and the silting up of the Forth being the two main objections which interestingly have both come to pass. Now managed by Strathclyde Regional Council, their lorries passed me by loaded with bales of hay for winter feed. SRC is one of the biggest hill farmers in Scotland and employs not only water engineers but shepherds, twelve in fact. Glenfinlas reservoir also produces £35,000 of electricity which is sold to the Hydro Board.

Cold comfort for the old retired shepherd I'd met near Brig o' Turk whose house was deep under the water.

Romantically the Ordnance Survey details the Silver Strand but search as I did in blistering heat I could not get JTR's position. There must have been more flooding.

Stalling going back to the hubbub of the Trossachs Centre and the collection of the big rucksack, I took to the hills above Brenachoile Lodge and found my kind of Trossachs. Just minutes away from that car park with rows and rows of shiny-backed insects where just six hours ago there had been nothing but empty white lined squares on black tarmac.

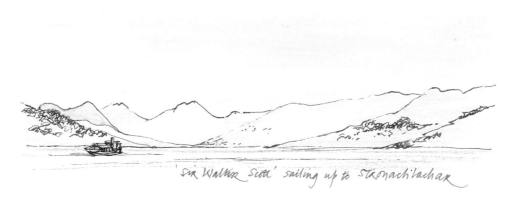

'Sir Walter Scott' sailing up to Stronachlachar

The air was so still I could hear the taped guide on the *Sir Walter Scott* telling for the second or third time that day the tales and legends associated with landmarks. 'And the Silver Strand where the Hunter first viewed the Lady of the Lake is now quite submerged.' I had hunted for nearly two damn hours for that spot. Should have gone on the tourist trip after all. But I would not have been sitting up that hill looking into the far blue of Stronachlacher at the end of Loch Katrine and trying to memorise lines from the little 1871 facsimile copy of *The Lady of the Lake* that I had bought in Brig o' Turk Post Office, would I? Even on that hot, hot day I could feel some of the shivers that must have gone up and down spines when the ballad was first recited in genteel drawing-rooms. Most of the countryside in southern Britain since the enclosures had become tamed.

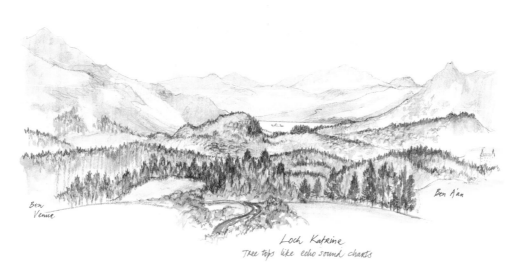

Ben Venue.

Ben A'an

Loch Katrine
Tree tops like echo sound charts

Imagine the excitement of discovering that the Highlands of Scotland were still wild.

As exciting as my own relative discovery that not all that far from the major tourist spots wildness can still be found. But ssh, don't tell anyone …

From Achray to Aberfoyle part of the 'hill path' still exists, winding its way through mature forestry.

Once past the main road and viewpoint at the top of the pass, the forestry tracks become wide and 'organised' with arrowed routes leading down to the David Marshall Lodge, a forestry information and leisure centre high above Aberfoyle. Beautiful mixed woods have myriad trails, all educationally signposted. Some purists believe in nature speaking for itself but I found the discreet panels of information and examples most informative. Like walking with a knowledgeable friend. Especially the living tree with a pile of sawn logs its equivalent weight at its foot representing the .85 tonnes each person in Britain consumes each year. Mind you, no self-respecting Rayburn would leave much else but ash from that pile at the end of a well-fired month but I suppose it was an urban estimate for packaging, printed matter, etc.

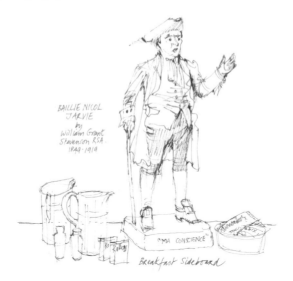

BAILLIE NICOL
JARVIE
by
William Grant
Stevenson RSA.
1849-1919

"MA CONSCIENCE"

Breakfast Sideboard

JTR Bailie Nicol Jarvie is the patron saint of the district; his arms, the red-hot poker wherewith he asserted the dignity of his bailieship; the inn is called by his name; you see him in the tea-cups, in the saucers, on the plates, and in the basin where you wash your face he is seen; and before mine host bids you adieu you fold him into your pocket with your hotel bill; while outside of the inn, attached by iron fastenings to an old tree, is the famous weapon wielded by the worthy bailie (at any rate, we are told so).

The Bailie Nicol Jarvie Inn is now the Hotel, and 'the hot poker', more like a bit of an agricultural implement, does hang from an ancient tree outside. The Hotel could only

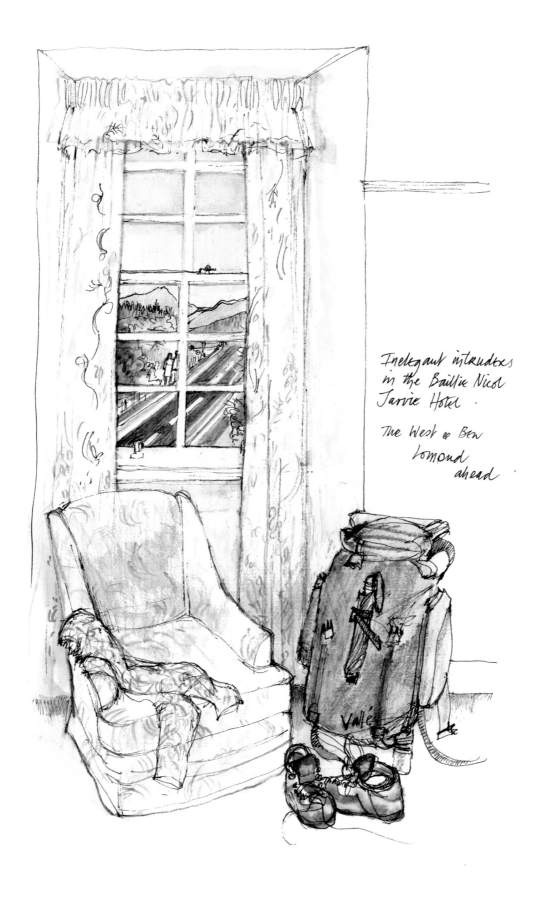

Inelegant intruders
in the Baillie Nicol
Jarvie Hotel.

The West of Ben
Lomond
ahead.

Vallé

offer a double bed and private bathroom. The past two days had been ones of unrelenting heat and twenty-odd miles of walking with that pack; staggering, latterly, over the hill. I took the room, my rucksack and boots incongruous in the chintzy satiny decor.

Aberfoyle is more upmarket than Callander. The Craignure Diner has pale *eau-de-nil* cotton table covers and a wide range of pastas. The athletes' feast, I told myself as I ordered seconds … A well worn Vivaldi 'Seasons' played in the background. Then the slushiest of Mozart piano concertos as the red wine hit the spot and I became obsessed with the young French couple sitting adjacent. Eating alone with a book is a wonderful guise for eavesdropping. One must remember to move the eyes along the lines and turn the page occasionally. There was something very unsatisfactory about their relationship. They ate haggis silently with just neeps. 'Non. Non – pas des pommes de terres.' How could anyone so young, female and French be so pasty and balloon-kneed and wear Dame Edna specs which she seemed to have difficulty seeing through? And he was so handsome with slicked-back dark sultry hair …

My double bed was calling. Mozart played on, high stringed.

Handel's 'Largo', the electronic version, brought me down to earth at the coffee stage. I left them looking at each other and smiling. How could he?

Solace in the Lounge Bar of the Bailie Nicol Jarvie was not forthcoming. The bus party was one of the Col. Blimp and Mavis variety. The women sat at the low little tables and the men came up for the drinks. 'So what's a girl(!) like you doing with a notebook?' accosted one canary-yellow-jumpered Blimp. What could he mean? 'Working,' I heard myself say rather abruptly, but with a smile. 'Ask a silly question and you get a silly answer,' a co-Blimp guffawed behind. They both moved off, ice clinking in their pudgy fistfuls of drinks; back to their 'proper' women who were no threat. One of the wives had on my flowery pants. I just didn't have the additional hair lacquer, support bra showing through the white lacey knit top and shackles of gold chains.

The bus drivers hugging the Snuggery told outrageous tales of the outright lies they told their passengers to keep them from getting bored as they cruised through uninhabited countryside. More likely to alleviate the drivers' tedium and encourage largesse of tips at the end of the trip. 'Did you know that those unexplained ruffles on the surface of Scottish lochs are evidence of water haggis swimming below the surface?' Less ingenious but much more lewd was 'The Cornflake Serial' in which the doubtful proclivities of 'The Sugar Puff' were stretched for miles. 'They believe the bit about the haggises you know.' All three drivers were from England. I think they believed it themselves.

Sitting alone at the edge of the big double bed debating whether to pierce a large blister on the inside edge of my little toe or not, I wondered what the hell I was doing in these awful places with such awful people.

John T. Reid had a lot to answer for …

I had been 'on the road' for thirteen days and the fourteenth day was all road and all sun.

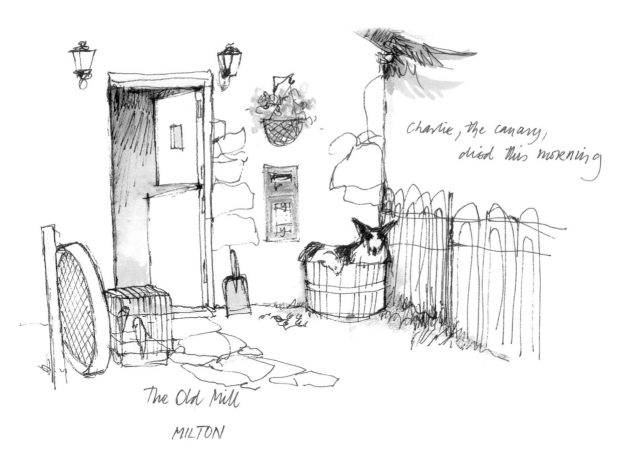

charlie, the canary, died this morning

The Old Mill

MILTON

I tried to pretend that it was 114 years previous as Col. Blimp and Mavis – she still had all that gold hanging off her – waved from the overtaking bus swaying Loch Lomondwards. At least I wouldn't be under the same roof as them that night.

JTR We have for a little distance the windings of the Forth on our left, and the dark steep brow of a Ben I incline to call Ben Dhu from its blackness – a liberty allowable when we find the stream under its shadow named Avon Dhu, on the left. The fields are laden with an ample crop of potatoes and hay; the cottages are weather-stained, and the large windows some can boast show how the south country is weaning our highlanders from their darksome rooms. Gardens by the roadside were clothed with wild flowers and weeds, among which an occasional garden rose shone in singular beauty … The hill beyond the river was crowned with a graceful group of Scotch firs; a cart passed, having a family and a large trunk in it, showing how thoroughly we were out of the coach and the tram route.

Well, John, speak for yourself …

It was strange to still be going up the River Forth, albeit on dry land. There is disagreement whether its source is Loch Ard or Ben Lomond. The Avon Dubh and the Ducharay Water flow from each location respectively and meet a few miles west of Aberfoyle. Their union the birth of the river that flows to the sea. Mrs Seabrook told me that it was still tidal at that point. Flooded fields sometimes. I find that somewhat fanciful

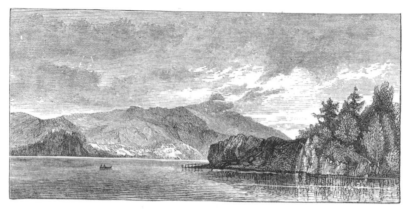

LOCH ARD.

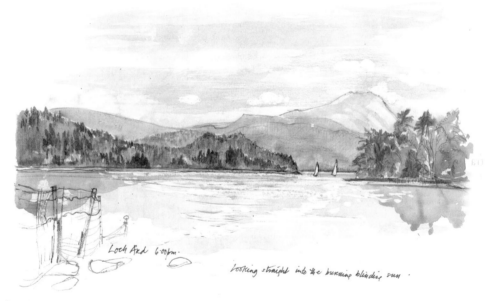

Loch Ard 6·00pm·

looking straight into the burning blinding sun·

but I am no geographer. Her name had maybe something to do with the conviction.

There wasn't much evidence of potato or hay crops, just fallow ground with seeding grass and ponies, and the mill is in a conservation area. How I longed for silver light and a gentle breeze and a passing cart or two. Maybe, like JTR, I would have made it all the way to Loch Lomond. I gave in at Altskeith, a miserly five miles from Aberfeldy, burst the blister and with it the heatwave, for in the middle of the airless night I woke to the sound of a heavy lugubrious summer wind rustling the trees outside the wide open window.

The morning was grey, cool and wide eyed. Indecision hung in the air but with promise of rain and less oppression. Ron of the Postbus would take my big rucksack all the way to Inversnaid on the bonnie banks of Loch Lomond. I felt ten feet tall and so fit as I stepped out light-footed to the end of Loch Ard, past Kinlochard and on to Loch

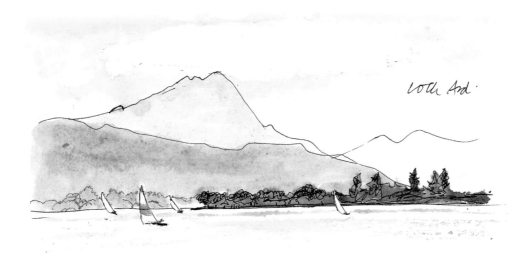

Loch Ard.

Chon. Here I threw accuracy to the rising wind and followed the roadless west side of the Loch.

One-hundred-foot pine trees, the oldest commercial forestry I had come across, blanked out any 'evanescent glimpse of Ben Lomond' of JTR's. There was a very old and trollish path, ridged with crisscrossing roots. The light filtered down green and the wind was high up at the tops of the trees; the only sound down below was the delicate aural tracery of the 'twee-twee' of little invisible birds. On the other side of the loch a family with a rubber dinghy made loud noise, every communication unnecessarily strident; bellows, screeches and yowls echoed round the hills. Like children in a big empty hall

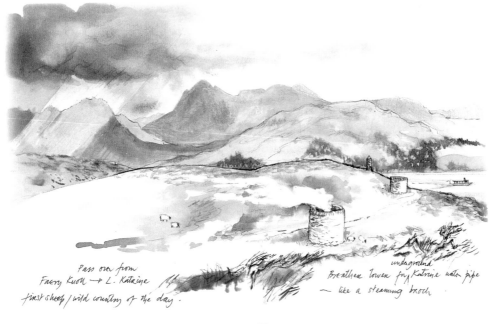

Pass over from Faery Knoll → L. Katrine first sheep / wild country of the day.

undaground Breathex Tower for Katrine water pipe — like a steaming broch

screaming territorial possession. Or were they just disguising their fear of the big wide open spaces around them?

Their jarring voices faded with every step that I took deeper into the other world of the wood that was fast becoming a forest. A little footbridge appeared in a clearing and to the left what seemed like a long open-topped cast iron tank between two tunnels; one coming out, the other going in to the hillside. Climbing up and peering in I expected to see a little train with Puck or the Erl King on the hotplate shovelling pinecones and acorns into the boiler. Instead a steady fast-moving flow of silky water, sometimes eerily slurping, ran on disappearing into the far black tunnel and under the trees on the other side of the clearing. A dinner's worth of a trout swam stationary against the current, occasionally jumping up for the midges that hovered above.

I had come upon the Katrine/Loch Arklet water supply system making its way to Glasgow. Not that long ago engineered (1909–1919), there is no sign left of man's scarring of the landscape. Farther along the path a circular stone and metal grille domed building, man high, stood incongruously, yet somehow quite acceptably, in another clearing. Like a sylvan urinal, watery sounds trickled continuously from below a down-spiralling stone stair guarded by an iron gate. Who would believe that fish were swimming deep down below these strange edifices and, even more unbelievable, below the roots of these tall ancient trees?

Somehow this private discovery was very exciting – there is no indication of a pipeline on the Ordnance Survey; for security reasons, I suppose. Every so often a sandstone marker, like a gravestone for a favourite dog, indicated the way to another breather tower in another clearing. The creepy subterranean gurgle of fast-moving water again. Not a soul in the world knew where I was. Not another foot-track on the path. I hadn't seen or spoken to another human all day.

I'm not ashamed to say I was in my element. The track in the forest crossed over that main road and zigzagged from the Faery Knoll, its very name compounding my fanciful and fancy-free mood, up over Meall Meadhonach to the wild and windy grey moor high above the north-west end of Loch Katrine. The tiny, tiny *Sir Walter Scott* still plied its tourist tack past the distant Silver Strand. Here it was just me and the mountains and – another breather tower. Twice the height of the ones in the forest, it had more the look of a gun emplacement. High on the hillside it eructed white steam which was snatched by the wind and torn into wispy shreds. A steaming broch. MacBeth's witches could have tapped me on the shoulder and I would have joined in with their dance round its granite perimeter.

Up there, on top of Glasgow's water supply it came to me that its citizens' annual pilgrimage to the Trossachs over the past century has not only been for the benefit of lungs and souls but to pay respect to the literal fountainhead of their existence, industrially and domestically. To say nothing of its properties as the very water of their lives – with or without distilled flavouring.

The Trossachs will never become industrialised or become a nuclear dumping

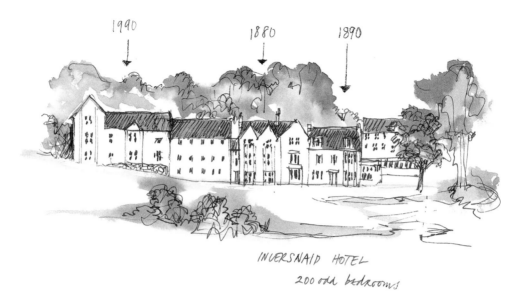

1990   1880   1890

INVERSNAID HOTEL
200 odd bedrooms

ground on account of all that water I could see from my eyrie vantage point. Those who live in the area have very desirable residences indeed. Little white cottages, very few and far between, were almost luminous in the pewter rain-laden light.

It rained the length of bleak Loch Arklet but the soaking was like a Baptist christening and rebirthing after eleven days of dust and despotic sun. That night on the news 'Drought in England' was the main item. Heavy rain fell continuously as I walked down the thickly wooded slope to Inversnaid Hotel and the big rucksack. It was late and there was no room, for which I was glad. Inversnaid Hotel was sold a few years ago by its local sheep farming owner who couldn't cope with the growing number of visitors, despite being on the remote side of Loch Lomond and served by the long narrow twisting road from Aberfoyle. The new owner has lurching tour buses come that way and up from Glasgow via Tarbet; cruisers take decanted coach parties across the loch to the hotel where they are processed in room after room of leather bench seats before being shunted off to minuscule bedrooms for one night. It's the new kind of intensive farming in certain parts of Scotland.

There is nowhere else to stay in Inversnaid.

I was lucky in my drowned-rat state to be adopted by a charming couple who host arts activity holidays in an elegant lodge up the hill from the tourist factory farm. It was the last day of a photography course and I was invited to a slide show of their best work. The tutor had given them specific insect study briefs.

There were lots of close ups; one stunning magnified shot of mating dragonflies, intensely turquoise with silver sequins – dew drops – clinging to a canopy of golden grasses as intricate and precious as a Fabergé jewel. The tutor was very robust in his criticism of everyone's work. This one was not 'as good as it could have been' for all sorts of lengthy technical reasons to do with apertures and light meter readings. The five men and one woman were very polite and supportive of each other's work. All the men came from the south of England: the woman was Dutch. None of them had been to Scotland before. 'The midges are unbelievable!' No wonder, crawling through Loch Lomondside heather and woods. As respite, the tutor had let them go off the previous day to the Bass Rock way over the midge-free East coast; a two and a half hour car journey to a waiting boat at North Berwick – just a quarter more of the distance I had taken fourteen days to walk. Edinburgh seemed as far away as Vladivostok to me. It was obscene that they could travel across Scotland as quick as that …

I must have been moaning on about road traffic. The Dutch photographer, who was a scientist, 'was fed up with the scapegoat of the car. Without them the human race itself is emitting far too many CFCs'. She went on to inform us that the natural gases from the humble cow as it 'burped at one end and er – you know what, at the other' was just as contributory to the 'hole' in the atmosphere as an aerosol can. She believed in bacterial survival. 'Sulphur-eating bugs, that's the answer.' I wondered if one could train midges to eat sulphur. What a lot of problems would be solved! We toasted the idea with more brandy.

It rained all night. Cataclysmic claps of thunder broke the monotony of the downpour. I dreamt of the collective fart of all the dinosaurs. Why has nobody ever blamed *them* for their contribution to the sorry mess the planet has got itself into?

At breakfast next day we all sat around the big table by the window looking out over swollen Loch Lomond. Ben Vorlich was wisped with cloud; the sky exhausted but brightening. Bach's Double Violin Concerto played softly in the adjoining sitting-room lined with books. 'My past,' said Linda who had been in PR with Michael Joseph, the publishers. Commuting had finally got to her and her partner.

Big Dad cat sauntered into the dining-room, rubbing against legs of chairs and guests. When there are no guests he gives a good-morning rub to the stuffed badger by the fireplace.

It was one of those quiet moments before the start of a new day, a new journey, new

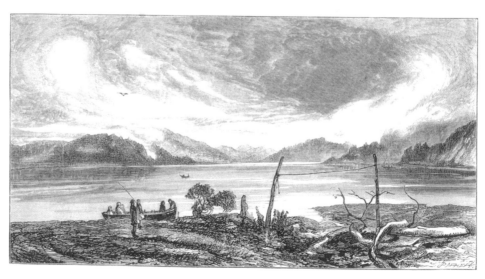

LOCH LOMOND.

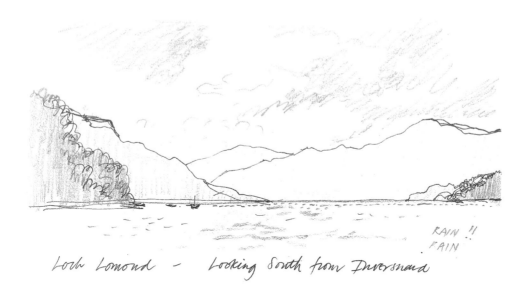

Loch Lomond – Looking South from Inversnaid

people. We would all be hundreds of miles apart by nightfall except for Lorna, her partner and Big Dad and the badger, alone in the Lodge till the next random assortment of visitors arrived.

One day, I thought, when I stop travelling, I will settle down in the house of my dreams and share it with others who will then move on when they have had time enough to stand still and look at the view.

JTR An early boat sailed westward, and I landed at Tarbet, and sought a homely lodging, thinking to settle down for some time; but rain – rain – rain was the song of morning, noon and night, and I saw very little of the pride of Scottish lakes other than its weeping, and learnt to sympathize with those enthusiastic amateurs who rush to spend their one fortnight of holidays in our Scottish highlands, and find St. Swithin at the head of affairs.

The West Highland Way – ninety-five miles of footpath from Milngavie by Glasgow to Fort William – goes straight past Inversnaid Hotel. It has to; the hillside is steep with oak woods. As I waited mid-morning for the boat to take me over to Tarbet a yelling group of young Londoners burst out of the wood from the south. As jubilant and thirsty as if they had walked all the way from London. They were pasty-white despite the heatwave July and looked as if they worked in shops that sold black leather jackets and silver skull and crossbone jewellery despite the brand new walking boots they all sported. Indian silk bandannas and leather-thonged wrists gave a Rambo nuance to newly acquired climbers' shirts. Trayfuls of beer were quaffed on the wooden tables and seats outside the hotel as determined shafts of bright sun kept the midges at bay.

A choppy wind chased the ferry boat over to Tarbet after a detour by Ardvorlich to

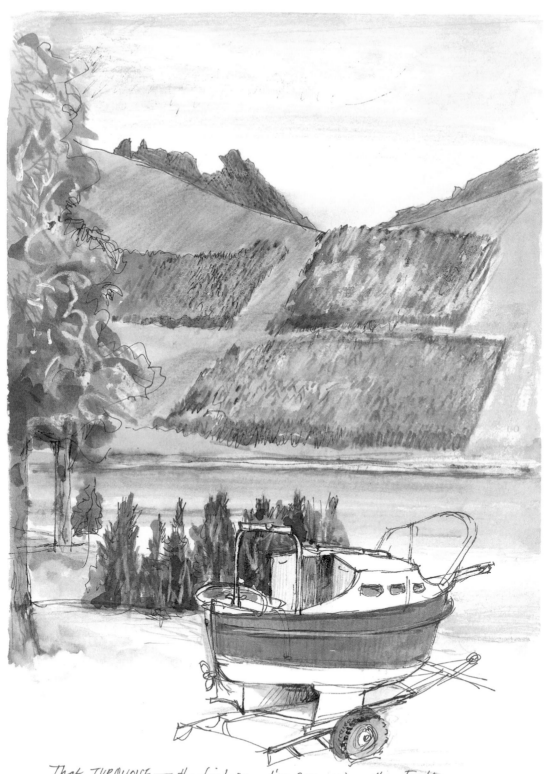

That TURQUOISE — the first sea I've seen since the Forth
a fortnight ago.
ARROCHAR

view the large rock in amongst a wild jungle and tangle of trees and boulders. 'CAVE' was painted on it in large letters. A group of Greek teenagers were told all about Rob Roy hiding there as he fled from the English by the tartan trousered helmswoman. The teacher in charge translated. They looked the way the young do on organised trips with token interest and then reverted to their own peer group landscape. Some of them started to sing Greek folk tunes so sweetly, and possibly nostalgically, as we puttered across the most famous loch in Scotland. What a pity the crossing was so short.

I kept my back turned to the blue-rinsed brigades waiting to embark from the crowded jetty at Tarbet until the last possible minute.

When I landed the violent assault to my wilderness-attuned ears of the past few days made me want to take the next boat back across the loch. It was a Saturday. Changeover holiday let day. The road streaming with arrivals and departures. A B&B sign said 'AYE SERVUS'. I doubted it.

JTR had hoped to sketch The Cobbler, a short walk to view from Arrochar, but the rain had never ceased for him. He quite unashamedly recounts that a 'kindly' Brother Brush 'allowed me to copy his sketch for my "Rambles" ' perhaps indicating that the artist as landscape illustrator last century was a recorder first and foremost and as such, poaching was quite in order.

At Arrochar, the smell of the sea! A west coast sea; the turquoise green of it. The sun had won the battle for the day and The Cobbler – and his wife – looked benignly down on a Quality Icecream booth by the shore.

It had taken me a fortnight to cross central Scotland from coast to coast. I was nearly done – in more ways than one.

The double nougat ice-cream slider tasted delicious.

JTR had taken the boat service from Tarbet down Loch Lomond to Balloch where an excursionists' train and 'a few hours steampower' landed him in Auld Reekie. If I had thought of this project just one year previously I could have done the same but the *Fiona* had given up the run. I took the early evening train from tiny Arrochar station instead, its Victorian waiting-rooms and overhanging eaves appropriate to the last stage of the journey.

Looking back over to the hills behind Inversnaid and treasuring their discovery, I remembered a bit of Gerard Manley Hopkins' poem 'Inversnaid':

> 'What would the world be, once bereft
> Of wet and of wildness? Let them be left,
> O let them be left, wildness and wet,
> Long live the weeds and the wildness yet.'

Unpublished in his lifetime, as was the rest of his poetry, the verse has a poignant relevance to today's great conservation debate. He was contemporaneous with JTR (1889). I wonder if the two of them would have got on well as travelling companions in

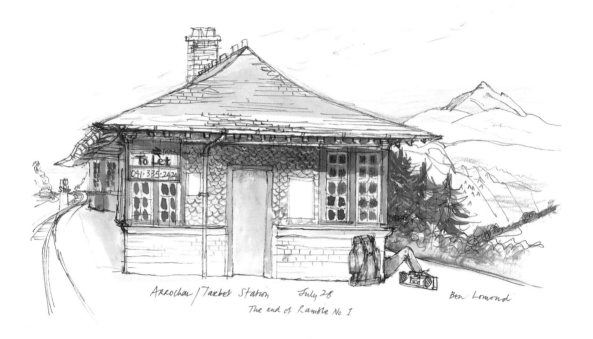

Arrochar/Tarbet Station   July 28   Ben Lomond
The end of Ramble No 1

the landscape they both obviously loved.

JTR and I had come to the end of our first Ramble. We had stuck together despite some
shaky moments.

The hills to the west were going a dusky blue as the train jogged high above the
contours of a sunsilk glittery Loch Long. I will never be in this exact same situation ever
again, I thought, looking over to the promontory of Gourock and the hills of Cowal
starting to silhouette in the sun-dying evening. As a child in that town I remember the
feeling of delicious unrest looking westwards at that very panorama.

Soon the view was passed. Back gardens of houses squashed up against the railway
track, then factory yards, tenements. Suddenly it was all gone. Left behind in the hills.
The Walk. The Ramble. How could the same person be sitting on this train?

A faint new moon was rising in the thin blue sky as we passed through Falkirk.
Travelling parallel to the Firth of Forth but in the opposite direction to the outset of the
journey, the now intimately familiar landmarks of Kincardine, Longannet, Grangemouth
edged the coastline. I even thought I could see the tiny inflatable dinghy and me in it
skimming up the silvery meadow of water. At Linlithgow I could make out the road I
had walked over from Bo'ness on that Sunday *so* long ago. I wondered if the young
invading cob swans were still being hounded backwards and forwards across the Palace
loch.

I was coming full circle. With a rucksack full of his story – and mine.

JTR went home to Edinburgh 'to rest for a couple of days … before making for the shores of Clyde'. He lived with his mother; no doubt she washed and darned his travel-weary clothes while he eagerly thumbed through his notes and sketches and planned the next Ramble.

I went to the Laundrette and bought an Ordnance Survey map of the Firth of Clyde in the newsagent's next door.

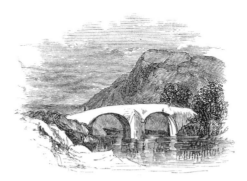

BRIDGE AT ABERFOYLE.

Ramble Two

Tuesday, August 4 – Monday, August 13

GLASGOW · THE CLYDE · BUTE · ARRAN · ARDRISHAIG
CRINAN CANAL · OBAN · STAFFA · IONA · MULL ·
COLL · TIREE

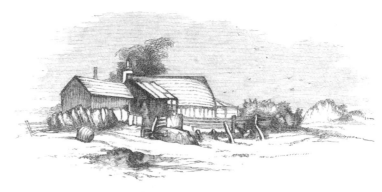

THE BOAT-HOUSE, BRODICK, ARRAN.

JTR A night of restless tossing, snatchings of brief seasons of sleep, and fitful wakings, preceded the morning of my departure for the West Coast. I heard the clock strike each successive hour, and I fear my mother fared no better, for she had promised to wake her (in ordinary circumstances) sleepy-headed son. At grey of dawn my place in Blanket Bay was vacant; the Rambler had left his moorings, and was scudding under full sail, with knapsack and umbrella, for the Caledonian Station at the west end of Princes Street. Nor had he to wait long there for the train running in connection with the sailing of the 'Iona' steamship from Greenock.

My night had been restless too with humid city temperature. The six a.m. news said that the heatwave was to go on. I walked from Newington to Waverley with minimally packed rucksack – I was getting the hang of this backpacking. I marvelled at my new found confidence and discovery – that of the anonymity of the walkers' uniform. I was going places, thinking and doing things I would never dream of in city civvies. Also, hot flushes are quite easily camouflaged with such exertion.

A young paper girl cycled past.

Bus stop queues were long with women of all shapes and sizes. The city day starts as so many homes do with the bustle of women. The sun was a red orange; burnt before the day had really begun. In the station short-sleeved policemen were gently waking rumpled carpets of young people on the mock marble floors.

The train to Glasgow was quiet. Does nobody go to work in Glasgow? Does nobody *work* in Glasgow? 7.45 a.m. August 3rd and the city centre seemed deserted. Those women again but not so many. The men stir earlier in Glasgow; and the women have more brassy outfits. Edinburgh's style and ordered architectural vistas restraining sartorial individuality and voluptuous vowels.

A beggar rooted about in a bin as I walked along the riverside. Edinburgh has its beggars, too, make no mistake. I remember the man with no legs, begging from his wheelchair and the younger man sitting on the pavement with his sad looking dog and a carboard sign saying 'Hungry and Homeless'.

Great drops of rain started to fall. The West Coast. Near to a seedy looking ship with a night club neon sign 'Tuxedo Princess' were a group of lags, lagerlags, with prematurely wizened faces and warped shoulders, toasting the new day. A young well-spoken Englishwoman was in their midst. She talked loudly about 'last night' and the millionaire that had slept with the group under the bridge. Was she doing sociological research? And who was the millionaire? Another philanthropist? Yet somehow she was very much part of the group and her loudness underlined yet another lost soul. She aggressively took her turn when the can came round; the men's rheumy eyes watched her every move.

A mild incident compared to that of JTR's musings on alcohol abuse en route to the West Coast. His port of departure was Greenock.

JTR Greenock does not seem a very inviting place for the pleasure-seeker at any time; in rainy weather its attractions are not heightened. It is ever associated in my mind with a scene I witnessed there many years ago. It was the evening of a fortnightly pay Friday, and the working people, who had spent a per-centage of their earnings in the public houses, were gathered *en masse* in front of the railway ticket office, to purchase tickets for the 'stand-up carriages' (carriages in which there were not seats), to convey them to Glasgow; they hooted, yelled, swore, crushed, and fought like fiends, and the depraved look engraved on many faces made one shudder. When we see sin unmasked now and again, and reigning even for a minutes unrestrained, we get a faint idea of its extreme hatefulness and loathsomeness. Surely the way of transgressors is hard, and stands out in striking contrast to the ways of the Lord, which are experienced by those who walk therein to be pleasant and peaceful.

No wonder Salvation was a Blessed Thing … Blessed indeed, dear John, given your own youthful misdemeanours … Remember the incident of the 'poisoned' shepherd?

JTR I had not in those days looked at the real aspects of the drink question – had not seen the responsibility that rests on each one to be guiltless in regard to that which is sapping our country of some of its brightest intellects, and killing numbers of her sons possessed of generous impulsive natures. And so, a brother artist and myself, starting for a painting campaign, had in our store a bottle of Highland whiskey, labelled by my friend, who was a Highlander, as a precautionary measure – 'Turpentine.' This bottle was the feeder of the pocket-flask, and the cup we used was sometimes used for real turpentine in cleaning brushes or like work. When wandering over the hills we met a shepherd, exchanged courtesies, and offered him a glass. He drank it gladly, asking no questions. The factor, who was with us, asked him, in Gaelic, if he knew what he had taken. He told him it was turpentine. The shepherd grew pale and left us at once, and tried to rid his stomach of the dread stuff, and thereafter went home to his bed, expecting to die. We called at the cottage at night, and found he was very ill, and it was not till the factor assured him he was joking, and that he had swallowed none other than the best of whiskey, that he rose from bed, and Donald was himself again.

John, your present temperance is admirable but, selfishly, I am comforted by your inclusion of that awful tale. It somehow excuses my necessary but mild intemperance after one of your punishing walks.

Housing conditions in Greenock in JTR's day were some of the worst in Britain. The Census of 1861 reported that 'In Scotland there are 7,964 houses without windows and 226,723 houses of only one apartment, proving that nearly one million of the people of Scotland, or one third of the entire population, are living in houses of one room.' The Smithston Poor House and Asylum was just being built in Greenock the very year that JTR rambled through. Despite, or rather because of, the heyday of the shipbuilding on the Clyde and the ever increasing commercial traffic through the port of Greenock, the area had become a magnet for unemployed, and especially the 'cleared' peoples of the Highlands and Islands. Conditions of work and accommodation were enough to drive anyone to drink. The first Temperance Society in Scotland was founded in Greenock in 1829. It obviously wasn't succeeding too well.

As I walked past my contemporary 'transgressors', cloaked in the anonymity of the backpack, I felt strangely more at one with the old lags' displaced condition than with the multi-hued raincoated and umbrella-ed Glaswegian families queuing to go aboard the *Waverley* paddle steamer for their day 'doon the watter' to Rothesay. This was as far as I could get by water. JTR went all the way in the *Iona* to Arran.

The *Waverley* is the last paddle steamer to be built on the Clyde. 1947 saw her launched from the Kelvin yard and she is now the last sea-going paddle steamer in the world, faithfully paddling the old route down the Clyde and out to the islands of the west when there are enough tourists to cram her nostalgic upper decks and saloons. A nearly full complement of 673 passengers cast off from the city dock this day, dark with continuous rain. Lights were on on the Kingston road bridge soaring over the murky river.

She moved fast down river, the comforting throb of her engines arrowing out wash to be broken on each bank side.

The tree-lined city embankments, riverside walkways and yuppiefied warehouse flats soon gave way to deserted shipyards. By the late sixties most of the grand old names in shipbuilding were no more. Our guide could point out one ship just completed however in Yarrow's yard. They had a Navy contract for F231 frigates.

'That's whaur yer Uncle Wullie works,' said a dad, proudly. We all waved at Uncle Wullie, in spirit if not in the flesh. The cold grey of the newly painted hull would soon be doing trials off the Isle of Arran. Would Uncle Wullie go for the ride?

An Air Canada plane came low over the river in line for Glasgow airport. I felt that the majority of the people on the *Waverley* were more familiar with that form of travel. Uncle Wullie's uncles and great-uncles long since departed Clydeside for the New World 'over the pond' and many times visited for holidays, with maple leaf tea-towels pinned up on Govan kitchen walls to prove it.

The *Waverley* puttered down the still narrow river like a little terrier keen to get to the open fields of the Firth and the sea beyond. Men on wharves waved, cranes flashed their lights, golfers on the port side, beyond the gold of corn beginning to catch the lightening sky, waved their clubs. Opposite, to starboard, the blue cranes of John Brown's, nothing moored alongside the bleak piers but two swans. But the giant meccano structures further inland were two half finished oil rigs, the guide reassured.

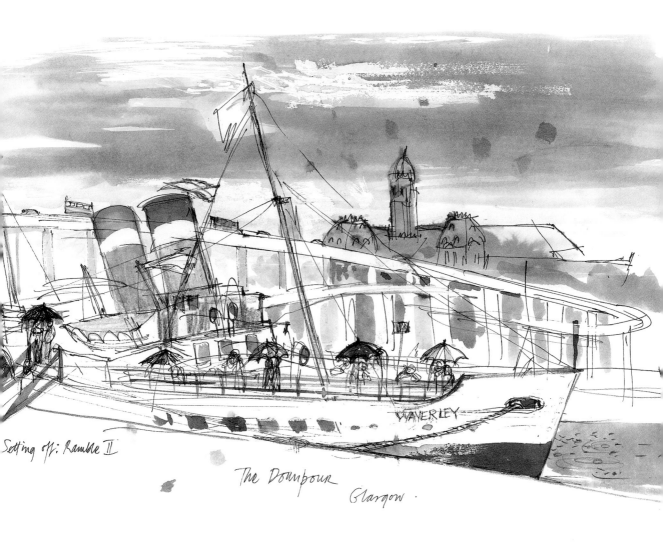

Setting off: Ramble II

The Downpour
Glasgow.

The river banks, increasingly rural with grazing Friesian cows, were thick with yarrow, appropriately enough, and Michaelmas daisies.

Somewhat incongruously, an accordian started playing 'The Northern Lights of Old Aberdeen' as we passed under the Erskine Bridge, thin and elegant as the still herons by the side of the now slowly widening river. It had started to rain heavily. 'Smashing Rothesay weather,' said one of the crew. The Glaswegians guffawed; the few odd American couples with see-through macs and dripping noses smiled politely.

In amongst Esso petroleum storage tanks on the north side of the river a high Cleopatra Needle by old fortifications marks the memorial to Henry Bell whose *Comet*, the first commercially successful steam ship, was launched on the Clyde in 1812. What a dynasty of beautiful, beautiful ships he started. The guide should have made us all stand to attention and salute.

A brisk wind was blowing up from the Tail of the Bank. Down below in the engine room it would be warm. I remember as a child growing up in Gourock almost living on ships like the *Waverley, Duchess of Hamilton, Jeannie Deans, Saint Columba*. In fact when older I was a snack bar attendant on the *Duchess of Hamilton* and fell in love with Harry, the student purser, as he with me. He emigrated to New Zealand. I still have his letters …

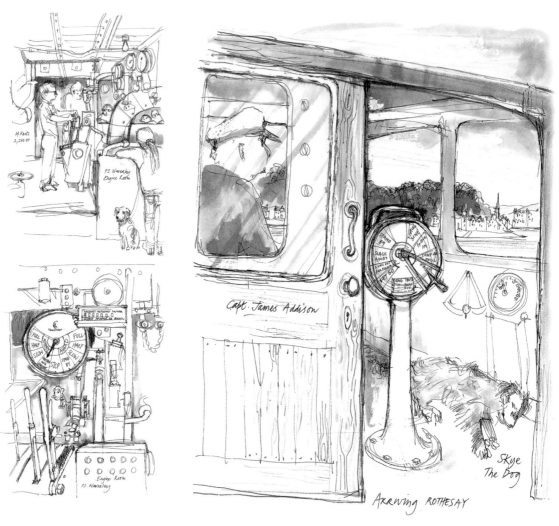

Capt. James Addison

Skye The Dog

ARRIVING ROTHESAY

The engine rooms and engineers of the *Waverley* and the *Jeannie Deans* however were fatal attractions too. And here I was, thirty-odd years on, still hypnotised by the great shafts of power, the paddle portholes thrashing like demented washing machines, the engines so straightforwardly mechanical they are almost comprehensible. As a small child my nose just tipped over the protective barriers. The engineers quite terrified me; like angels in hell with their white overalls. Then came embarrassing memories of adolescent elbow lounging over the self-same barrier. Now at last a brazen middle-aged hussy I enveigled my way right into the engine room, sweating with delight as I sketched shining brass, rachetted levers and big end bearings. Through the communicating voice tube I was invited up to the bridge. Thirty years' worth waiting. I had never had such elevation before.

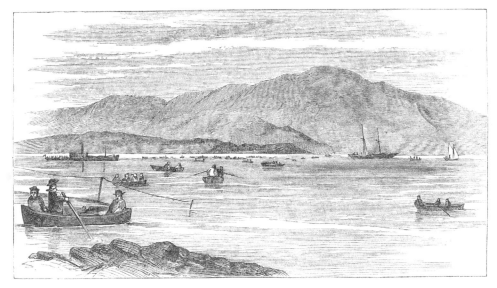

ROTHESAY BAY.

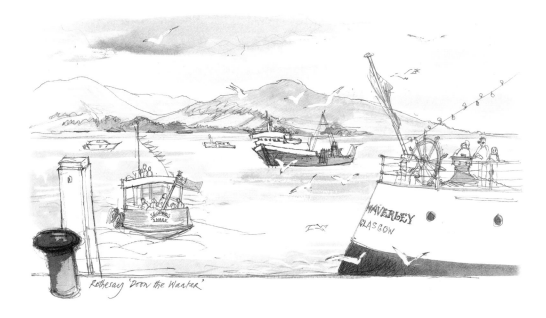

Rothesay 'Doon the Watter'

JTR The sail was only too short, and after rounding Toward Point, we steamed slowly into Rothesay Bay, whose shipping and surroundings brought to us manifold reminders of city life: it was a strong contrast to the quiet of the Arran hills towering heavenward above the encircling wreaths of mist. ... All spoke here of man's work – his enterprise, his pleasure; stately hotels vied with one another, handsome shops displayed in their windows all the luxuries one might expect in the great cities of the realm. There was considerable shipping traffic; many wheeled vehicles mingled with the throng of foot passengers. There were untold numbers of pleasure boats ... There was a museum on the southern shore, and the coast was lined by terraces of comfortable villas; a band-stand occupied a prominent place on a new promenade ... and at dusk a large crowd thronged round to listen to the music ministered to them by a company of musicians that some call in Scotland a 'brass band'.

The island abounds in pleasing scenes, and a season may be well spent there by those who desire to live near city comforts. The 'Iona' – D. Hutchison and Company's famed steamboat – calls each morning on her way to Ardrishaig *viâ* the Kyles of Bute and Loch Fyne.

JTR and I parted company at Rothesay; he to go on to Arran on the *Iona* and me to zigzag over there via Wemyss Bay and Ardrossan ferries. He made his way to Bute a few days later.

Our approaches were from very different angles in time and geography but almost identical in impression. After a disastrous period of neglect when Glaswegians preferred the Costa del Sol to this island of Bute abounding 'in pleasing scenes', the 'stately hotels' and 'comfortable villas', though older and a bit worn, are sprucing themselves up as the visitors, still almost exclusively Glaswegian, are coming back. Fleets of modern-day replicas of those old boats might grace the waters of the Firth of Clyde yet.

The car ferry to Arran was full of tourists and, being Friday evening, city commuters who made a determined beeline for the bar before the weekend golf louts took all the elbow room. It is a short crossing to Arran. The queue stretched far out of the bar into the companionway and the mood and manners were reminiscent of the Greenock fiends JTR took such exception to. He would have been quite appalled at the class of some of these 'fiends' with city suits unbuttoned and slack ties askew.

We were enumerated off at Brodick which is still the 'tourist centre for exploring the island, and is in daily communication with the mainland ...' A friend collected me and whisked me away to a quieter part of the island. Her home nestles by the foot of a burn; and she is a Sister Brush and the weekend was full of her friends, music, long walks and talks. But nothing could ever compare to the delights of JTR's landlady and accommodation ...

JTR As we neared Arran the clouds became denser, and in turn cast deep shadows over the Firth and the Arran coast, or were lit up with a glow of intensely bright sunlight … On landing I sought for the cottage occupied by the Duke of Hamilton's piper, in which some friends had found most comfortable quarters the season before. I found it preoccupied by a little company of artists, either professional or amateur, who made use of the rainy day by camping in the coach-house to sketch from its shelter a fine group of trees … The piper's little girl was mounted on horseback, and dispatched to Brodick in quest of a lodging, and returned with the news that there was a spare room at the 'Boat-house'. The Boat-house became my roosting-place while under the shadow of the mighty mountain of the wind, 'Goat Fell.' The lady of the house loved to be called by her Christian name, *Martha*, and she was not without traits in her character we are prone to associate with the name. She was

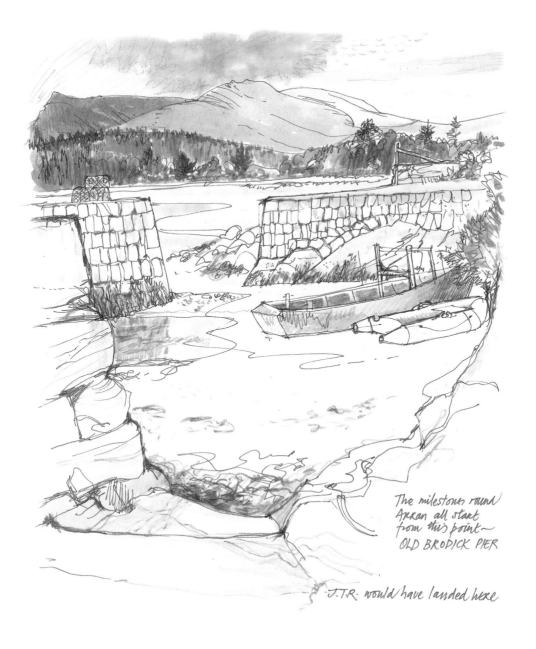

The milestones round
Arran all start
from this point ~
OLD BRODICK PIER

J.T.R. would have landed here

careful and troubled about many things. In the summer season her troubles were born of her prosperity. Like the woman famed in the bairns' rhyme, 'who lived in a shoe, and had so many children she did not know what to do,' Martha in her Boat-house kept so many lodgers – the cooking of meals, making of beds, and washing of linen for such a host made her often remark, 'I have so much wark, I dinna know what to do first'; and then she had a husband to work for. 'There's poor Archie, he canna dae a han's turn for himsel', and I've to earn every bite o' bread he eats.'

Yet Martha was a woman of courage, and she succeeded nobly in satisfying her hungry lodgers with wholesome fare, and spreading for them sheets a prince might fold around him … Her castle was quite unique in regard to construction, and the site was a novel one. It was built so very near the sea that it had narrowly escaped being carried away in high tides, and doubtless would have been altogether afloat but for its having a foundation of some two feet and a half of stone.

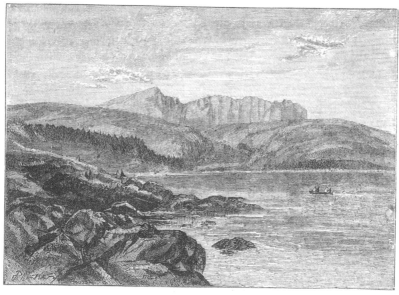

GLEN ROSA MOUNTAINS, FROM BRODICK BAY, ISLE OF ARRAN.

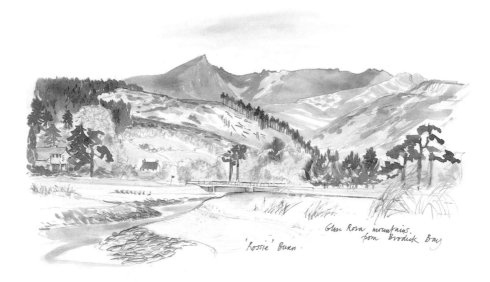

'Rossie' Burn.

Glen Rosa mountains.
from Brodick Bay

Dear old Martha had much of the milk of human kindness about her; she had pensioners who shared with her such things as she had: one was a lame robin redbreast, who came and sat on a bush opposite the door till he was fed; another was a pigeon whose cot was quite a mile away: she too looked for a meal on every visit … From the sketch my reader will discover why this sea-cot was called the Boat-house: an upturned boat forms the roof, and under this roof is the but and the ben, the kitchen and the parlour, each boasting its own snug bed-box. The kitchen had one small window, the parlour two, one looking out over Brodick Bay, the other inland; joined to this main building were various outhouses, each having a door, a window, a box-bed, a small deal table, a candlestick, and a wash-basin of its own: these were let for the most part to single gentlemen, though now and again she had also lady lodgers. The surroundings were full of interest: in the foreground we had Martha's pig-store, where she kept a varied assortment of china and earthenware; it also was roofed by the remains of an old pleasure boat; Martha's cabbage garden and potato plot, and Martha's hen-house, where the roosters were alike honoured by having a boat-house of their own.

I tried and tried to find out who Martha was. So often on this project even the oldest locals interested in what I was doing had no memory, actual or handed down, of the people mentioned by JTR. Conversely their own recorded tales of well-known characters of that era, JTR makes no mention, like Muckle Kate in Brig o' Turk. The Highlands and Islands were vastly more populated then and 'characters' must have been two a penny.

Martha certainly takes some beating. I would have loved to have stayed in her Boathouse despite the eight-inch snail with head and horns buried in a roll of butter in the larder in the morning and his relatives 'who had a provoking way of paying nocturnal visits, and wandered between the wooden walls and the loosely fixed paper that decked the walls …'; the family of mice and the 'sagacious hen' that laid her eggs in the corner of the hole in the wall designated as a cupboard.

I found the site but only the snails were visible in the sandy dunes at the edge of the golf course. An old trading smack hull showed its bones further down the beach. Hamiltons built these boats here last century and my own Crawford forebears from Corrie worked one of them, the *Betsy Crawford*, back and forth to Ardrossan. Did they know Martha?

Harvey Pitcher, doing research on nineteenth-century Arran writers and painters and especially on the wealthy Muir family who rented houses for many years on Arran, has given me this delightful little gem. 'Alice Muir,' he writes, 'was a homeopathist and in 1878 treated old Mrs McNeil at the Boathouse in Brodick so successfully that two years later the latter presented her with an engraved tumbler glass.' It's *got* to be Martha! Despite Harvey Pitcher's reservations as to Martha's ability to afford such a gift, I'm sure it is just the kind of thing she would have engineered as a token of thanks. Possibly JTR got it for her in Edinburgh? He might even have engraved it.

It is just as well that I am not a serious researcher of times past. I got a bit carried away with Martha and dallied in the Arran Heritage centre over long – 'Everyone wants to know about the past and *it is too late.*' The elderly female attendant almost shouted. I thought she was angry with me. But no. 'If only I'd listened to the old folk telling their stories.'

Do we ever?

JTR At the Boat-house again another ramble simmering. I unfolded to Martha my design of starting at dead of night for a walk round the north of the island. This she protested against

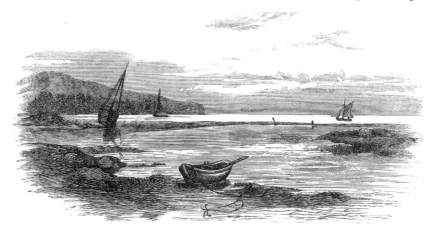

DAYDAWN, BRODICK BAY.

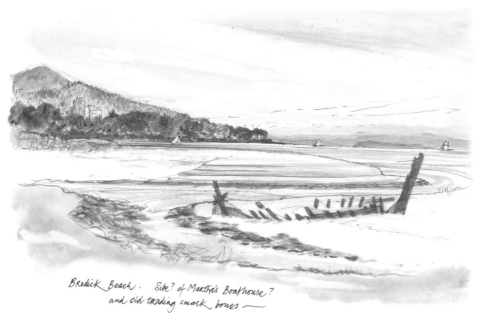

Brodick Beach. Site? of Martha's Boathouse?
and old trading smack bones —

very strongly, on the ground that she had known many missed and some murdered who essayed to travel round that way in the night; not that she thought such dark deeds as robbery would be perpetrated by any of the islanders, 'But you see, sir, the island is very near the sea, and all sorts of men are sailing round about, an' when they've spent all their own earnings on drink, it's hard to know what they'll no' do to try and get more.'

So I was persuaded, and planned a start at dawn.

I wasn't very faithful to JTR's timings and routes whilst on Arran as my own 'landlady' had powers of persuasion, too, in a different kind of way. Fitting in with her hectic social agenda I was most conveniently dropped off and picked up by car.

Staying with friends on these kinds of wanders can be very disorientating. Prior to Arran I had walked long days sometimes speaking to no one and moving through completely new landscapes. Every impression sharply registered and the thread of my progress and purpose unbroken. And that anonymity, that protective aura, intact. Like the writing on the wall, the hand having writ moves on …

Arran I have known since childhood; my hostess not only a friend but a colleague. No room for cyphers here. And no early nights either. But it is good to be reminded of who one is in relation to others who know a bit of one's past; where one 'is coming from'. After a while, travelling alone can lead to a loss of identity. First meetings are not followed up, relationships not developed. That of course can be one of the joys of travel. But as in all things a balance gives the best of both worlds. Are all travel writers but schizophrenics, indulging in their disease?

It was early evening when we visited Corrie. Alison was performing with the Inglewood String Players as part of Corrie Capers Week. I had to come along. I was glad that she was not taking part in the Mini Marathon though the Lantern Workshop looked fun.

The warm gold interior of the wood-lined church was the venue for a 'Come and Bawl your Hearts Out' hymn singing celebration. The audience stood jampacked. The old familiar hymns from childhood comforted everybody. In between the Players played – to give us a chance to get out breaths back. There was a charming and I thought authentic baroque quality to the musicians' solos. 'A scratch group, literally,' apologised Alison afterwards to myself and her other house guest, a Dutchwoman, en route from a healing course on Iona. As the Dutchwoman and I waited for the musicians to gather themselves she commented on the sea symbols of fish and anchor in the nave.

'Christ was a Pisces,' she said, assuring us that she had read several books on the subject explaining the importance of the fish in Christian religion.

'Well, all I can say is that there is a whole lot of bloody sheep as symbols as well in the Christian religion,' said Alison as she packed up her 'baroque' fiddle. My hostess was not a believer, I'm afraid, John.

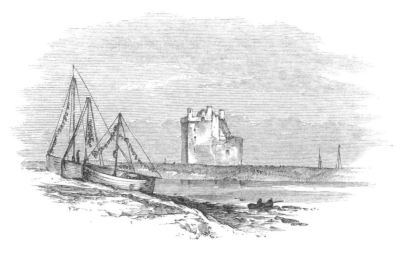

LOCH RANZA CASTLE, ISLE OF ARRAN.

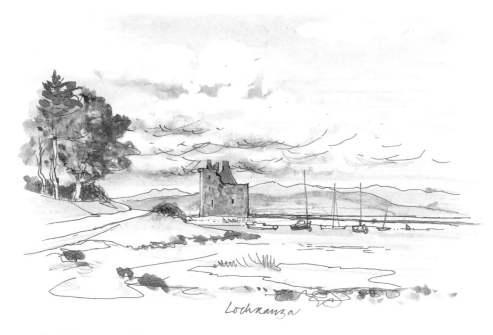

Lochranza

JTR Loch Ranza opened to us a complete change of scene: there were houses, a church, an inn, and even the old castle was allowed to retain its site, and guide the fishers in their homeward course. The fishing-boats had landed the catch of the night, and were spreading their nets on the tall masts erected for drying them over …

My fifteen miles' walk had whetted my appetite, and therefore I looked with no angry gaze on Ranza Inn, and, despite the large company of tourists airing themselves outside, I made inquiries for breakfast, and was told it would not be ready for an hour (it was now nine o'clock). This hour I spent in sketching Ranza Castle.

By this time the families staying there for summer quarters were out for a forenoon walk: mothers, nurses, playful youngsters – some with towels for the bathing, others with picnic baskets, making for the cliffs or the shore. A lone grave, the resting-place of one who had died at sea, lay at a point of land under the shelter of a rugged knoll: the grassy mound was decked with a cross of white stones, and at either end an unhewn rock was placed to mark the spot as sacred; and on the taller stone was a square patch wheron the remains of an inscription that bore a roughly-drawn cross and an anchor, and the fact J. M'L. died at sea – all else defaced.

When JTR returned to the Boathouse that night he 'had walked thirty-five miles, and had given a place in the sketchbook to eight subjects.' I had been quite spoilt by now and anyway I had had my fill of walking alongside modern-day roads, so I took the bus to Lochranza. Arran buses have printed timetables but, as in all islands, clocks are set to boat times and it was a long wait. The boat was late because the train was late …

At eighty-three, Miss Kerr is one of the oldest inhabitants in Lochranza. The Post Office said that she wouldn't mind a visit. I was wanting to identify JTR's cottage sketch. Her parents would have been children when he wandered past their door. She is cruelly twisted with arthritis but her spirit is livelier than a young lass's, more concerned for an old friend in Lamlash who has the same complaint – that dread West Coast damp – and is quite unable to move. 'A terrible thing, that. Living on her own and her such a great walker.' She was quite unaware of any comparison to her own condition. Old Ranza, a very large and mostly white collie, sighed by her chair as she hummed and hawed at the cottage sketch. 'It's either *Seaside Cottage, Fair Dell* or *Braeside*.' We looked out over the bay to the houses directly opposite. 'Now who you should speak to is … ' And she reeled off several names and exact addresses and sent me on my way: Kerr ('Everyone is related to Kerrs'), MacMillan, Mackinnon, Lowe.

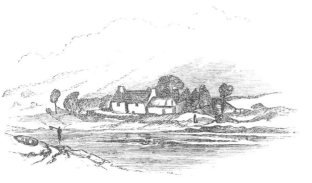

COTTAGE AT LOCH RANZA, ARRAN.

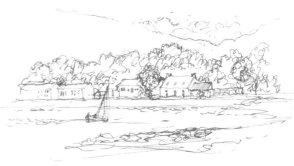

BRAESIDE – 'Only one to have byre to the one side'

The whole afternoon was spent meandering in and out of the welcoming homes of Miss Kerr's ageing contemporaries. All a ploy on her part, I'm sure, to help pass their day. 'It must be *Braeside*,' said Mrs MacMillan. 'It was the only one to have the byre on the right side.' They all remembered the days when Lochranza was daily served by pleasure steamers and all the houses filled with 'the gentry', the locals decamping to huts and sheds in back gardens. Lochranza has been ignored in recent years since the only crossing to Arran is now at Brodick. But a ferry over to Claonaig on the mainland of Argyll runs from Lochranza in the summer and the tourists are coming back. 'But we don't have many holiday houses lying empty for the better part of the year,' said one local, proudly. There is a kind of insularity at Lochranza cut off from the Corrie side by the great glens and hills of Sannox and on the other side by the long wild uninhabited coastal stretch to Catacol.

It is interesting that JTR noticed J. McL's graveyard on that wild shore road and that it was defaced. There is only one tall stone standing now and no white cross on the cairn-like mound of loose stones. A hand inscribed concrete block says 'A Sailor's Grave. Here lies JOHN MCLEAN. Died Aug. 1854'. I met the middle-aged son-in-law of the man who, a generation ago, had carved the block. Why so much effort so long after the event? 'Don't know,' he said dismissively, and turned to the tele on the wall in the Catacol pub. End of story. Sometimes you meet locals that are brimming with tales to tell the tourists. Like well primed pumps – but in need of a 'top up', just a wee one, of course – they latch on to the wide-eyed visitor. Others quite obviously can't stand the repeated and endless questioning.

J. McL died at sea of the plague. He had made his best friend aboard promise that he would not be buried at sea – something he had a great fear of – but on land. The ship steered into Lochranza; the inhabitants had heard of the boat with plague aboard and would not allow the body to be brought ashore. Even the dead in the graveyard denied his soul peace for fear of infection.

Under cover of darkness, the friend took the body ashore and, on that lonely west-facing beach far from human habitation, the shallow grave was dug.

I still wonder at the curt response to my query. Is there still a residual guilt in Lochranza about J. McL?

The surrounding short-cropped grass with magnificent sunset views and easy vehicle access makes the spot a favourite stopover for campervanners and tenters. Do they know who lies beside them the long night through, under the overhanging cliffs recorded in the Guinness Book of Records as having the only sunless spot in Britain, summer or winter?

JTR Early in the day these westward-looking cliffs were in shadow, and a grateful shade it proved, for the sun's rays were exceedingly powerful. Sandy bays invited the bather to plunge in the clear cool waters; boating parties found no breeze to fill the sail, and rowed lazily around the coast. A solitary fern-gatherer was filling his basket with specimens. A wooden mansion was quite an inviting residence: it consisted of the saloon of a large ship that must have been wrecked in the neighbourhood.

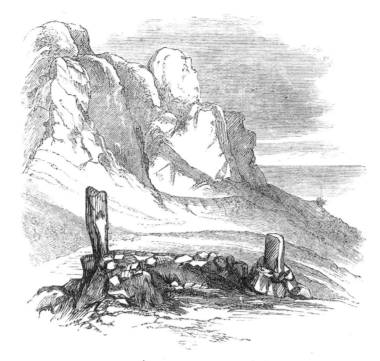

SAILOR'S GRAVE, WEST OF ARRAN.

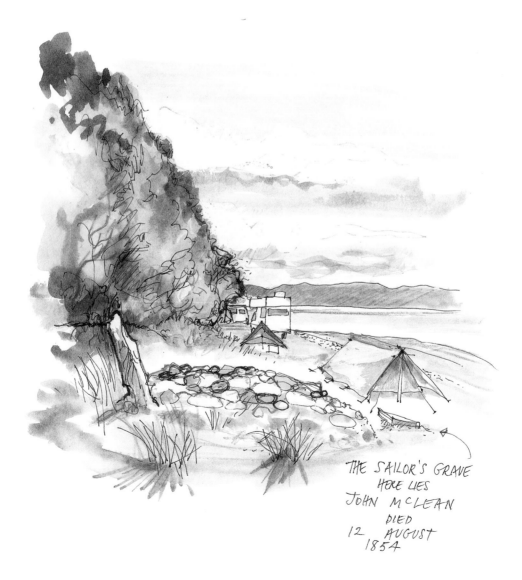

THE SAILOR'S GRAVE
HERE LIES
JOHN McLEAN
DIED
12 AUGUST
1854

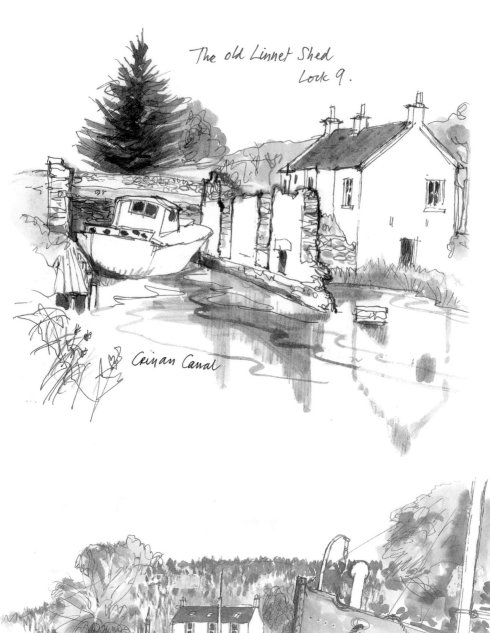

The old Linnet Shed
Lock 9.

Crinan Canal

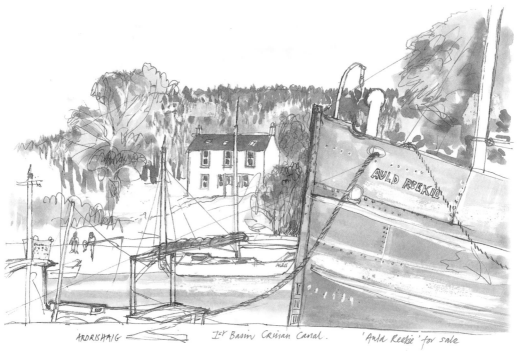

ARDRISHAIG   1st Basin Crinan Canal.   'Auld Reekie' for sale

Of the wooden mansion there was no evidence and no folklore to confirm. Neither are there any sandy bays on that coastline, the sand having been extracted for the development of the Sloy Hydro scheme on the mainland.

How transitory are the most apparently substantial things.

JTR travelled on to Bute on the *Iona* and thence through the Kyles of Bute to Ardrishaig on Loch Fyne where passengers transhipped for the continuing boat journey through the Crinan Canal to the open seas and islands of the West Coast of Argyll. I hitched a lift on a Cal Mac van from Claonaig to Ardrishaig. Well, it was a sort of a boat journey, the van belonging to the shipping company that monopolizes the western seaboard.

JTR The goods are sent on by large waggons, and meet us at Loch Crinan; while the 'Cygnet' or the 'Plover' puffs along right merrily, and we sit down to have a quiet look at the bonnie bits of scenery that are everywhere meeting us. Just on the hill-side above the starting-point is a little cottage – one of the large family of rural homes that adorn the Highland hills. The young kilted boys and tartan-dressed girls used to run a long distance on the canal bank in healthful rivalry, and were oftentimes rewarded by having money thrown to them. There are fewer runners now: whether the halfpence have not flowed so freely from the pockets

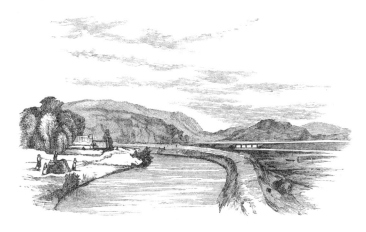

CRINAN CANAL.

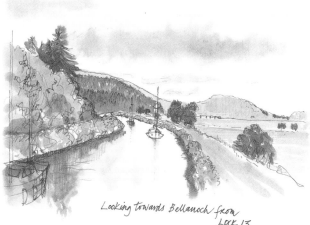

Looking towards Bellanoch from Lock 13

of the tourists, or the youthful population has decreased, I cannot tell. A larger number of bigger girls and women were in waiting at one of the locks, where the passengers are politely informed they may walk for a mile; they had large pitchers and small jugs, and we are all favoured with pressing invitations to have '*sweet* milk.' Sometimes a more matronly dame may preside at a table whereon is a large basin of curds, jugs of cream, a number of strong dessert-plates and horn spoons, and a goodly array of oaten cakes; so you may thus have curds and cream in the land of brown heath – and if lovely scenery lends a zest to, wholesome fare, you should not fail to patronize this vendor of good things.

No passenger boats on the canal these days. I decided to walk as far as Bellanoch where a friend would pick me up for that weakening hospitality again – a dear old Sister Brush who shames me with her eighty-year-old energy, integrity and artistic confidence.

A delicate silence accompanied me along the towpath. It was one of those West Coast days where the damp drizzle dulls all sound and activity. But I was light and free. Early morning coffee in the Ardrishaig Hotel helped find the holiday people with car only too happy to take the big rucksack to Crinan. Slowly the seaward houses sank below the level of the canal; to begin with parallel to bedroom windows, finally above roof level. The path became more overgrown with honeysuckle, convolvulous, montbretia and brambles. Hawthorn and lime trees thickly blocked the canal edge; every so often big iron rings set in stone lay half hidden, redundant in the long grass. By Cairnbaan only three motor yachts had puttered by.

It always seems to be the yachtie women that walk in between the locks, their men seriously at the wheel. Maybe they just like the exercise. I wish they would buy all their groceries from the Cairnbaan Post Office as they meander past. If they don't it will soon be another broken link with the past. The old varnish-crinkled wood lining is very exposed as the shelves are sparsely filled. The place has the feel of a museum. Old cigarette and washing powder advertisements proclaim products long gone, their successors in limited supply. The Postmaster, third generation, is well aware and proud of the uniqueness of his Post Office but wonders at its future. The honeypot of Inveraray lures the car-based tourist past as the main road is on the opposite side of the canal. The dwindling traffic of commercial boats spells further doom.

'They go in there to Inveraray on a bicycle and come out in a Jaguar.' The Postmaster was referring to his retailing competitors not the tourists.

By delightful coincidence I spent the evening in another wood-lined building but with more positive conversation. Betty had met me at Bellanoch, whisking me off to a venison dinner at her friend's at Ford. The little tin house had been built for the friend's father-in-law who had been the captain of the steamer based on inland Loch Awe. The little house, its walls cosily cluttered with treasures of old photos and watercolours was perched up on a hill directly above the old pier, its verandah giving a Raj-like quality and view on life. We talked of old days and new ways – and living alone. And how we coped with the return to our homes at the end of a day or a trip away.

'I come in the door and do something immediately,' said Sheila. 'Just love coming in the door. Silence!' said Betty. I said I hated it. 'Maybe that's why you still have to wander,' said Betty.

In my homeless state, I listened to these independent old ladies and vowed to remember both tactics when my time came.

For the time being there was no problem. JTR and I had a new door to walk through practically every night.

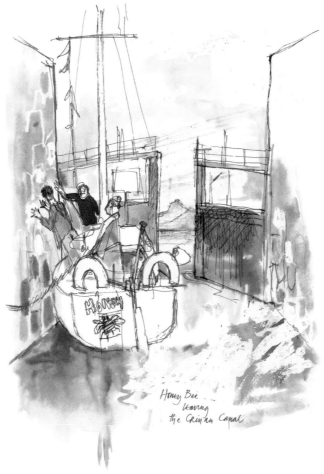

Honey Bee
leaving
the Crinan Canal

The journey from Crinan to Oban was quite hair-raising. Authentic reconstruction found me hitching a lift in the sea lock of the canal. Sadly, the beautiful old yacht *Honey Bee* was only going to Cruibh Haven but they keenly solicited around the basin on my behalf. They came up with a 230-horse power sports cruiser happy to have me aboard. The *Honey Bee* had taken ten hours from Troon on the Clyde coast to Ardrishaig; the cruiser two hours.

'The pencil could not go fast enough over the paper, so quickly changed the scenes.' JTR wrote that as he was sailing through the Kyles of Bute on the solid *Iona*. I don't think my boat even had a name. 'The Gas Guzzler' said its cheery owners, David and Karen from Northumberland. They had never been on Scottish waters before and planned to go round Skye. Navigation seemed to be after the style of painting by

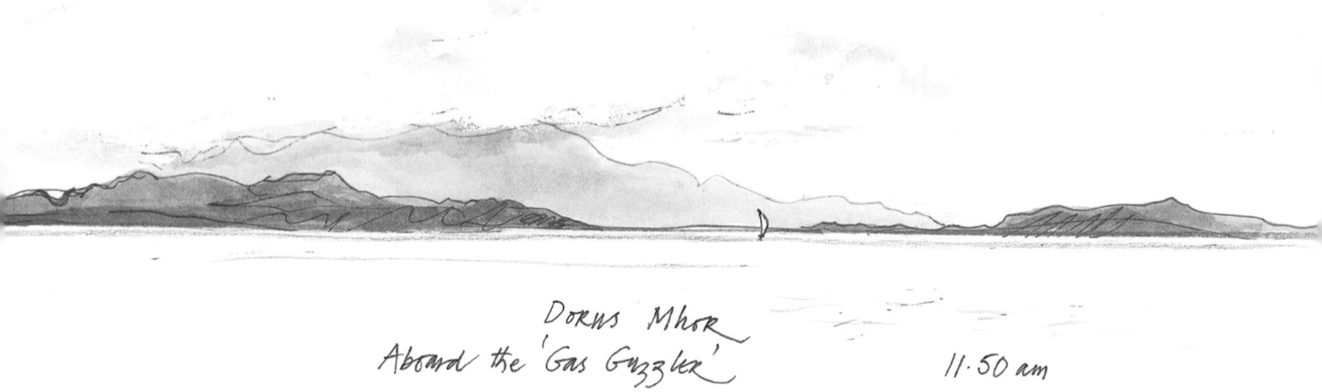

Dorus Mhor
Aboard the 'Gas Guzzler'

11·50 am

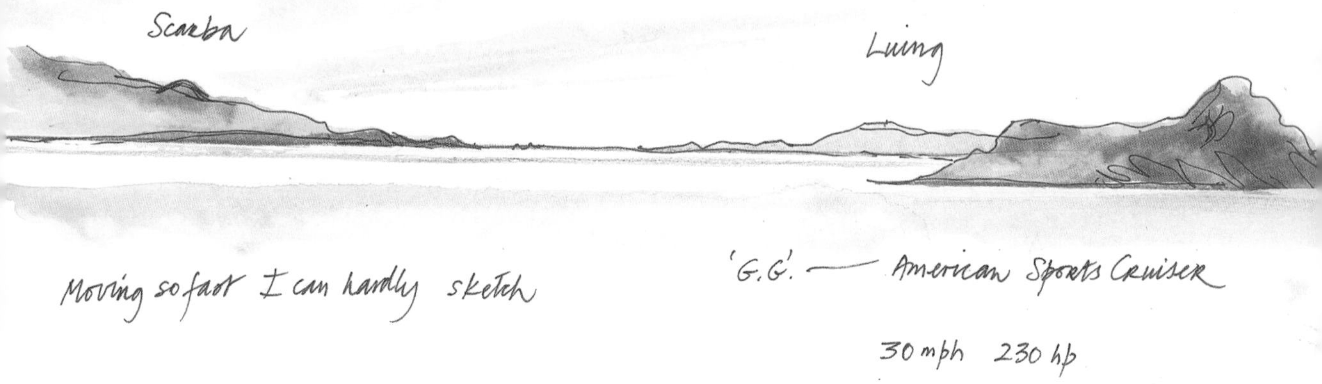

Scarba

Luing

Moving so fast I can hardly sketch

'G.G.' — American Sports Cruiser

30 mph   230 hp

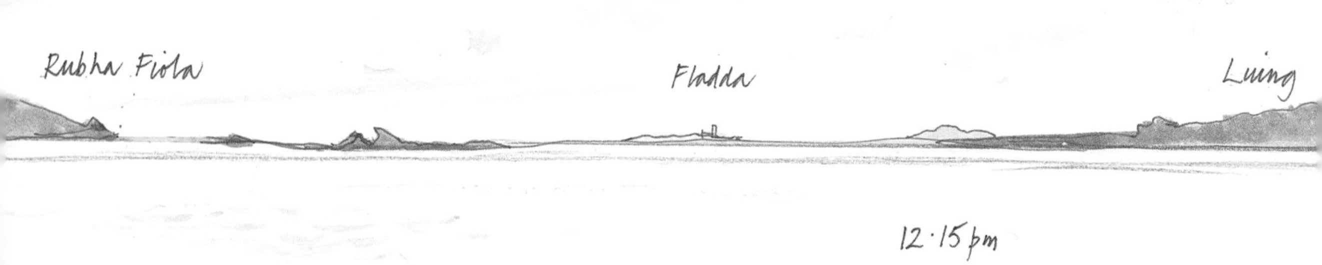

Rubha Fiola

Fladda

Luing

12·15 pm

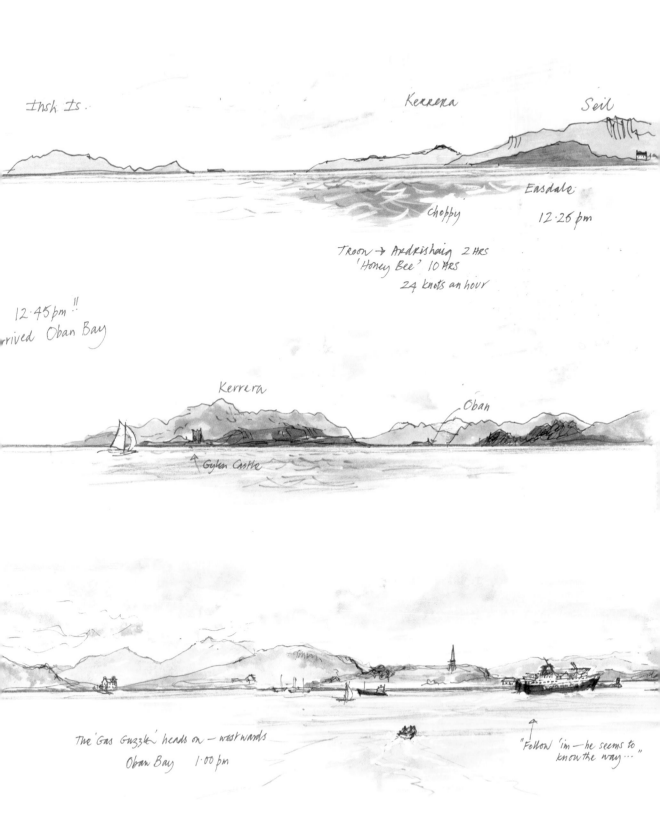

Insh Is.

Kerrera

Seil

Chobby

Easdale

12·26 pm

Troon → Ardrishaig 2 Hrs
'Honey Bee' 10 Hrs
24 knots an hour

12·45 pm "
rrived Oban Bay

Kerrera

Oban

↑ Gylen Castle

The 'Gas Guzzler' heads on — westwards
Oban Bay   1·00 pm

"Follow 'im — he seems to
know the way ..."

numbers. 'It's all great fun,' said Karen burying her head in flapping charts. David smiled with enthusiasm at the car-like steering wheel of the boat. The previous day's drizzle had given way to sun and wind. We scudded over the Dorus Mhor which was conveniently quiescent, its frothing tidal step lurking in the depths. The Northumberlanders hadn't heard of the Dorus Mhor. Or maybe my accent was incomprehensible. Conversation was limited by the roar of the engine and the thrash of the bow waves.

We flew to Oban, really.

Suddenly I was climbing up the long ladder of the North pier, the rucksack being roped afterwards. Tourists clicked away with cameras as I hauled myself inelegantly over the top. Feeling very scruffy and a little bereft, I watched the Gas Guzzler cream out of Oban Bay north and westwards. '*He* seems to know where he is going.' They followed a large outgoing Cal Mac ferry.

It had all been too fast. Oban was a different kind of noise and fat bare-armed people wearing far too much white and doing nothing but staring. At me.

I later learned that David and Karen got no further than Tobermory. Thank God – or the Mishnish Hotel. Even the most experienced of sailors get waylaid in Tobermory.

JTR When the steamboat touches the pier, you are met by a throng of canvassers from the hotels and private lodging-house keepers, and not a few of the holiday residents, who look out eagerly, in the hope of mayhap meeting friend or acquaintance or notable traveller.

The *Oban Times* of August 9th, 1876, faithfully recorded the comings and goings of any 'notable' travellers in the area. 'Mr G. W. Wilson of Aberdeen, the celebrated photographer, is on a professional tour of the West. There are many oil and watercolour artists busy at work in all parts of the Highlands just now – several of them being at Iona.'

You can read the actual old newspapers in the offices of the *Oban Times*, not a microfiche in sight. A rare treat nowadays. Shelves of leather-bound copies (£300 each to bind) are accessible to all. 'But the 1861 to 1865 papers are kept under lock and key,' warned the owner, implying that those that I freely but reverently leafed through might have to have similar protection one day.

A century ago the *Oban Times* was an international newspaper. The copy that JTR must surely have bought contained careful if long-winded analysis of world events as well as local news. 'WAR IN THE EAST' weirdly echoed the very headlines of a 114 years later. I say 'echoed', as all history does repeat itself. The circle ever full of wars and counter wars. Servia, or Serbia, had been invaded by the big bully boy of the time, Turkey. Austria and Russia were poised for intervention and the English Consul had 'been instructed to inform the Servians that England (sic) will be glad to tender her services'. Servia declared against mediation. As I write Serbia's slow burning fuse of bitterness from the Second World War is soon to ignite in open war against Croatia.

Nearer to home, the *London Letter* reported the elevation of Disraeli to the peerage 'for reasons of health', also that 'the number of lunatics in England and Wales on the first of January last was 64,619, being 1123 more than in the previous years.' Scotland preferred to keep such private matters to herself, obviously.

There was typhoid fever in Croydon and demands for sewage system improvements, a 'great fire' in Clerkenwell and the mysterious death of a French tailor in Tottenham. Five thousand agricultural workers had met in Walsham in Norfolk demanding the vote on grounds of paying taxes. All this English news in the *Oban Times*! If the impoverished crofters of the Highlands and Islands and their 'young kilted boys and tartan-dressed girls' that ran alongside canals and coach routes 'rewarded by having money thrown at them' had had the ability and opportunity to read that last item, the Victorians might not have travelled through their territory with such confidence … But the natives were friendly except for a few incidents in Skye. Another item assured us that 'Mr Cook was personally conducting one of his Highland Tours'.

And just to prove further that things never change, the Oban Town Council were arguing about a slipway and boat park and whether to set land aside for an Esplanade …

JTR A steamer leaves Oban on certain days for Staffa and Iona: it goes by the Sound of Mull round the north of that island, and returns by the south. To lovers of the sea it is a great treat, and affords scope for varied tastes. The route has been described to death and … I am inclined to be silent till I reach some spots where fewer pens have essayed to give to the world their portraiture, allowing the sketches engraved to leave my mite of tribute alike to the noble natural architecture of the Isle of Caves and the art treasures in the Isle of Ionic Crosses.

Many artists are now drawn to it, and find that it has other attractions than the records of the burial of kings: they love to paint the children who come to meet the tourist with wave-worn pebbles from the sacred isle.

Staffa, Iona and I never get on well together in the height of the tourist season. I know exactly what JTR meant in saying 'the route has been described to death'. His route is the exception to the rule nowadays. Buses for Staffa and Iona wait at Craignure on Mull for independent foot passengers from Oban, bottlenecking with the tour buses that disgorge from the giant frogmouth of the Isle of Mull ferry.

An earlier ferry had got me a front seat in one of the waiting buses. The bus driver washed the windows as a classical music tape played from his dashboard. Four drivers smoked and gossiped in the neighbouring bus. 'OUR BOYS GO IN' front page headline in the *Sun* lying beside one of them. On my driver's seat was a *Telegraph* with front page headed and devoted to the 'Kuwait Crisis'. How many times in the months ahead was that heading to coyly vacillate between 'crisis', 'situation' but never actually say 'war'? Inside the *Telegraph* was an advertisement for Sky Television: 'Watch History unfold with

Live Bulletins on the Hour.' A true theatre of war in every home. How glad I was to be homeless.

The *Oban Times* was more preoccupied with a West Coast sickness scare and a photo of a policewoman with holiday stray dogs, Rusty and Scoobie. Scoobie had found his way onto the Mull ferry but had not enjoyed the trip and was mightily relieved to be found by his owner. Rusty looked out with a baleful eye from the front page. Nobody had claimed him.

Mendlessohn was seasick both ways on the trip by boat from Oban to Staffa. Dave, waltzing us along the undulating peat based roads of Mull, said he was giving us wave action practice before embarkation at Ulva Ferry.

The intense blue sunshade strip at the top of the vast front windscreen gave a false impression of the day. It was actually rather grey and windy outside.

Packed like sardines, the motley crowd of tourists, me included, masochist that I am, could not land on Staffa. We circled several times in the over-laden boat. One of the two crew, the braver, told us it was on account of the work being done on the new landing stage that access was impossible. A large helicopter buzzed overhead, a cement mixer hanging like a spider from a dragonfly. 'But you must have *known* this before we set off,' said a very irate Italian. The publicity material promised landing, weather permitting. The weather was fine, if grey. With deft mastery of the English language the Italian went on and on about misrepresentation. The crew decided to go in by the entrance to Fingal's cave. One jumped ashore onto the hexagonal topped columns. The ever present ubiquitous swell, even on the calmest of days, heaved the boat sickeningly up and down. Like a voyeur I watched the land-based crew try to decide on the easiest 'platform' to land the now very silent Staffa baggers. We were moored for a minute, then 'Let's all get the hell out of here,' said the man in the wheelhouse and like lightning the young lad untied the rope and jumped aboard as the boat reversed astern.

There was a six-month-old baby en papoose on board. I'm continually amazed and yet secretly admiring of the intrepidness of travellers – or is it ignorance?

The Italian was demanding his money back.

Behind us the nearly finished landing jetty scarred the primeval lump of fantastic volcanic and sea-wrought basalt rearing out of the sea. Like the opposite of cosmetic surgery it was a layering on of disfigurement, a wart.

And I always seem to have bizarre experiences on Iona. At the height of the season …

Trying so hard not to weep at the demise of the old Post Office now replaced by a kit construction for other uses, I walked robotically to the cathedral like all the other tourists.

Sometimes I so hated JTR for putting me in this position. I did not like retracing his dynastical tourist footsteps. But in all dutifulness there is a bonus. So Calvin said. JTR would have admired my sense of duty.

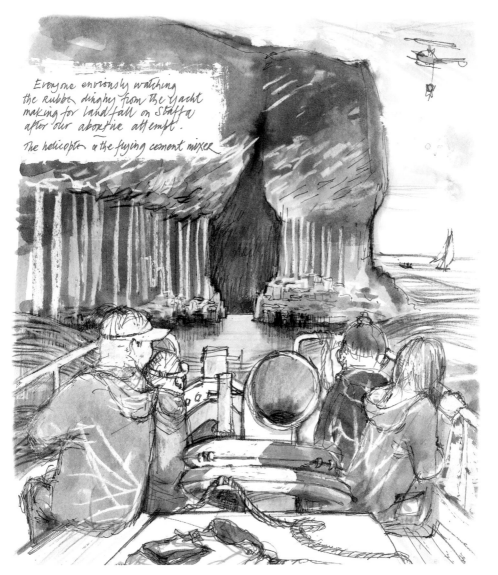

Everyone enviously watching
the rubber dinghy from the yacht
making for landfall on Staffa
after our abortive attempt.

The helicopter a the flying cement mixer

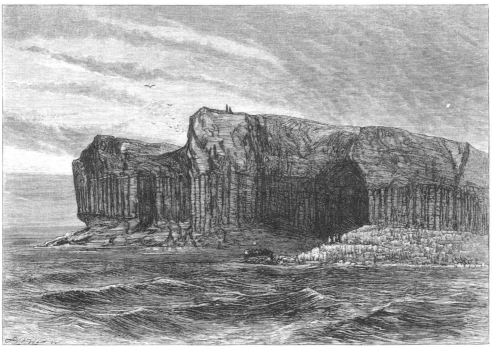

STAFFA.

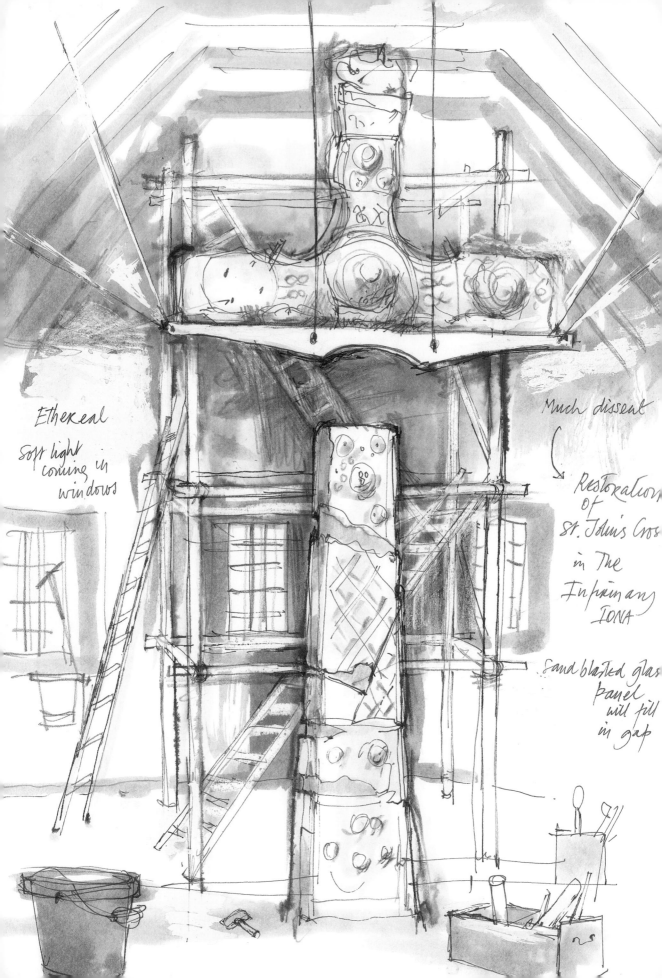

Ethereal

Soft light
coming in
windows

Much dissent

Restoration
of
St. John's Cross
in The
Infirmary
IONA

Sand blasted glass
panel
will fill
in gap

The bonus was stunning. A choir from Soweto was performing in the cathedral. We sat in the packed aisles, the building's relative simplicity a delusion for what was to follow. Shrieks and whoops heralded two loinclothed South Africans who rushed in from the side cloisters with spears and animal skin tabards. Women in a riot of beads, bandannas and provocative bustles followed to centre nave. Rock Gospel vibrated through us all, the light from behind the altar silhouetting the blackness of the men's skins. John, what would you have made of it – the tremendous celebration of beat and sound? Not even John Knox or Ian Paisley could have competed.

I recognised Aaron in the audience. He was working on the restoration of St. John's Cross in the Infirmary. 'Much dissent as to reconstruction,' he said, taking me beyond bounds. I felt so privileged to see the semi-fractured religious edifice so beautifully linked together with sand blasted glass and aluminium supports. In the seclusion and safety of the Infirmary, its potency is assured.

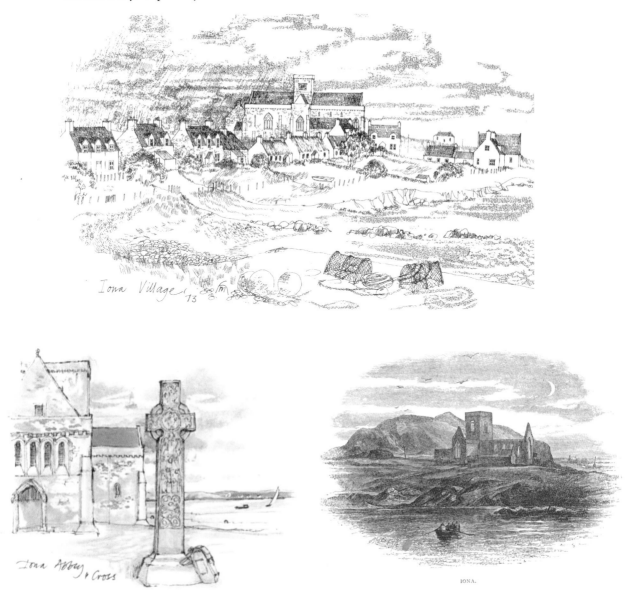

Iona Village

Iona Abbey + Cross

IONA.

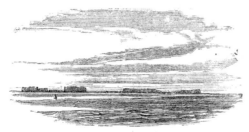

FLADDA.

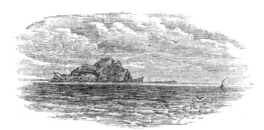

LUNGA.

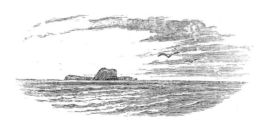

DUTCHMAN'S CAP.

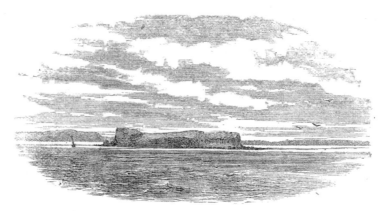

STAFFA.

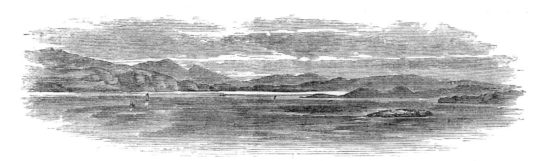

OBAN SOUND.

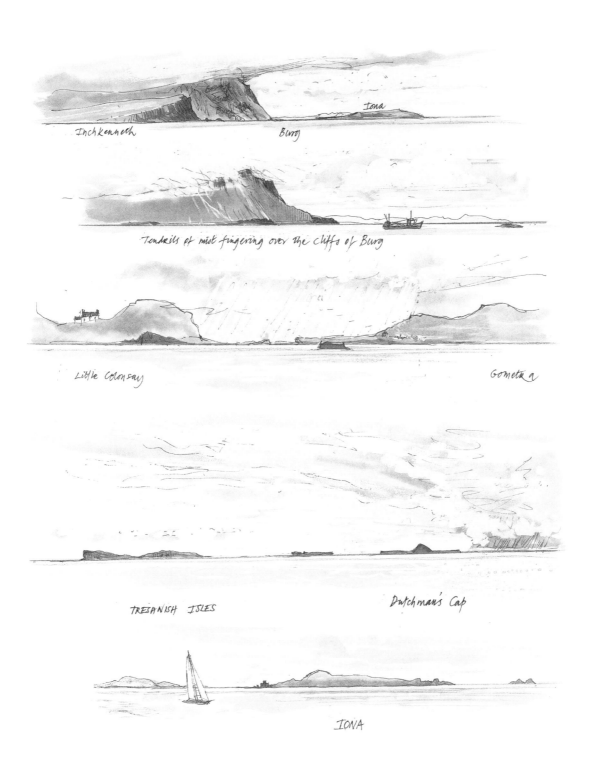

Inchkenneth   Burg   Iona

Tendrils of mist fingering over the cliffs of Burg

Little Colonsay   Gometra

TRESANISH ISLES   Dutchman's Cap

IONA

Mull does not feature large in JTR's text but there are several engravings in his book of the island. During his round trip 'described to death' the boat would have called in at ports on the way and the passengers would have had time to wander whilst goods were unloaded and loaded. There was no *Honey Bee* or *Gas Guzzler* to replicate the sea route for me, so buses and hitches and foot slog gave me more time on Mull than was strictly accurate. But who was caring?

Unfortunately it was classic summer weather. *And Sometimes It Rains*, a tourist book of Mull in the Tobermory bookshop, said it all. Sitting in the steaming restaurant the rain and condensation dribbles on the upper half of the window competed with the lace curtains on the bottom half. Through both intricacies, bright yellow, blue and red-hooded anoraks, like monks *en fête*, wobbled along the sea front. Somehow the visual jarring of primary coloured wet weather gear is less offensive in the brightly painted Main Street of Tobermory, especially in the rain. A large extended family tribe, all brand new Barbour-outfitted from the boots to the hats, looked almost threateningly military and morose by comparison.

They were all Italian (no, not related) and from the luxury cruise ship, *Hebridean Princess*, moored in the bay. Some local retailer would rest easy in his bed that night.

It was the kind of day that worms deep down in the earth, drown and float to the surface.

Knowing the curator of the Mull Museum helped – and hindered – the tracking down of the spot for JTR's sketch of the 'Fall near Tobermory'. I was determined it was at the burn that came down by the distillery at the edge of the town. He was sure that it was at

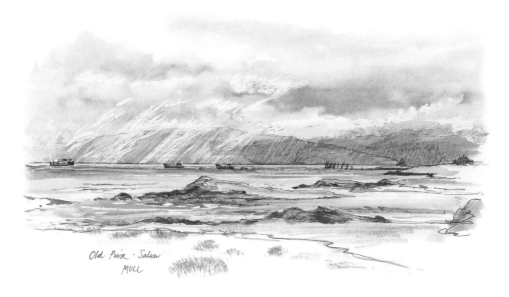

Old Pier · Salen
MULL

Aros. With so much tree growth over the years it is impossible to identify the bare rocks of the engraving.

As we tunnelled our way through the steep rhododendron-canopied paths at Aros, Alistair said the rain, the humidity and the terrain reminded him of his 'spell in Assam during the War. Just needs a string of natives bearing head bundles and brollies to come up the footpath.' Maybe this is why so many ex-colonials retire to Mull, I thought.

We were both very wet and still not quite in agreement by the end of the day. But curators have keys to museums after hours and a big deep bath of unlimited hot water back home where wives have dinner waiting.

By the end of the evening, Alistair and Hilary's enthusiasm and background knowledge had almost convinced me. Alexander Allan, of the Allan Shipping Line, had inherited the Aros Estate on his father's death in 1874. He became a permanent resident and devoted his life, with time off for sailing, shooting and fishing, of course, to the improvement of the area. In 'Our Portrait Gallery' from the *Oban Telegraph* of the times, his profile is exemplary. 'With his business training and keen sense of duty, he makes an admirable country gentleman; on all Boards, on all Committees, on all Councils, in politics, and generally in affairs, he is to be counted on and dependend upon; he brings an admirable sense of rectitude and a very kindly heart to bear on public business. He is a Conservative in politics and a Free Churchman in religion.'

Of course JTR would trot along the shore to have a peek at Aros – and maybe the great man. He must have been the talk of the town.

In the Museum there is a little booklet published by the Tobermory Branch of the WRI on the occasion of its Golden Jubilee. It records the memories of a Miss Marjory Mary MacKinnon of Rose Cottage, Tobermory, born there in 1864. She would have been a young lass of twelve as JTR strode his way Arosward. Her memory picture of Old Tobermory is dated 1874. She describes a lively thriving community that would not always have necessarily kowtowed to Mr Allan. There was a strong merchant class whose aspirations were no less than his.

Tobermory was not only a trading centre but an administrative 'capital'. The Crown officials of Sheriff and Procurator Fiscal were based there, as was the Courthouse. The Mutual Improvement Society studied Shakespeare and the topics of the day. Miss MacLean had a waist-length mannequin, 'very beautiful', in her shop window uncluttered with posters and advertisements of local events. For the bellman still existed as the means of such communications. There were concerts and balls.

Even the Poorhouse had an air of prosperity about it. The inmates wore a uniform of pale blue, the girls with white pinafores.

Inland from the boom development of Tobermory there was real destitution in the crofting community, however. In the *Scotsman* of December 8, 1877 there is a chillingly inhuman extract from a Special Commission report on the state of the Highlands which deals with conditions in Mull. Torloisk is mentioned, where the estate had the irritating

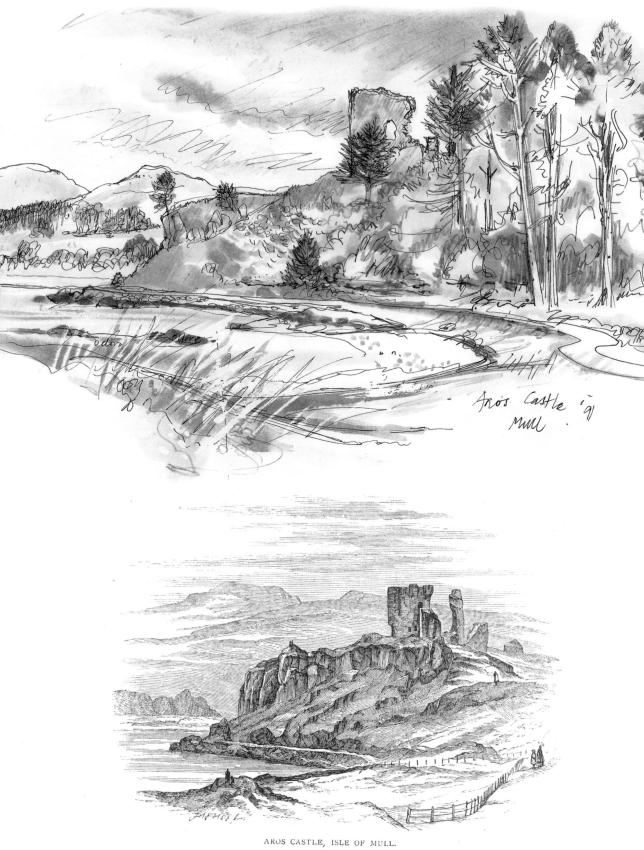

Aros Castle '91
Mull

AROS CASTLE, ISLE OF MULL.

90

problem of the crofters that would not leave. 'It is apparent that a step has been made in the right direction … the property will soon be entirely under comparatively well-to-do tenants. In no season,' continued the report, 'were the crofters able to sustain themselves entirely by their land. Never at best able to make both ends meet they have become very badly off indeed since the last rise in rents … Of their own inclination the people will not apparently leave the place … they prefer to stay on, meeting calls upon them by small accommodation bills, thus gradually impoverishing themselves and making their prospects cheerless.'

I wonder how much JTR and his fellow Brother Brushes knew or understood of the genocide their land-owning peers were guilty of? All that development and philanthropy disguised hard commercial policies. Was that what all the passion for landscapes and pretty rural images was about – 'they love to paint the children who come to meet the tourist with wave-worn pebbles from the sacred isle … ' Looking the other way?

In blissful oblivion, I'm sure, JTR boarded the *St Clair*, 'a Glasgow trader, that calls at many ports with merchandise and does a lively trade in the transport of cattle.' The *St Clair* had been launched just five months previously and her spick and span shiny newness must have added to the air of wealth and progress.

JTR   Before she reached the precincts of Iona she made the round of the Sound of Mull, called at Tobermory … sailed up Loch Sunart, got on board part of a flock of sheep at Salen Pier, landed them at Croag in Mull; and now we made for the Isle of Coll, – the 'Sandy Coll' Sir Walter speaks of. We had a bachelor party on board, who were out for a little merrymaking: an island marriage ball had wooed them from the desk of the counting-house, and having had a taste of the free air of these parts, and being good fellows well met, a few more days of healthful roving have a gleeful appendix to the gaieties of the wedding … We had in addition to this party, – a doctor coming to visit his mother, who lived in Coll; a young Englishman with a fishing-rod, who had left a medical practice for a few days, to whip the burns of Coll and breathe the fine air; a minister's wife; a retired minister and his wife, both in delicate health; the fiscal of Tobermory, who had a farm in Tiree; the Chief Constable and Sheriff Clerk from Mull, who came to investigate a case of suspected cattle poisoning; and a young Glasgow teacher, who came to be guest of the Fiscal aforementioned.

JTR did not land on Coll but sketched part of the village from the *St Clair* as she hove to in the bay for disembarking passengers and goods. In 1876 the population of the village was 129. It is now 85 and the population of the whole island a mere 179. In 1841 numbers peaked at 1500. The potato famine of 1846 and the clearances, slowing up but still grinding on, had the 1871 Census figure at 723.

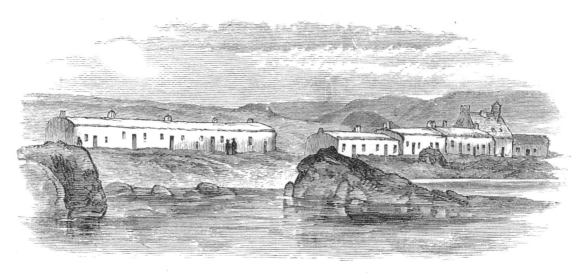

ISLE OF COLL.

These two-and-a-half-room cottages built in 1820 by the Estate still stand. The large house at the end is still the shop but with an added provision – the Coll Bistro. Only three of the houses are permanent homes of locals, the rest holiday houses. Not of incomers, though. Each house has a living link with Collachs of the past. The rellies (relatives) are proud to make the distinction.

Betty MacDougall, local historian and folklorist, was able to work out what families would have been living there in 1876. MacKinnons, MacInneses and MacDonalds predominated. The fifth house from the left belonged to the latter. Katina MacDonald, widow of one of their descendents, lives there at the present time. 'Aye, it's a dark street in winter,' she says.

But the contrast of summer, with the street (the only thoroughfare from pier to shops, Post Office and hotel) filled with visitors, cars, yachties, locals, the odd sheep or two, and the rellies – all packed into the tiny cottages makes both seasons of the year worth waiting for. Katina puts out her best potted plant on a stand on the pavement in the summer.

JTR It was Saturday evening as we neared the low-lying reaches of sandy shore and the outlying rocks of Tiree, and the sun was setting peacefully as our steamer came alongside of the stone pier at Scaranish Harbour, and we saw a sand-environed bay with some veteran sloops fixed in the sand – no more to mount o'er the waves of ocean, and spread ample sails to the breeze of heaven – left there, I am told, because it would not be deemed lucky to break them up. I got a room in the inn, and despite the windiness of the house and the army of earwigs that people it, I was very snug: a friend who has been there in winter gives amusing

particulars regarding the draughts that are vocal as well as felt in this palace of the winds;
he found it necessary to nail up his bed-room windows with many plies of blanket, and thus
to allow day and night to glide unnoted past, for all was dark – yet were not the breathings
of the winds hushed!

High on the tideline just below the Scarinish Hotel on my Sunday morning saunter
before breakfast were four pages of the Bible washed up. The Book of Judges, pages 16 to
20, limp but clear. 'Then went Samson to Gaza and saw there a harlot, and went in unto
her.' What a bizarre beachcomb …

I had hired a moped in Tiree, there being no bicycles left, and like a multicoloured
Batman Snoopy in my Mary Quant cape arrived at the Balemartine Baptist church for
morning service. The island had responded particularly to the fervent missionary work of
the itinerant Baptist preachers in the early years of the century.

The young and kindly bearded Reverend had tissue creases of sad worry round his
eyes. Membership has dwindled from a peak of 160. There were attendances of five to six
hundred at the time of the 1873 religious 'Revival'. And Balemartin was not the only
Baptist church in the island; there was another at Baugh and 'stations' at Balevullin and
Balephuil, many of the congregation having to stand outside. JTR notes that 'credible
witnesses gave accounts of many marked cases of conversion' during 'the Revival'.

Ignorantly, I thought he was referring to the great Catholic/Protestant divide. 'No,'
said Donald, son of Tiree Baptist cloth, 'Conversion from *Sinfulness* to *Godliness*.'

It took a poet, John MacLean of Balemartine, to query the phenomenon. Like the
Brahan Seer who prophesised that 'two false preachers would come across the seas to
revolutionise the religion of the land and the Highlands would be overrun by ministers
without grace', he was distrustful of this new religious energy. Some recognised in the
American evangelist Moody and his vocalist Sankey the manifestation of those 'two false
preachers'. Despite minority reservations, Moody and Sankey were rapturously received
in 1874 in Inverness, Campbeltown and Oban after international success in Edinburgh
and Glasgow to mention but Scotland.

I have a cynical notion that all religious revivals spawn from times of extreme
economic disparity. As I write Billy Graham is back in Britain again preaching to crowds
of thirty thousand. Tiree, along with many other towns and places, is having tapes of the
events played in Baugh and Balinoe Hall.

Meanwhile the number of beggars in our city streets increase.

JTR Monday was spent among the people, sketching one of the bays, the fisherman's sea-side
hut, the farmer's house, a Druid stone that is the only representative of what had been a
Druid circle – the base of the others remain in the ground. There are still very many families
in Tiree who pay no rent, and these have a settlement of their own, called 'The Moss,'
where some very poor creatures dwell, and must have but a miserable livelihood. I was led

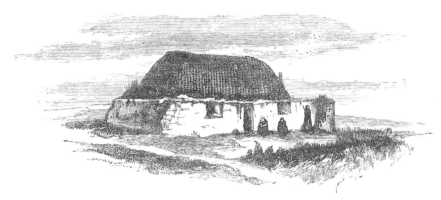

FISHER'S HUT.

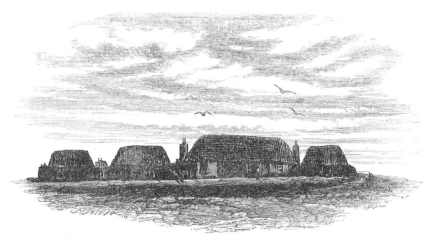

TIREE FARMHOUSE.

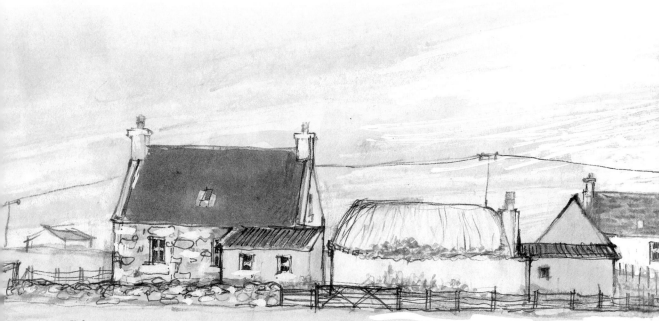

Tiree.   Marigolds on the thatch.

thither by the fiscal, who knows them well and is kind to them. The people of Tiree were very kind, and I had to take tea with a family who had good English, and invited me to come right away and remain their guest while I stayed on the island. Other cottagers the teacher from Glasgow visited gave him a proof of their kindness; they presented him with a large basin of milk: he took a drink of it, and would have left the remainder, but they signalled to him to drink it all, and the old man stood opposite the door to prevent his getting away till he was obliged, in answer to Gaelic gesticulations, to drink all the milk that was in the basin.

The families that lived rent free on the Moss had a price to pay – infill of the boggy terrain for the Duke of Argyll who owned the whole island. Nothing for nothing.

Old Sandy at Crossapol, with a fierce mane of white hair like Bertrand Russell, still 'fumes' when he remembers the eight innocent Tiree men arrested in 1886 at a Land League meeting at Balephuil.

A great number of crofters had gathered to discuss the partitioning of the good land of Green Hill but the Duke's factor and the police arbitrarily apprehended the first eight to hand. They were not activists in the movement – some of them might have been from the Moss and come to watch the barney – but all were sent to the jail in Inveraray and then taken to Edinburgh for prosecution. Most of them had no English and those that did could not possibly cope with the linguistic circles that no doubt would have been run round them.

All this head of steam must have been boiling up at the time of JTR's visit and yet he seems not to have been aware of it. It was not until the twentieth century that visual

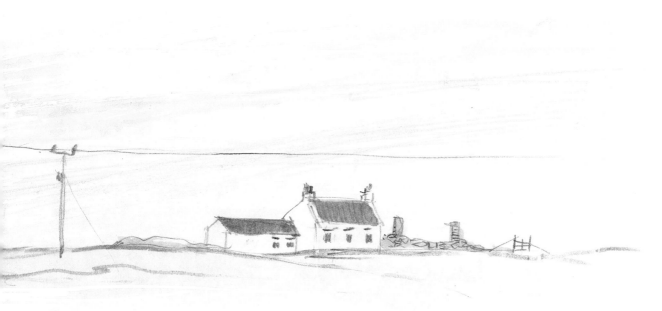

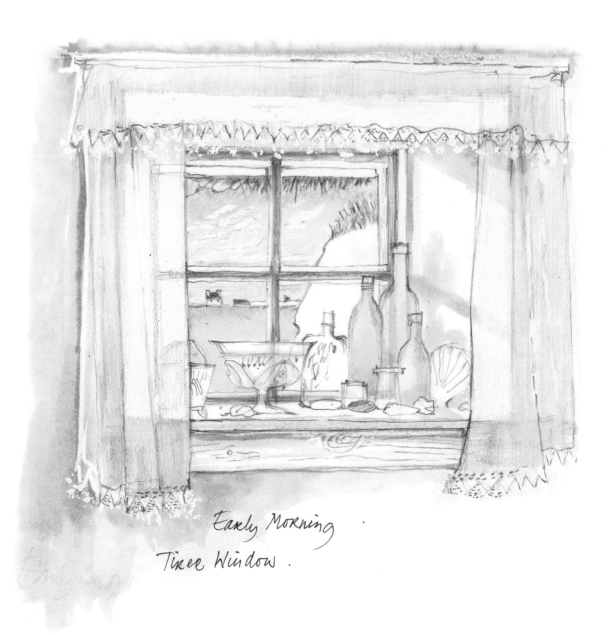

Early Morning

Tiree Window.

artists started to look *into* the landscape of the Highlands and Islands and try to say something about the lives of the people that lived through those times. Writers, poets and bards had been telling the stories for centuries but it was not until the Victorians that a visual interpretation was recorded and that was essentially romantic and ill-informed. We repeat these images of the Highlands and Islands to this very day.

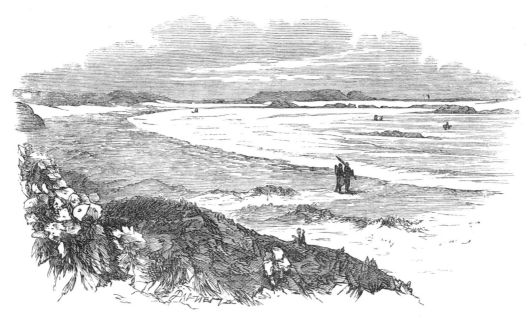

A SANDY BAY, TIREE.

Thankfully there is less Gothic exaggeration of the landscape but the images are too often limited to natural forms without any human comment. Why, in a contemporary painting of Tiree, is a kithouse not in the foreground, only a thatched or blackfelter cottage? JTR was sketching contemporary architecture. Why don't we artists 114 years later?

I hated sketching those council houses at the foot of Stirling Castle but who knows, in another hundred-odd years those houses could be as romantic as the tenements of Scotland Street in Glasgow or the crofthouses in Tiree.

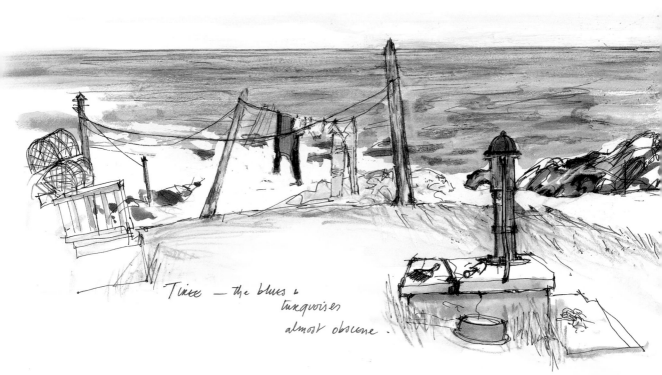

Tiree — the blues &
turquoises
almost obscene.

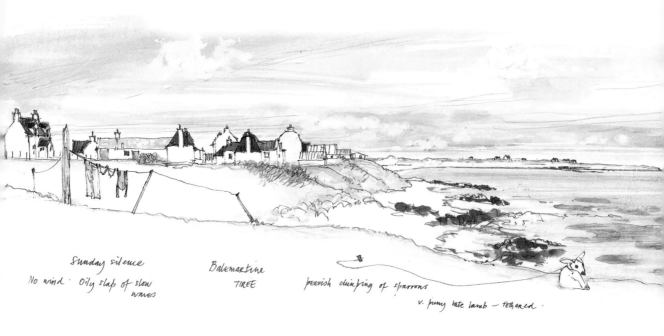

Sunday silence
No wind · Oily slap of slow
waves

Balemartine
TIREE

peevish chirping of sparrows

v. puny late lamb — tethered .

The waves slurped oilily as I sketched Balemartin. A late puny lamb was tethered by a washing line and sparrows chirped peevishly. Sunday silence. Yet I knew big Sunday dinners and family get-togethers were behind the closed doors. It was at times like this that I felt very small in the landscape.

Returning to Edinburgh after Ramble Two was to Festival City. Coming in by train to Waverley I tried to identify with those tourists 'seeing' Edinburgh Castle for the first time. This conquering by seeing – tourist empiricism.

I was getting tired. I had lost the excitement of the first Ramble to the Trossachs which had all been new territory. Ramble Two was over very familiar terrain. But maybe JTR was making me look further into that familiar landscape …

Ramble Three

Wednesday, August 22 – Friday, August 31

OBAN · BALLACHULISH · GLENCOE · FORT WILLIAM ·
CALEDONIAN CANAL · INVERGARRY · FORT AUGUSTUS ·
LOCH NESS · INVERNESS

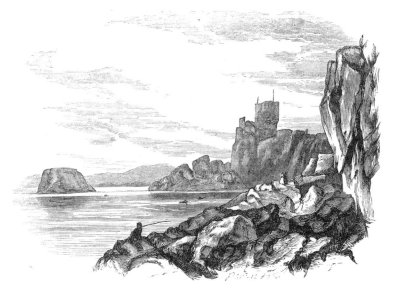

DUNOLLY CASTLE, OBAN.

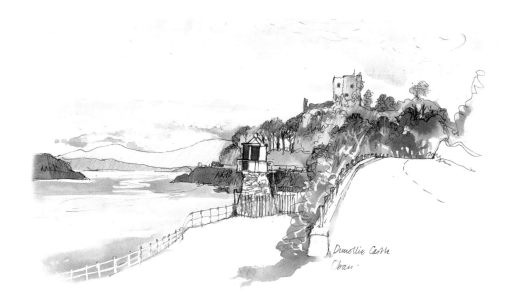

Dunollie Castle
Oban

JTR Oban Pier is again the starting-point from which the 'Clydesdale,' the 'Clansman,' or another of Hutchison and Company's well-equipped steamboats start to bear the traveller out of Kerrera Sound, past Dunolly, past Dunstaffnage, across the opening of Loch Etive, round Lochnell Head within sight of the Lady Rock, Duart Castle, and the mountains of Mull; having on the right the mountainland of Lorn, whose ever-changing forms fill the mind with admiring wonder; on our left the Isle of Lismore and the coast and far-stretching hills of Morven.

JTR was heading for Glencoe and the Caledonian Canal.

I'd decided to relax and just go along with the 'package' that he offered. Oban was full of other packagers. Two elderly Irish ladies, sisters, linked arm in arm, asked me where they were. 'Oban? Oh!' Yes, they knew where their hotel was and the bus driver was a laugh but they were outraged that Irish money was not 'taken here'. Despite this they had a wonderful tranquillity in such a foreign place, so far from home.

No boats to Ballachulish for Glencoe but I island-hopped instead up Loch Linnhe and walked the roadless east coastline of Lismore pretending I was on a boat. It was another still island day and I could hear the sounds of a motorbike and chainsaw on the mainland. The coast was rough country and the big rucksack a burden in the muggy atmosphere.

Only the ferryman on the Oban/Lismore boat knew that I was aiming for the northend ferry to mainland Port Appin. For once I was not travelling along a public road and here I was thinking about falling and having a broken ankle and nobody knowing to look for me. I'd never thought like that before. It was an uncomfortable feeling.

Set back, uncared for amongst bracken at the edge of an arable field, was a short-armed Iona cross, a monument to 'Waverley Arthur Cameron of the Oban Times' drowned in 1891 whilst his sailing boat foundered off the coast – erected by his sorrowing father. Such graves, despite their isolation and neglect, are very touching. J. McL on Arran – and there was another to come on another Ramble.

Of course I got the ferry to Appin and a lift to the very pier south of the narrows of Loch Leven where JTR landed.

JTR An omnibus awaited us, and we got ourselves and our luggage stowed therein or thereon; but a place in the hotel omnibus does not guarantee that you will find a corner in the house. An eager throng approached a lady who in great style bids you begone, for her hotel is full, while the ostler outside advises you to try again. 'She is only a woman, you know, sir, and a little nervous. Say you'll sleep on a sofa or a table, and you'll be all right. You see, she is a little put about when so many come all of a heap.' One old gentleman took the advice, pleaded his cause with the head maid, and got a place. I preferred to cross the ferry to the hotel on the other side, and found there was a spare bed though not a spare room.

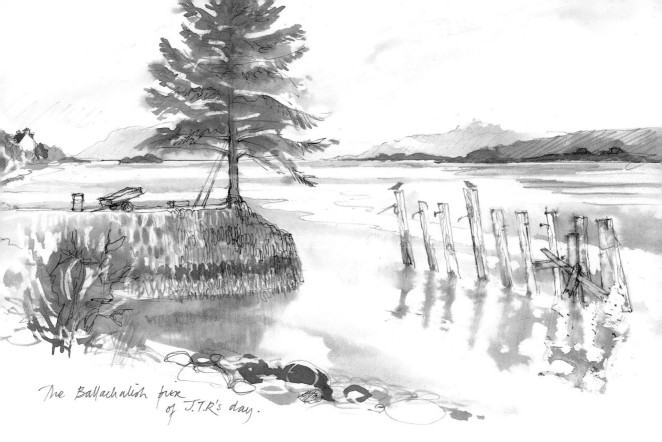

The Ballachulish pier of J.T.R's day.

My room-mate happening to be a policeman, I was at a loss whether to look upon it as a special honour or a special precaution.

I preferred to cross the bridge to the hotel on the other side on account of cost and no accommodation for singles at the Ballachulish Hotel. A spare room with no room mate was available, thank goodness, at the Loch Leven Hotel. Travelling accommodation seems to have been very casual and limited for JTR on occasion, more like hostelling. I was soon to have my own experience of room mates, however.

All was silent down by the slipway. The Ballachulish bridge overpowering above. I can remember the swirl and flourish of the ferry boats at full tide race like young girls dancing coquettishly, flouncing their skirts to the side.

Breakfast and my book of the moment, Paul Theroux's *Kingdom by the Sea* – I was now travelling with two male companions – was infiltrated by a monologuing female of middle years. She sat bushy-tailed for the day at a table with two men, one her husband ('You'd think I'd know by now after thirty-eight years what he likes for his breakfast'), the other a distant cousin, I decided. Both had been dragged on a Highland holiday from leather-button cardiganed Surbiton, I also decided.

She was telling them what they had watched on the breakfast news. 'Scottish Television News. I mean, it is sort of *local* as well, isn't it?' I think this was a redeeming feature. Don't they have local TV news in Surbiton?

Saddam Hussein had just held a press conference with the hostages. 'One woman, *very* articulate – from Jersey, I think – said how *wonderful* it was to see her husband!' Mrs Surb gave a tinkly laugh. What on earth was articulate about that?

'They all looked very scared.' 'Mmmm,' mumbled the two men through their cornflakes. 'Margaret', the name said with loving intimacy, 'used the words "disgusting", "repulsive", "revolting".' Another tinkly little laugh. 'It's almost best to just forget about it all, isn't it? Do you want marmalade on your toast?'

Did her husband know that this was his 13,870th breakfast with Mrs Surb?

The walk to Glencoe passes through the re-landscaped slate quarries of Ballachulish and St John's graveyard where many of the workers are buried, their beautifully copperplate-inscribed slate stones facing the site of their earthly toil. 'This grave was earth's limit, Heaven is our home.'

The Ballachulish Slate Quarries were opened in 1693 and worked continuously till 1955. Peak production time was in 1880: 16 million slates quarried by 600 men. They worked in crews of four or six, striking a bargain with the quarrymaster for their own section of rock face. They bought their own tools and powder, and were paid by the number of slates they made. The quarry provided the heavy gear and engines. Still embedded high on a rock is a tangle of telephone wires and a ceramic insulator. What messages would have passed along those lines? 'Summer must have come. I see the artists making for Glencoe. There's a tall one chatting up Minna and Brenda.'

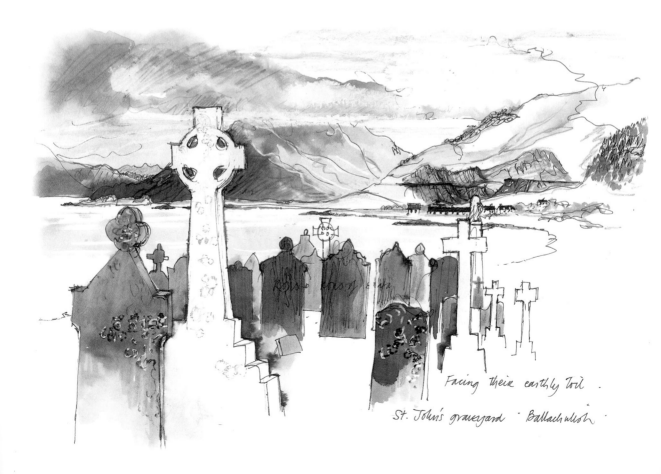

Facing their earthly toil.
St. John's graveyard · Ballachulish.

JTR The extensive slate quarries, and the long rows of cottages occupied by those who work there, are a strongly-marked feature in the day's walk; while many of the walls are entirely composed of slates fixed into the ground and placed upright: in the churchyard many of the tombstones were slate slabs, with painted inscriptions.

As I walked along the road that skirts the southern shore of Loch Leven, I met two fair ones, a Minna and a Brenda, walking leisurely, having as companion a jackdaw. He hopped close to my feet and waited till I presented him with a bun all to himself, and he had hard work nibbling it and taking it along with him to his home. Many of the cottagers in the neighbourhood keep one or more of these quaint pets.

Oh, John, *what* a Highland Romantic you were! And faithful seeker of Scott imagery. Minna and Brenda are the two heroines in 'The Pirate' who had become fashionable shorthand reference for rural femininity.

During the subsequent break in Edinburgh from JTR and this Ramble, I, in a desultory yet pragmatic mood, went to see 'Scotland's Pictures', a National Gallery exhibition relating the history of Scotland's paintings. There was Minna emphatically immortalised on canvas in Orchardson's 'Queen of Swords' telling me to keep going.

I saw no Minnas or Brendas in Ballachulish that day, maybe a Kylie Minogue in the supermarket, and nobody had any folk memories of tame jackdaws. How sad such a general habit should have no other record.

Walking on up to Glencoe I saw a canary at a window with an 'I Love Ballachulish' sticker on the base of its cage.

JTR 'did not see the glen to the greatest advantage; the weather was too fine.' The weekend was under a heatwave according to the *Oban Times* of August 25th, 1876. The same weekend in 1990 was identical and sketching was a tedium of narrowed eyes against the glare.

JTR I met a man in the glen who seemed to know every spot, and gave me the Gaelic namesof all the corries. He described to me the glen in a storm – the darkness that mantles it,the springing into life of untold hosts of runlets, the careering in mad fury of the burns as they break through and tower above the channel wherein they are wont to flow; theshowers, the careering of the clouds, the thunderings and the lightning-flashings, and the artillery of the winds, as the air-gusts meet the peaks and explode in the hollows of the darksome corries. He pointed out to me the 'Thief's Corrie' – a dismal place onlyaccessible at one point – that point the apex of a rocky and almost perpendicular water-course; he said one man could hold the pass against five hundred, and I inclined toagree with him.

The Thief's Corrie is now popularly called Hidden Valley. JTR's informant was translating from the Gaelic. At least JTR did not then rename the spot as so many others of his class and time did. In Ballachulish an old man, who had no recollection of the jackdaws, told me, 'We all have our names for these mountains but they call them different now.' A slight exaggeration but I knew what he meant.

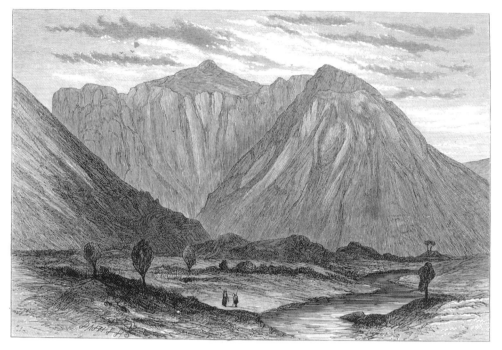

GLENCOE.

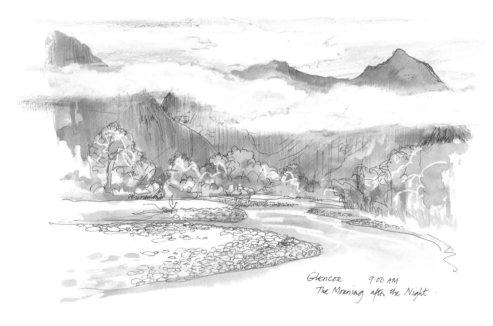

Glencoe   9:00 AM
The Morning after the Night.

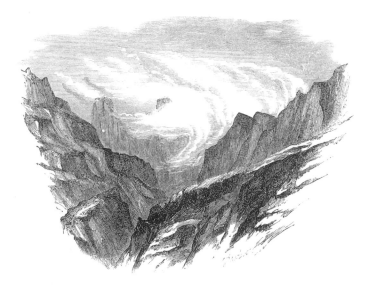

CORRIE AT GLENCOE.

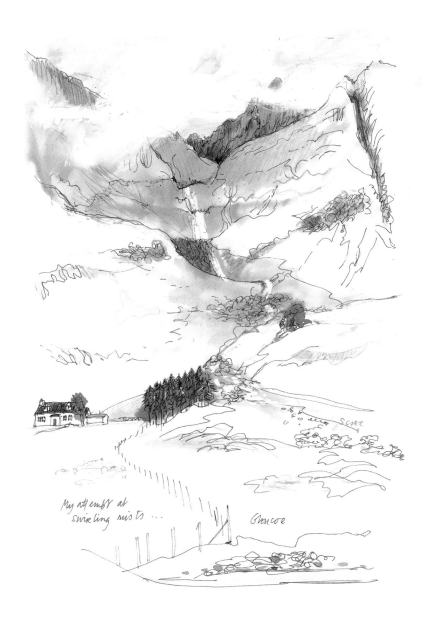

My attempt at
swirling mists ...   Glencoe

There is no one living in the Glen now to glean information from, save the National Trust Rangers and a tenant farmer. There are no slow-moving herdspeople, pedlars, travellers. No working indigenous community linked with the wild landscape or the people who walked, warred or survived in its past.

Everyone is in fast-pressing cars with instant 'Information' to be had in an ugly Visitor Centre, a blight on the landscape, if ever there was.

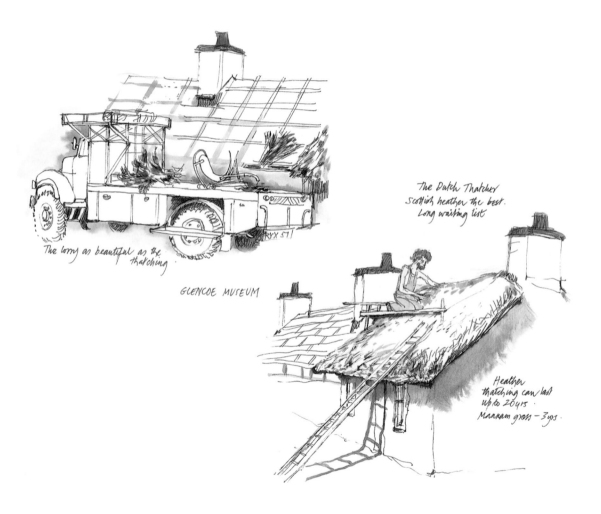

The lorry as beautiful as the thatching.

GLENCOE MUSEUM

The Dutch Thatcher
Scottish heather the best.
Long waiting list

Heather
thatching can last
up to 20 yrs.
Marram grass – 3 yrs.

I did meet a man in the Glen, the farmer, distraught with the number of sheep and lambs already killed on the road. 'And the summer only half way through.' Signs pleading for slower driving seemed to have no effect, he said. He was truly considering hanging the next carcase from a gibbet at the side of the road. 'But the environmental health would be on to me … '

JTR I walked the glen many times, and looked back on the few trees, lying far in the hollow, that grow near the place where the massacre is said to have begun; while on either side were deep rock-lined, tree and fern-fringed chasms, leading into seclusions and bleak mountain summits, one could spend long hours exploring. I then returned to the little inn where I had ordered dinner to be ready at an hour early enough to allow me to walk back to Ballachulish in time for the calling of the steamboat on its Fort William route. The landlady was going out to see the workers among her hay some miles down the glen; her man-servant (the Hermit of Glencoe) drove, and she asked if I would come with them as far as they went. The Hermit lives in a small slated cot, with a very tiny cottage window in it, in one of the loneliest corners of the glen. He is about the inn all day, speaks broken English, and in acknowledgment of any kindness will show the suppleness of his old bones by standing on his head for a little time.

Sundowner time found me at the Clachaig Inn (JTR either went there or to the Temperance Hotel in Glencoe Village on the edge of Loch Leven) after twenty-odd miles wandering and walking. It was a Bank Holiday weekend, the hotel small. And nowhere else till the village, three too-far miles on down the road. There was a youth hostel but I have never joined and part of sticking with JTR was dependent on the extra comforts of hotels and B&Bs.

I ended up in a bunkhouse: 'Women to the left at the top of the stairs, men to the right, if you're bothered about these kinds of things.' The £4.50 'paid now' included a blanket with the bed, cooking facilities and a shower. I had no food with me and, exhausted by the day's walking and my mismanagement of the day's end (no sundowners that night), I went to bed early, in the room to the left, planning a stupendous breakfast the next morning in the first hotel en route for Fort William. Nobody else was in the room.

Loud Clachaig Inn climber revellers woke me clambering up the stairs. It was dark. Happily drunk they tried to whisper when they saw 'a body' already in the room. Wobbling torch lights sorted out packs and bedding and within seconds of lying down all three men were fast asleep. And snoring.

Now if there is one thing I absolutely cannot stand, it is snoring. I lay rigid, willing myself into the exhausted stupor that I knew was there waiting to engulf me again. I tried to relax my tightening nerves with mind pictures of the most beautiful landscapes of the Rambles. I tried to separate out the harmonies in the snoring.

I decided to sleep outside.

There was enough starlight coming in the window to make out the dim shapes of bunkbeds and rucksacks. I had just stood up, fully clothed by the doorway, when one of the harmonisers stopped with a snort and a wakeful chomp of his lips. I froze as he fumbled for his torch and, stark naked, staggered to the door. 'Eh – just going for a pee,' he said, shielding the necessary appendage for such an activity. 'Eh, so am I. After you,'

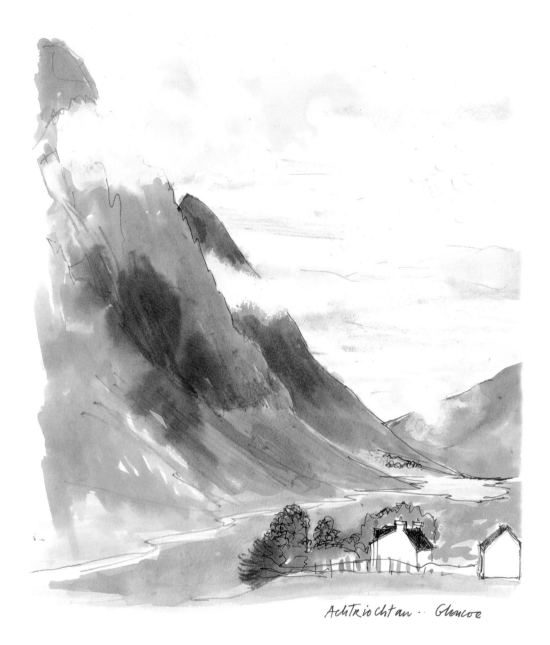

Achtriochtan · · Glencoe

said I. He nearly fell down the steep stairs. I waited till I heard him go into the bathroom, grabbed all my gear and tiptoed out of the house. His mates snored on, oblivious. They would never believe his ghost story in the morning. And I certainly would not be there to confirm or deny it.

In theory it should be an idyllic experience sleeping out on a still starlit night at the height of the summer. For two reasons it is not: midges and numbing cold. I had no sleeping bag but always carry an orange plastic survival bag in the rucksack. Almost suffocating myself with a minimum breathing aperture on account of the midges, I also started to condense inside the bag. Drops of freezing cold water soaked my twitching body. It was a nightmare. Or worse. I was awake.

Above, the canopy of cruel brittle stars showed no indication of softening with a glow from the east for hours and hours. Eventually I walked the night away, twice hiding in the ditch of the old Glencoe road as lagerlout cars – I could hear their maleficent approach down the glen – tyre-screeched past. It was the only time I was ever frightened on any of the Rambles.

Dawn found me stretched out on the bench below the War Memorial in Glencoe Village soaking up the first warm rays of sun and waiting for the shop to open. Of course primitive man was a sun worshipper. His nights were hell.

'Scandalous,' the early bus party members must have thought as they swung past. 'Sleeping rough by the War Memorial. Shouldn't be allowed.'

I worked out that I had walked thirty-two miles the previous day and night.

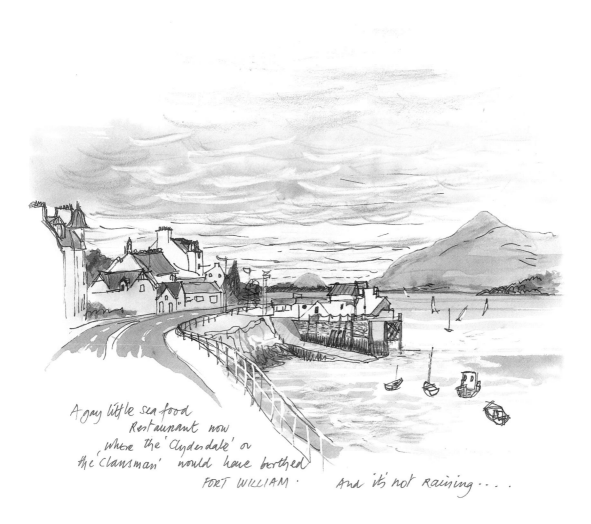

A gay little sea food
Restaurant now
where the 'Clydesdale' or
the 'Clansman' would have berthed
FORT WILLIAM.   And it's not raining....

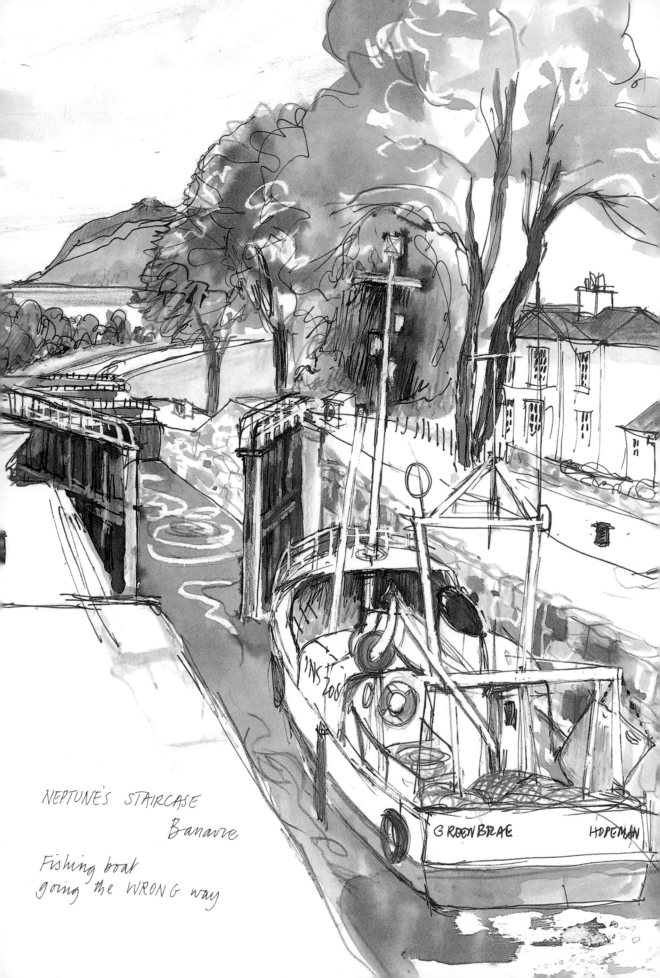

NEPTUNE'S STAIRCASE
        Banavie

Fishing boat
going the WRONG way

GREEN BRAE   HOPEMAN

After Glencoe JTR travelled to Fort William by boat then trans-shipped at Banavie to the Caledonian Canal steamboat. He was heading for Inverness ultimately but made several sketching forays westward from Laggan Locks.

I *knew* that I would get a lift on a boat going up the canal. Such optimism. I had missed, early morning, the *VIC 32*, one of the few working puffers kept afloat by an enthusiasts' club. The Corpach lock-keeper suggested a German yacht waiting to ascend Neptune's Staircase, the eight locks from sea to the first stretch of canal. 'It'll take about an hour and a half. Maybe longer because of maintenance. And then they'll spend the night not much further on.' The last lockings are at the ridiculously early hour of 4.30 p.m. to give the lockkeepers time to finish duties before their tea.

I did not fancy approaching any of the holiday cruisers – a bit like knocking on a caravan door and asking for a bed. No, I wanted a working boat, a fishing boat. 'You're too late. They all go through first thing in the morning. They want to get through the canal in the one day. Saves time and that's money.' It costs about £187 to take a fishing boat through the canal – one way.

So I walked alongside the quiet, still canal. Occasionally the cruisers, usually in twos, chugged past. Trails of misty Lochaber rain came down from the Nevis mountain range and the round purple heather-clad hills of Glen Loy.

At Moy Bridge the young fat cheery lockkeeper – or rather bridgekeeper – 'Only one in the country', was happy to chat. The bridge is open most of the day as access is only for farm traffic. Soon the canal was to be closed and emptied for repairs. 'We try to save the fish.' He'd noticed that the geese had just arrived in the back fields. He was a nice young man bemused by the 'city folks that go down the canal then back up again. Seems stupid.'

As he talked a flying ant landed on his large beer belly. It was delicately, unselfconsciously removed and set in flight again.

Next day it rained very hard and the leggings were worn for the first time. No, there were no fishing boats coming through that day. The canal men at Gairlochy advised me to

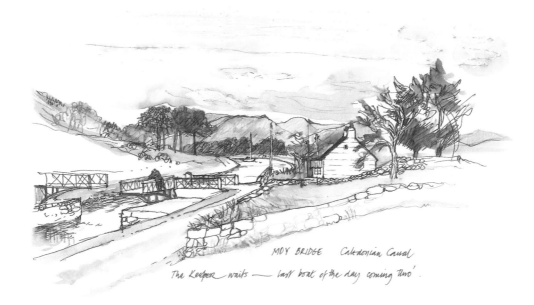

MOY BRIDGE   Caledonian Canal
The Keeper waits — last boat of the day coming thro'.

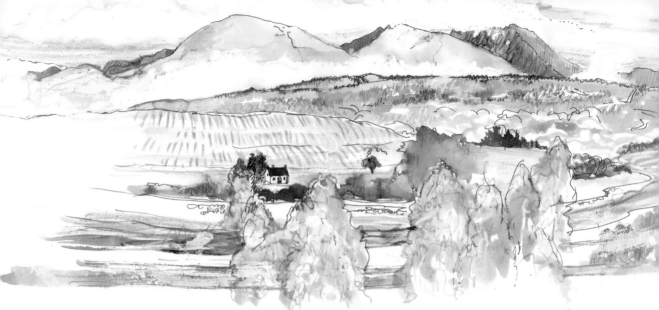

Nevis Range from Gairlochy
The river & canal side by side

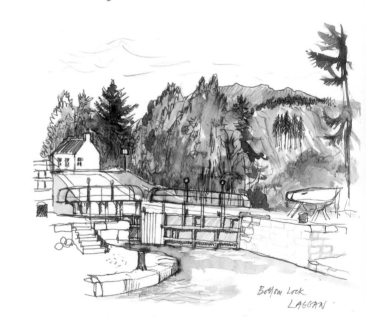

Bottom Lock
LAGGAN

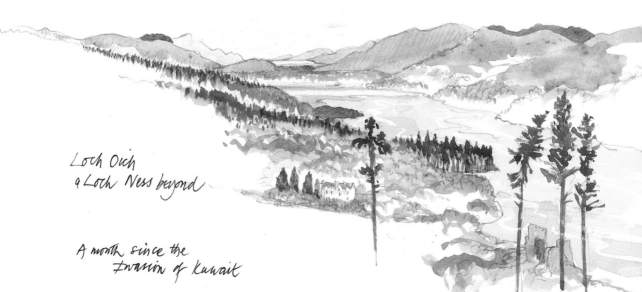

Loch Oich
& Loch Ness beyond

A month since the
Invasion of Kuwait

keep to the south-east of Loch Lochy and follow the disused rail track to Laggan instead of the forestry road on the other side.

The track kept high above Loch Lochy. Now the cruisers' engines abraded up and over the hills, their clackering drone in need of silencers. The sun started to filter through and silver the loch. A regatta of little boats fanned out behind the cruisers and yachts, one with a multi-coloured spinnaker. How sun can instantly change mood and temperature. The umbrella became a sun shade high on the hillside.

The green swarded track alternated between old military road and the disused railway track foundations to Fort Augustus. Sometimes the track was exposed, other times tunnelled by rhododendrons and very overgrown. A padlocked deer gate told me this was not a public path. But it was. Thousands of feet had tramped this route in times past before railways and military invasion. All over Scotland – and the world – are tracks like these, conveyor belts of pedestrian history. My boots were by each indent of pressure keeping the route and the spirit of those who walked before alive. Padlocked gates sever the thread.

In confused, time-warp sympathy, the ghost roar of a train came up behind me. It was a freak soundwave reverberation from the thrum of passing cars far below on the loch side. The ghosts followed me on and off to Laggan Locks and into a liquid gold evening walk over to Invergarry, to the west of the canal and Loch Oich. I broke off branches of deep purple cherries, devouring enough vitamin C for the rest of the length of the canal if walked it had to be, waving their thick-leaved wands at the flies, as I plodded the day's last few solitary miles.

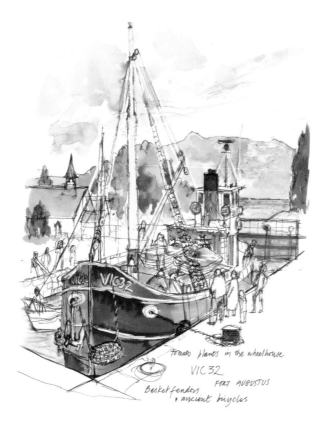

Tomato plants in the wheelhouse
VIC 32
Basket fenders   FORT AUGUSTUS
+ ancient bicycles

Next day it was rain. Again. Good for the fishing, though the River Garry is at its best from February to May for the spring salmon. So I met no one on the riverside path, soft-cushioned underfoot with years of leafmould. Psychedelic green moss and bright yellow rhododendron leaves submerged in pools like goldfish reminded me of Aros on Mull. A tiger, benign, would be pleasant to meet. A rotting rustic hut gave shelter from the monsoon and there I decided to forget about JTR's sketches at the sheep farm by the Laddie Burn many a mile on.

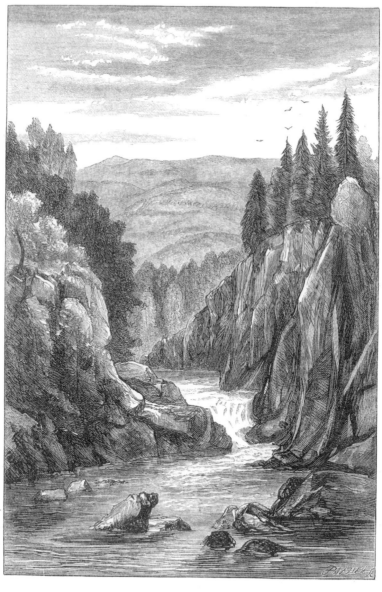

ON THE GARRY, INVERGARRY.

Standing in the Invergarry pub with Scotch broth and whisky, I learned the sheep farm and shepherds were no more. 'Just forestry. Maggie Thatcher's fault.' That woman has a lot to answer for.

There is a most delightful walk the full length of the south-east side of Loch Oich, parallel with the old railway line, shored up in parts. Like in the Trossachs, the mountain bikes leave their marks but I did not meet any. Towards Aberchalder the track goes up high into rocky grottoes; below, the railway duct is black, canopied by trees. And always the edge of the loch and the lap, lap of its waves a stone's throw away.

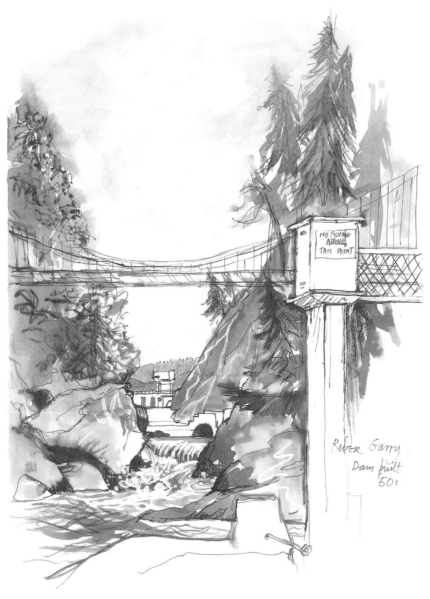

River Garry.
Dam built
50s.

The loch ends at Aberchalder and it was back to the canal for the last haul to Fort Augustus and Loch Ness. The morning's rain had given way to a lush golden evening. Walking back alongside the canal again was familiar and reassuring. We would get there. Each slow curve of the waterway showed another glittering stretch with no end, however. Hazily cradled between the blue-ing mountains and hills of the Great Glen faultline, I *was* the canal flowing inexorably northwards.

During the day four low-flying military jets had blasted down the Glen. A common practice. Now in the special silence of summer dusk, sibilant with drowsy leaves and little waves, another ear-rending arrow of black flew past. The Kuwait 'Crisis' was all of a month old; I had thought all our military might was in the Middle East.

The only thing that kept me going on the last lap of the journey was the rhythm of my steps. I was very tired. Too tired to even stop for a bramble.

That night on the television Saddam Hussein patted Western hostage children's heads. One blonde-haired little girl was chucked under the chin; she winced.

JTR On reaching Fort Augustus, when the steamer is being lowered in the locks towards the loch, tourists have time to look about them. It will soon be known as a centre of Roman Catholic influence, for a large monastic institution is in course of erection on the site of the old fort. It looked dismal enough when I saw it, as if given right over to darkness. It seemed altogether deserted: no martial coat was seen, no sentry on guard, and many of the ancient walls were being pulled down.

The 'large monastic institution' is now a well-maintained Abbey and private school. Watching boats being lowered in the locks is still the major tourist activity. This tourist was watching too, from early morning. *All* morning. That fishing boat had to appear. No tracks on either side of Loch Ness, just the main trunk road north on one side and a tourist road on the other. The canal walk was over.

Unquestioning faith is not always rewarded. But some things you just *know* will happen. And there she was, a bit dented and definitely in need of a coat of paint, a Peterhead prawn fishing boat, nudging her way into the topmost lock.

'You'll have to ask the skipper,' said the young lad with a strong north-east accent, a gold earring and stud in one ear. His hair was blond streaked, stylishly short at the back but with swinging forelocks. The pale middle-aged skipper emerged from the bowels of the ship as the second mate, another young lad, ticked the engine over from the wheel house. I do not know who was more apprehensive, them or me.

I know enough about men and boats to behave immaculately with them and stood where placed until the serious show business of the lock manoeuvres was completed and we were full straight ahead in the ruffled unconstrained waters of Loch Ness heading for Inverness. Everyone relaxed for the two-hour journey. The skipper showed me round. We came to an agreement; sketches of his boat seemed fair barter. And the bottle of whisky.

From the wheelhouse the high-railed bow made it impossible to see immediately ahead. 'No use for canals or this kind of water. At sea it is fine.' I had an instant picture of this docile boat now chugging at nine knots with a following wind on a choppy but inland loch, far out in the North Sea bucking and corkscrewing, the bow sickeningly below the waves as often as not.

Two windsurfers, like rainbow-flashing kingfishers, cut dramatically and dangerously back and forth at right angles to the blind spot of the bow. A taunting display of leisure time frivolity right in the face of a working man's day.

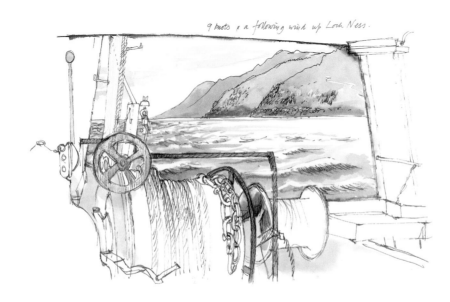

9 knots & a following wind up Loch Ness.

The boat had had no luck on the West Coast. 'Misjudgment on my part,' confessed the skipper. Tiredness stitched every worry line of his face. He spoke and looked like an end of term lecturer of some provincial college English Department. This man was not the average prawn boat captain.

'Talks funny,' colluded the crew down below. 'Not quite the two shillings, the skipper.'

The little blond Adonis was watching television. Since school, which wasn't long ago, he'd worked as a butcher, 'squeezed a heart in a sink and got blood all over – sickened me', and latterly as a – guess it – hairdresser. This was his first job at sea. Naw, he would pack it in once they got back to Pee'erheed.

The second mate had just finished preparing breakfast. It was well past one o'clock. 'Never eat before now. Especially when fishing. Only eat when the work is over.' Standard bacon, sausage, tomato and eggs were garnished with fried potato scones, beans and buttered white sliced bread. I had to have my share as the two lads ate theirs and watched 'Neighbours'.

The skipper called from the bridge on the intercom to come up. A big splodge of blue, green and yellow dots was registering on the echo sounder. 'Marine life,' intoned the skipper. 'Deep down. Big lump.' With a depth of 121 fathoms (726 ft) at this point it could hardly be a family of trout out for a finny stroll, he remarked. His strange turn of phrase evoked no response from the lads; neither did the unusual image on the screen. 'Your breakfast's ready,' said the second mate, taking over the helm. Whatever it was on the bottom of the loch it was no more strange than the atmosphere on that boat.

Scuds of rain gave way to sun as we got near to the end of the loch. I sat high by the bow like a proud salvaged mermaid as we entered the canal at Dochfour leading to Inverness. What a way to return to the city I had lived in for ten too-long years and had left with but a rucksack on my back only a couple of months previously. Couple of *months*? What a strange void-like thing time can sometimes be. It seemed years.

For all that following wind the boat was stuck at Muirtown with only one lock and the sea gate between it, the Moray Firth, and home that night. It was 4.30 and tea time for lock-keepers. As the skipper sashayed the boat into her overnight berth the young hairdresser cheekily tightroped along the taut stern rope, showing off. The second mate was up front securing the temporarily slack bow rope. The hairdresser's was a feat of great dexterity and he revelled in his prowess. Maybe that was where his future lay …

In slow motion, however, the stern rope slackened and the hairdresser was teetering, valiantly to begin with, but inevitably out of control and doomed to a watery safety-netless future. The stern of the boat continued to swing round to the spot where he had fallen in. The second mate was shouting hysterically. I was paralysed on the canalside, mid pen stroke, sketching the boat for the skipper, then running towards the stern where the young man was swimming for his life out of the narrowing gap.

He made it. 'Fucking bastard!' he shrieked at the wheelhouse as he dragged himself up the slimy wall, earrings gleaming. I lowered my eyes once I knew he was all right.

It was definitely time to say farewell, and stepping down from the canal at that point I found myself on the very street of my son's house. A short walk through urban Inverness and a knock at a familiar door.

'Hi, Mum!'

Like as though I had never left …

JTR There are many good hotels in Inverness, and also good private lodgings. It has annually a very gay season during the days of the Highland games, when balls are held, for at that time from far and near there is a gathering of the clans: the games were instituted with that purpose, and have continued to draw together year by year Highland chieftains and men of note, and ladies of rank, accomplishments, and beauty. Many notable marriages have been arranged at these meetings.

Inverness has also had of late years its annual Christian convention. I arrived there during the last day of it, and heard Dr. Barnardo pleading eloquently on behalf of the

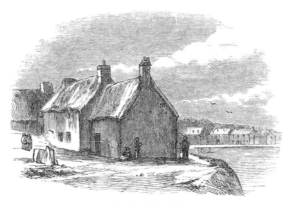

INVERNESS COTTAGES.

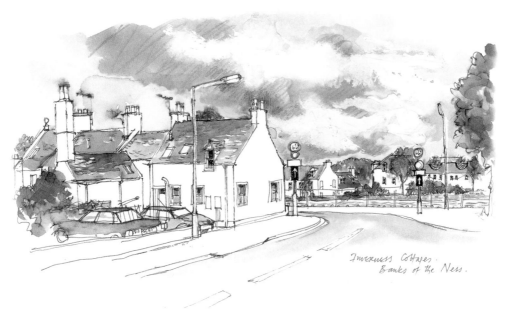

Inverness Cottages.
Banks of the Ness.

children he labours so unweariedly to rescue from the streets of our great cities, and also saw a gathering of the colporteurs gathered from the north and west, to get a word of encouragement in their laborious work of carrying pure literature into the homes of those who in numbers of instances live beyond the reach of the minister and the bookseller.

The newly pedestrianised High Street was full of locals and tourists, the former proud of their new identity, the latter indulgently at ease. 'A street party would be fun,' said a Highland lady 'of rank' in front of me to her companion who wore a dog collar. 'All towns look the same nowadays until you look up at the buildings above and the scenery beyond,' he grunted. Yet he was right. What price progress. Instead of fights outside the Market Bar they are outside McDonald's and the protagonists are years younger.

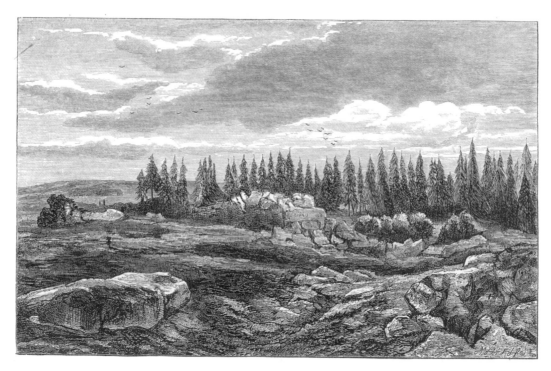

CULLODEN.

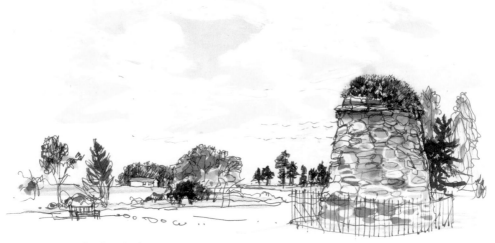

The CULLODEN Monument — like a breach with the beginnings
of a gorse busby or a lop sided Tam O'Shanter
A Red roofed kilhouse the only enemy on the moor these days.

In the *Inverness Courier* (price 3d) of that early September week in 1876 the usual wide-ranging local and international topics were aired. Rain had set in after the heatwave and there was an infestation of jelly fishes in the Moray Firth. A thunderstorm in Cambridge had struck a public house, demolishing the upper portion of the chimney, splitting the rest down and finally striking the landlady and knocking out all her front teeth.

J. MacKenzie MD Inverness was counterblasting the efficacy of smallpox vaccinations, the disease 'being beyond *our* control'. Mr Melvin, Bookseller, Union St, had 2 public and 4 bedrooms to let in Academy St for Northern Meeting Week. And a 'Lady residing in a healthy part of Inverness near the school wishes a LITTLE GIRL to live with her. Love of children more than remuneration is her object. Good references required and given here and in the South.' Imagine placing that kind of advertisement today.

The editorial dealt with the 'Eastern Question'. It noted an enlivened parliament during recess. 'Everywhere meetings are held to discuss the Eastern Question … The public is awakening to the fact that our Government has blundered in its treatment of Eastern affairs.' Touché. Meanwhile Dean Stanly is reported saying that 'the settling of the rights and claims of the various races and creeds in Europe and Asia is a task too serious to become the monopoly of any one party in the State.'

JTR In passing through Inverness, do not grudge to halt a night to visit the islands: if the night is moonlit, revisit the scene, and see it under the mellow beams. Another place within easy reach is Culloden Moor; the railway will take you within a few miles. You will have a real country walk and a fine view of Moray Firth and Loch Beauly by the way, and mayhap a little seven-year-old will lead you through curious windings among a forest of the future.

His 'forest of the future', bar a few outcrops, has been felled and logistics of the battle have been more comprehensible at the Visitors Centre. He gave a moody farewell to the scene which 'left many of our kilted heroes on the field cold and stiff'. I did not stay long.

JTR never referred to world events. I suppose it was not the done thing for a book of Rambles. Was he interested anyway? I doubt it. Religion, not politics, was his base line. And a passion for 'more national art: all our Highlands and islands are teeming with histories and traditions, manners and customs, and scenes worthy of the life-labours of our most gifted sons, yet few care to venture into this field.'

He was referring, of course, to his Brother Brushes, who exhibited annually, as did he, at the Royal Scottish Academy in Edinburgh. One of its founders and fourth President in 1864 was Sir George Harvey, celebrated for his canvases depicting Covenanting times and scenes of everyday life in the Scottish landscape. JTR was a devotee of his work and *Art Rambles in the Highlands and Islands* is indirectly dedicated to him. Harvey died in the year of the Rambles. 'It needs a born Highlander to understand aright our Scottish Highlanders,' goes on JTR, 'and to gather from them all the lore they know, so as to give us pictures that will live on in after ages. The Covenanting pictures of Sir George Harvey are the very near realization of that which I refer to. His heart breathed alike in sympathy with the men and their land.' Sir George was born in Perthshire.

Sir George's paintings are little known today except by those specially interested in the genre. Poor old JTR's quite unknown. The RSA's records lists forty-eight paintings and watercolours exhibited by JTR from 1865–1886. I have still to find one.

Of all JTR's contemporary Brother Brushes the one that has stood the test of time in not just an historical context is William McTaggart. He was the son of an Argyll crofter and although mainly concerned with landscape and seascape he was the first Scottish artist in the 1890s to place people in that landscape without sentimentality. JTR was not around to see the beginnings of political comment in Scottish art; his life took a new path far removed from the galleries and drawing rooms of artistic Edinburgh. His theory, misjudged with Harvie, has been proved correct, however, with McTaggart.

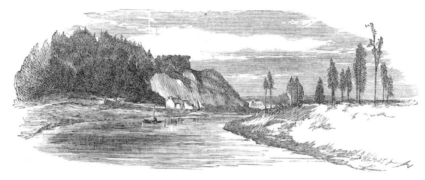

CALEDONIAN CANAL.

Ramble Four

ISLE OF SKYE
PORTREE · SLIGACHAN · CORUISK · STAFFIN

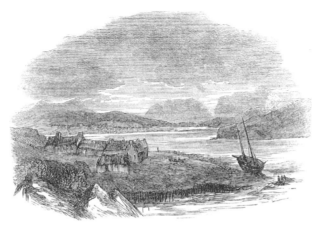

PORTREE BAY, ISLE OF SKYE.

JTR chose to reminisce in his chapter on Skye on several sketching visits to the Misty Isle from the comforts of his Edinburgh home. So I cheated too. A house-sit on the island for the MacLachlans at Camus Lusta in the Waternish area, where The Book was first found, gave me the luxury of motorised instead of pedestrian pursuance of Mr Reid Esq, save one memorable walk and a few hill scrambles. I became a car driver again *widely* overtaking walkers and cyclists, and made forays of comfortable detective work returning to my cornucopean base, some of the victuallings within you will learn about in the Lewis section.

Portree has long been the commercial centre of the Isle of Skye. The National Bank was built as early as 1830 and in JTR's time there was a comparable expansion of its administrative function just as today with all branches of government represented within a hand's throw of the Square. A Telegraph Office was opened in 1872 and the Portree Hotel was all of one year old, though JTR stayed with the Postmaster and family.

The first Ordnance Surveys of the island were being undertaken in three sections: Portree/Dunvegan, Staffin/Quiraing, the Cuillins. Maps however were not published till 1884/85 and JTR makes reference to the use of guides for mountain walkers. In 1836 a Professor James Forbes made the first recorded ascent of Sgurr nan Gillean with Duncan

MacIntyre, a local forester, as guide. Duncan must have been the mountain man of the day, for the previous year he had been engaged by the Revd C. Lessingham Smith to take him from Sligachan to Loch Coruisk, climbing in Harta Corrie on the way. And that was the beginning of Skye's climbing industry.

In 1882 one of the debates held in the YMCA in Portree was entitled 'Are the visits of tourists as a whole beneficial to the Highlands?' What a pity the local library did not have a record of the evening's discussion. Word for word with today's arguments? But maybe not, for on each side, one for, one against, were 'Mr Graham (merchant) and Mr J. Nicolson (merchant).'

Whilst scrambling about in the Quiraing the impression was of a giant stalagmite Disney World maze filled with wandering families in soft shoes and yet more babes in papooses. The serious climbers would not be seen dead with such riff raff. Munros are no longer the fashion. Corbetts, if you must, but the new bagging fashion is to find mountains that only the cognoscenti know and take at least a day's walk to get into. And then they don't say where they have been, if they are wise.

JTR The Coolin Mountains have a mighty power in drawing forth emotions of admiration and awe, and the appreciation of John MacWhirter's pictures of 'Coiruisk' in all its stern sublimity, by all classes of people, discovers a much more general appreciation of the grander aspects of nature than we would credit the ordinary picture-loving public to possess. It was seeing his picture of 'Mountain Silence' made me long to see the darksome mountain-girt lake in its weird lonesomeness with an intense longing.

And here we artists, not only writers, must admit to part of the blame for the popularising of the wilderness areas.

MacWhirter, though settled in London from his middle years on, was a Scottish painter whose best work was in the tradition of landscape painting traced back to the early seventeenth century. Landscape is not an old word in our language. The Shorter Oxford English Dictionary lists it orginating about 1602. The Russians had no word for landscape till the French arrived with 'paysage'. In our day it seems incredible that the landscape was at one time of no consideration to artists – and maybe the people in it.

Slowly the exterior background settings for religious paintings, the major activity of artists in the seventeenth century, took on more detailed contours and established geographic as well as topographic influences that we still see in some forms of landscape painting today. The Italians, and the Dutch, surprisingly, were the first true landscape painters, the Italian countryside always their source of inspiration. These images behind religious, secular or allegorical subjects as the century moved on, greatly appealed to the English. The Grand Tour of Italy was like what National Service used to be to the young men of our country. Except that it was only the wealthy that did their two years. By the end of the century landscape painting for its own sake was established.

Claude, the seventeenth-century French painter who spent much of his life in Italy, formulated a set of rules for landscape painting that became *de rigeur*. His foregrounds were blue-ey dark, far distance hazy and atmospheric with light. By the eighteenth century his fascinating contortion of viewing the English landscape was all the rage.

As though their own countryside let them down compared to that of Italy, the wealthy English had with them when travelling a Claude Glass through which they viewed the passing landscape from their carriages. It even tinged the foreground with blue and in its distortion made the landscape look just like a Claude painting. Nature imitating Art ...

This style of painting was obviously very popular but thankfully the English developed landscape painting away from the picturesque reaching their apogee with Turner and Constable.

By the nineteenth century England had become *the* nation of landscape painters although a large proportion of her artists were Scots who, tempted like their lairds a century before, had moved to London for prestige and remuneration.

Landscape painting is flourishing in Scotland today, artists resident, their subject matter possibly more valued than it has ever been with so much 'green' and wilderness awareness. Each age has its style. We now look at the gothic exaggeration and moody drama of Victorian landscapes and we learn of their romantic yearnings. I wonder what future generations will see in our contemporary landscape paintings. A countryside that is no more? We landscape painters might 'sell' the landscape but we also preserve it. And often at great expense to ourselves. I am thinking of all that walking again.

JTR Our way led us out of sight of the bay, [Portree; JTR has picked up a 'preacher of the Gospel'] and we were within hearing, and also could trace, the rocky stream that coursed seaward from the mighty mountains that form the Coolin range. I endeavoured to paint a picture of this scene, but again and again legions of midges drove me from the spot: I got a phial of essence supposed to keep them away, but alas! in vain. I have yet to learn an effectual protective against the midge. I believe tobacco-smoke is the most effectual, but to one not a smoker it would require to be a case of hiring another to the office of smoking away the midges – a work many would gladly undertake, for tobacco is looked on in the Highlands as a very great good, almost as essential as the whiskey ... We rested quietly and most comfortably in Sligachan Inn, than which I cannot imagine a better retreat in the early summer of late autumn, either before or after the great throng, who, coming from north and south to it in the height of the tourist season, make it a place of stir. Its proximity to the crags of the mighty Scoor-nan-Gillean, or 'Crag of the Young Men,' and to the stream that is fed by the waters that gather on its massive ramparts, are a great attraction.

After breakfast we left the inn and got on the track, which, with care, need not be lost sight of in good weather, except in haze or severe rain ... On the westward side of Heart o' Corrie a path is traced winding up the hill ... This is the path generally chosen by visitors going to Coiruisg, and once the hill-top is reached, the guides are quite contented to allow the visitor to see a small corner of lake. Those who know better will not rest contented with such a meagre peep of a lake so singularly grand, but will round the hill rather more than another mile to the west, and when the dark lake is full in view, sit down to drink a long look from that favourable point of view.

The more remotely JTR travelled the wilder became his place-name spellings. 'Heart o' Corrie' is Harta Corrie on the Ordnance Survey map. A perfect example of anglicising. 'Sorry, er, what did you say? Ha-er? ta? Oh, *heart* of the corrie.' And a scribbled note eventually gets printed for posterity. Nobody seems to have taken on JTR's corruption, however.

I walked to Coruisk from Sligachan and on to Camusunary and Kilmarie with a young American friend who had never been in this part of Scotland before. Or done such a walk. At the Bad Step above the sea beyond Coruisk I wondered at my lack of responsibility. It was getting dark but in a beautiful silvery still way. There was a long haul ahead. It was the one shared walk of the Rambles and I had forgotten the golden rule when introducing someone to the hills, never to stretch them beyond their ability.

There were no Disneyland walkers over that part of Skye. The nearest place to park a car was seven miles ahead or eleven miles behind.

Dianne was quite unaware of my sickening misgivings at the Bad Step and rightly so. She was in awe of the mountains around. 'I get the impression the landscape has suffered. Ancient. Wise. Mature.'

Was she hearing, in the gentle wind, eddying along the purpling coastline, the ghost lamentations of the thousands of sgitheanachs that had ended up against their will in her country over the Big Water?

A heron scraiked below the steep slabs of stone that chuted down into the sea. One false step and we would be down there too.

At Camasunary the bothy for walkers by the sea had a driftwood firelight glow coming through the window. We passed like wraiths zipping our anoraks against a colder night wind coming down from the deep indigo silhouetted mountains. Stars were coming out. The headtorch stumble down to Kilmarie and pies and Guinness back at the Sligachan Hotel on the way home ended Dianne's 'Maimorable day'. We had come back like the full circle of our route, intact.

The 'Glamaig Water' etching is in fact the Allt Daraich coming down from the corrie to the south of Glamaig and there I found one of the most reassuring sights of the Rambles. I could not *see* the ravine and its bald cliff edges on account of the trees and shrubs that had reached a confident maturity despite long years of unprotected infancy and adolescence. My notebook list includes rowan, oak, birch, Caledonian pine, hazel, holly, round-leaved willow, cherry (gean), aspen, dog rose, juniper, ivy, berberis, rhododendron. And honeysuckle twining up the birch.

The day after the walk to Coruisk turned vicious with cold winds and icy rain – the Jekyll and Hyde of the Hebrides, one day Greece, next day the Falklands. In Portree the

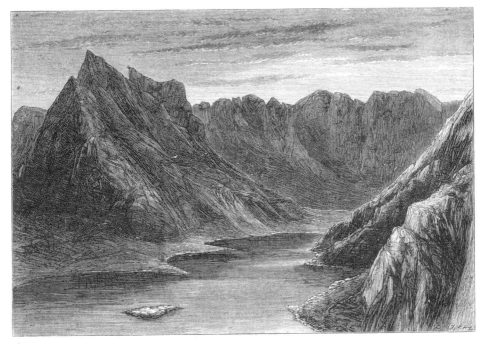

LOCH COIRUISG.

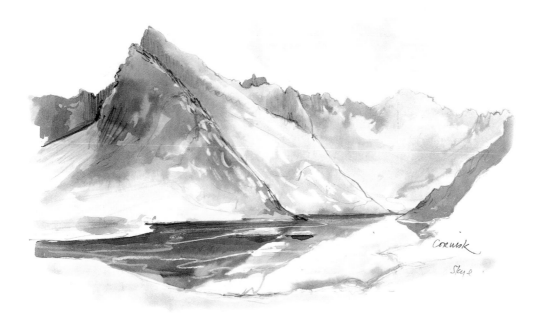

Coruisk
Skye

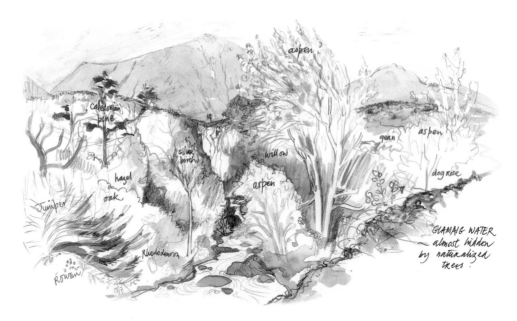

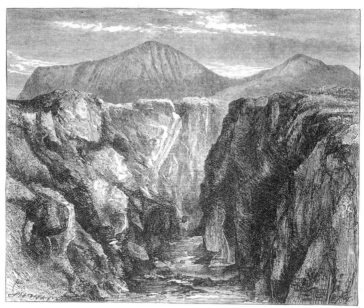

GLAMAIG WATER, ISLE OF SKYE.

locals in the shops were all saying 'Well, that's it then. Not long now. Winter's coming.' There was almost a note of relief in their voices. The wind whistled up round the corner past the supermarket to Stormy Hill. There in a tiny traditional house flanked by council housing lives Mrs MacKenzie.

Skye, again, had given me a unique link with JTR.

JTR There is a road on the brae-head, Portree, where you can see a number of very primitive cottages: it is known as 'Stormy Hill.' Certain it is, in stormy weather, from any point of the compass you will have a blow on Stormy Hill, and it does further seem as if it were tenanted by those who in the voyage of life have weathered storms quite as real, – long sickness, pinching poverty, and mayhap, in some cases, that very terrible malady when it becomes chronic, a disinclination to regular work ... As they are for the most part Gaelic-speaking folk, it is difficult to learn from themselves much of their true circumstances; but there are friends in Portree who would gladly assist any soul who would like to be helpful to the dwellers on Stormy Hill. You would marvel to know that even in that locality Sectarianism has raised its voice. I am told there are two sisters who dwell under one roof, and cannot speak to one another, for the one is a Free Churcher and the other is a Baptist; and that one gave to the other cause of great offence, having put cream in the tea of the other when such kind office was not desired.

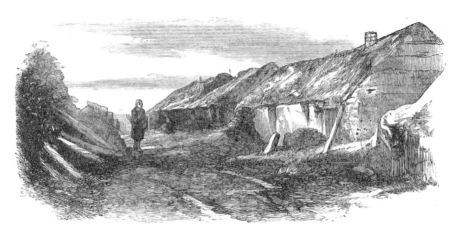

COTTAGES, STORMY HILL, SKYE.

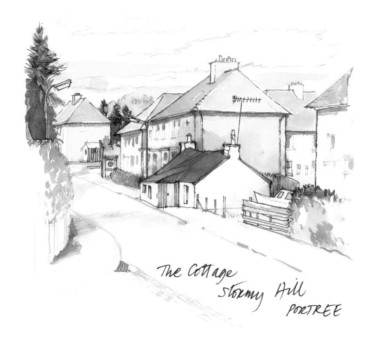

The Cottage
Stormy Hill
PORTREE

When I fought my way up the brae and saw all the council houses I almost turned back, dismissing the possibility of there being any evidence of older architecture. But there it was, The Cottage, its porch right over the pavement to the gutter, red reflectors for night traffic on its corners, pedestrians having to detour on to the road before regaining the pavement again.

'I hear people passing and saying "How on earth do they allow a porch to be built on top of the pavement?" Don't they realise the porch was there fifty years before the new road …?' said Mrs MacKenzie, a hint of exasperation in her voice. The black tarred roof had been 'like that for as long as I can remember.' A widow, now in her eighties, her husband was brought up in the house by his grandparents. In the late 1940s when council housing was planned, Lord MacDonald allowed the old houses with resident tenants a reprieve from the builder's bulldozer. Only two of the originals survived, the other less incongruously surrounded and more 'improved' thus lacking such character, nearer the braehead.

'If the council houses hadn't come, we'd not have had electricity, water or the phone for all these years.' Mrs MacKenzie did not mind the houses so close. 'Just get an awful downdraught in the chimney sometimes.'

She said she knew nothing of a sectarian feud in the old days of Stormy Hill but if she did it was not the kind of thing you discussed with strangers, I sensed. Or dwell on the kind of poverty that JTR described. We wondered at the 'pinching poverty' that could have cream for tea.

Mrs MacKenzie proudly showed me her minuscule immaculate palace, the walls almost thicker than the passageway. A leg of something simmered in a pot on the stove, as tasty and traditional as her grandmother-in-law's, I'm sure. And there certainly was cream and more for tea.

For all my love of landscape, nothing would induce me to spend weeks painting the Needle Rock in the Quiraing and certainly not in JTR's era when hazards were beyond mere midges. I leave Skye returning to Inverness with his account very similar to my own experience barring the missiles and the guides and honestly think once again that the number of visitors to some 'beauty spots' in the Highlands and Islands were far in excess of those of today.

Maybe phenomena like the Needle, a pockmarked warty old erect penis with a tuft of grass on its tip, do not hold the same attraction these days. I certainly have not met another Brother or Sister Brush that has been compelled to study it for *weeks* on end …

JTR In company with an English artist, I climbed up the steep hill-side for many successive weeks to paint the Needle Rock.

It is not a desirable place to paint pictures in, inside the Cuiraing: the silence and the

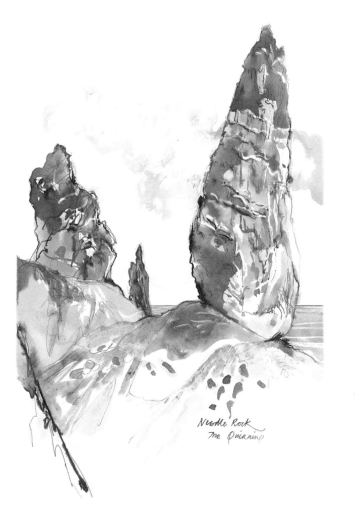

Needle Rock
The Quiraing

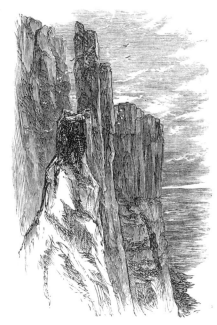

OUT-STACK AND THE KILT ROCK, STAFFIN BAY, SKYE.

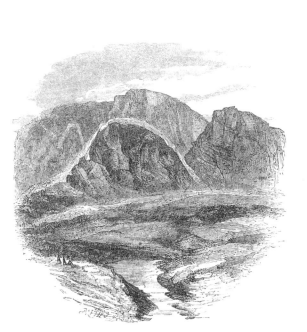

OPPOSITE THE CUIRAING.

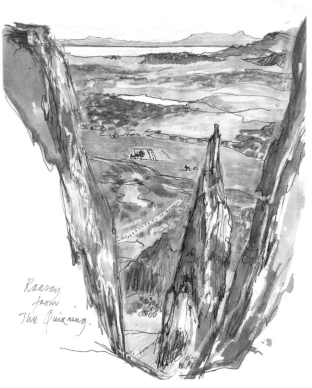

Raasay
from
The Quiraing.

grandeur awes you; and the sheep above where we stood had an uncomfortable habit of loosening with their feet stones that came with an ominous crash near to us, and some shepherd lads, much less excusable, thought it good fun to threaten to, and likewise to perform, throwing stones near us. I will not suppose them guilty of a direct intention of striking us, particularly if they had any idea of the danger of such a proceeding, for the cliff rose much more than a hundred feet above us, and even a very small stone would have fatal effect by striking the head. We had tourist visitors of every age and family, and some quaint scenes were witnessed on the upgoing – many of the native children (and one who in a few years after might be called an old man) found it a profitable, and I doubt not, too, a pleasurable work, leading the tourists to the top. We noted how shrewdly the man was found paying attention to the member of the party who looked most likely to be the paymaster.

Ramble Five

DINGWALL · KINLOCHEWE · TORRIDON · GAIRLOCH · DUNDONNELL · ULLAPOOL

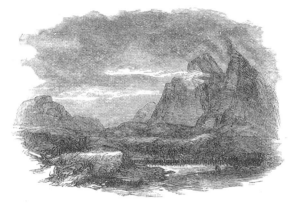

IN GLEN TORRIDON, ROSS-SHIRE.

JTR On our way from Inverness to the west we went out of the train at the Muir of Ord of cattle-market fame. It was the day for the sale of sheep, and we saw many little lots under the guardianship of shepherds and collie dogs; eager buyers were going from group to group, judging their respective merits – now taking a hold of a sheep to feel his weight, and noting the quality of his fleece. The market was principally composed of lambs of varied breed and from many diverse parts of the country.

By now it was October and the month of the sheep sales. Some things never change. Muir of Ord Mart is no more, but Dingwall serves the purpose almost identically. Pens nestled alongside the wall of St Clement's Parish Church, carparks jammed with Landrovers and their brash modern progeny, Subarus and Toyotas. The smell of sheep hung in the atmosphere soaking into sawdust and Harris Tweed alike. Buyers from Oban, Skye and Ullapool, with gimlet eyes, hung over the railings marked with farm and estate names – Belmaduthy, Morvich, Torgormack, Glastullich, Lochrosqua, Kintradwell and Erribol.

Prices were not good for the tup sales. 'Been too many good tups over the past few years. There's a glut now,' said one rueful farmer. £20 was all he'd got for one beast. The £30 subsidy per sheep would maybe keep the bank manager quiet for a while. 'But the subsidy is being withdrawn next year. Bloody EEC.'

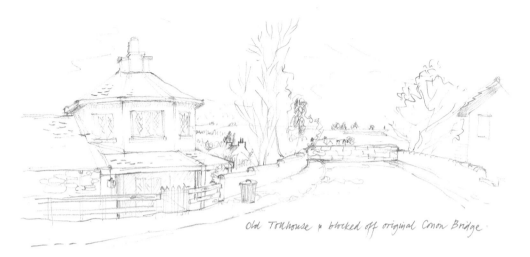

Old Tollhouse & blocked off original Conon Bridge.

Wives in good thick skirts chattered between auctions. 'Are you getting on holiday?' said one, relieved that the end of the farming year was at hand. 'No,' said her friend, 'it's the sheepdog trials next.'

After Muir of Ord JTR got off the train at Conon Station as did I, and walked down by the river to sketch from the Telford bridge of 1809 now replaced by a modern version built in 1969. The old tollhouse further upstream by the site of the totally removed old bridge is a very desirable residence with ubiquitous modern coachlamps at the door and surrounded by bungalows built 'where groups of fine cattle were grazing on the rich grass', that made JTR 'covet the power of the animal painter.'

Dingwall was the start for the journey into 'the great western wilderness'. Lochs Torridon and Maree were his next sketching locations.

JTR Magnificent subjects they are; but how are they reached? Fortunately, or unfortunately, that is easy work now: the iron horse speeds you along, you steam under the shades of Knockfarrel, which has on its summit a very fine vitrified fort; past Strathpeffer Wells, Castle Leod, Lochs Garve and Luichart, through Strath Bran, till you reach Auchnasheen, where you change steam for horse-power, and get a little exercise in patience, waiting in the drizzling rain till the horses are rested, re-yoked, and ready for starting. One Highlander was in a fix regarding his dog: he would not pay the fare for his collie; the official threatened to take him – the dog – as a hostage; Dugald warned him Prince would 'grip him' if he dared. The poor dog seemed to know all about it, for in fear and trembling he waited behind his master, hanging his tail most ignobly. It ended in the fare being paid with a very bad grace. Our mail gig party consisted of the Highlander who owned the dog, a woman with a very large bundle, a young man just home from his studies at a school in Germany, going to join a family party at Gairloch, and two men I would judge to be shepherds, possibly coming from Muir of Ord after selling their sheep. Our driver got the mail bags stowed away, and made his horses strike out in good style. We had ample occupation watching the play of the clouds over the sides of the hills, and the bits of rugged moor and moss and flowing stream that enlivened the way; but at a turning within some three miles of the inn of Kinlochewe, as we were about to pass the east-going mail gig with its complement of travellers, our driver jerked the horses into a ditch, which upset our machine and broke one of the springs. Fortunately nobody was hurt. After the horses were released from the machine and the ditch, we walked leisurely to the inn, only regretting that the clouds hung so heavily over Loch Maree that it was completely obscured.

In that week's *Ross-shire Journal* it is reported, amongst other items like the 1,522 soundings taken by the Channel Tunnel Company – 'Greater progress in the formation of the Company has been made in France than England' – that Sir Kenneth S. MacKenzie, proprietor of Gairloch, was promoting the welfare of his tenants by offering to defray the costs of mail delivery. Sir Kenneth was the half brother of Osgood MacKenzie who created the famous gardens in Inverewe. Osgood was the same age as JTR and it is a pity that JTR did not continue northward from Gairloch and possibly meet this incredible man whose life and family chronicled in *A Hundred Years in the Highlands* gives such detailed insight into the times.

Suffice to say JTR was travelling through territory totally ruled by a very wealthy network of families who, politics aside, were more in touch with their peasantry than their less isolated land owning peers. The railway only went as far as Achnasheen in 1876. It goes all the way to Kyle of Lochalsh these days turning southwards from Achnasheen, leaving the wild vastness of Wester Ross accessible only by the motor car, a later and more threatening penetration.

My mail gig was the post bus from Achnasheen to Kinlochewe, horse power converted to cylinders and passing places obviating diversionary tactics with oncoming vehicles.

I and the one other passenger viewed the landscape through the grille dividing us from the driver, the mail, bottles of milk and newspapers. My fellow traveller was going to a reunion with school friends at Torridon. Brought up in Kinlochewe, she had left thirty years ago and never been back even though she lived in Tain only sixty-odd miles to the east. I could tell that this was a big event in her life. 'My man said he wouldn't mind looking after the kids.'

I met her later in the pub, shiny-eyed with memories. Things she had 'never thought about until now!' Like riding bareback on the ponies on the other side of Loch Maree and taking the boats out on the loch. 'Nobody bothered where we were.' How *could* she have forgotten? She remembered helping in the hotel kitchen when she was ten but *nowhere* near the Bar. The Aberdonian housekeeper was very strict. Despite such professional guidance this plump middle-aged woman laughingly recalled 'being legless at the Village Hall dances, all at the age of thirteen. Best forgetting that and all the half bottles in the backs of cars but, you know, I never took to the drink in adult life.' She sipped a coffee while I nursed a double brandy.

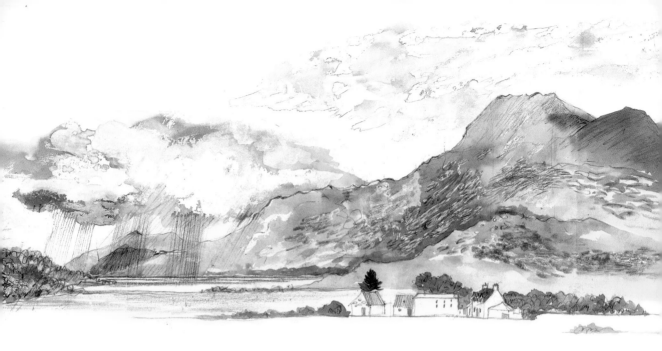

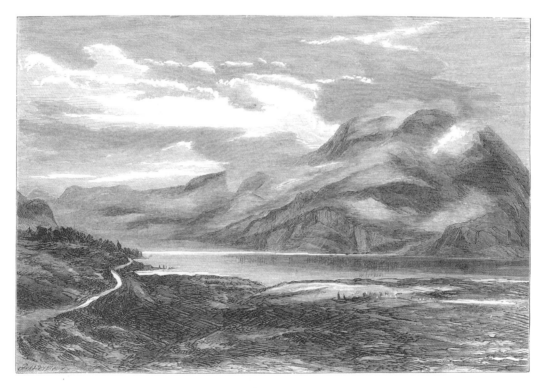

LOCH MAREE.

The sketchbook and notebook pages for the day are almost indecipherable with rain drop splodges. Drifts of rain came up Loch Maree as I plowtered wet and chilled along the lochside to find the spot for JTR's 'Loch Maree'. By four o'clock car sidelights were on, small-eyed in the gathering gloom. The season was over. The visitor centre at Aultroy was closed. Through cobwebby windows I saw a relief model of the surrounding mountains and a large vacant video screen hanging from the ceiling. Redundant until next year's visitors.

Now I felt more in tune again with JTR's travels. No gimmicks to explain the landscape. At least he was spared that.

I love more than anything JTR's 'fortunately or unfortunately' reference to travel improvements in the area. He must have understood what that meant. What ambivalence that man had brought out in me …

At the Kinlochewe pub, all the talk was of the Countryside Commission's just published report 'The Mountain Areas of Scotland' recommending that Wester Ross have National Park status. Should it be so decided, the first thing under review will be the road system, which just about copes with the present traffic. Improve it and the door is open to summer invasions like that of the Lake District. At least there is no M6 so near. But who can tell of the future.

Everyone I spoke to was against the widening of the roads, especially the steep pass down into Kinlochewe. 'They go fast enough as it is,' said one local certainly not averse to the many material improvements in his lifestyle compared to that of his parents without electricity and all that that facilitates.

Crofters were very apprehensive of the possible changes. 'National Parks are run by management boards that dictate the very colour of your window frames.' They manage people in the environment, as well as colour schemes it seems. Someone maintained that the land owners would be immediately involved in these management groups. 'They don't want their hills covered with people.'

'They are covered with too many stags, that's the problem.' 'Hinds must be culled in greater numbers,' said someone else. 'The clients only want the trophy heads of stags, you see.' They all agreed it was better to make steps on the eroded paths scarring Beinn Eighe and keep everyone on the one track.

JTR I cannot express to you the charm that hangs about a mountain like Ben Each as the mists swathe its rocky sides; they rise, they fall, they whirl, they soar as on wings of light, they cast shadows, they give grand mystery, and anon reveal some hidden dell, some great bare precipice, or perhaps display a glowing patch of verdure … I expect each one will take from these misty illusions, creations congenial to his own mind. I do not envy those who only see in them the messengers of evil tidings, forebodings of rain, and who think the landscape is devoid of loveliness because the sun does not shine – because there is not an Italian sky overhead, and that the open car or gig he travels in is not a Pullman car. We had not only the glories of the mist-workings on the sides of Bens Each and Leagach on our right; we had Ben Lair, which was now and again seen with the deep cloud-shapes falling over his rocky summit and his tree-lined base.

JTR was obviously in foreign territory. His mountain spellings are very idiosyncratic but no doubt faithful attempts to transcribe local pronunciation. For instance he wrote Leagach (more as it sounds) for Liathach; yet Each for Eighe (pronounced ay as in play) seems to have no phonetic parallel.

The warden's wife at the Beinn Eighe Nature Reserve told me the no doubt apocryphal tale of a traveller in Northern Canada laboriously taking down phonetic notes from an Inuit pointing to various landmarks in his territory. Back in civilisation the explorer finds that the translation reads, 'Don't know what that is called' and 'Don't know what that is called either'.

They better get the spelling right before the hordes arrive in Wester Ross. Look what you started, JTR, with your Rambling. And what I sustain with mine. The changes they are a-coming. Adaptation the name of the game. Deer are no longer upset by bright red anoraks. 'Khaki greens are the worry,' advised a local, on the brandy as well. Mrs Tain ex-Kinlochewe had long ago retired to bed. It was left to us alcoholics to sort out the thorny problem.

FREEDOM TO ROAM MUST BE GUARANTEED was the headline in the *West Highland Free Press* the following day. That was just what I had been doing for the past four months innocent of impending restrictions. Will my rambles be as arcane as JTR's one day?

'7.10 am on the dot and my husband will give you a lift to Torridon,' the woman in the council house opposite the hotel had said. I stood waiting in the pre-dawn dark watching house lights go on. Garden birds roused themselves bravely, far off a cockerel said it was the new day and buzzards with peeinging whistle arced over the slowly silhouetting mountains. It was freezing cold.

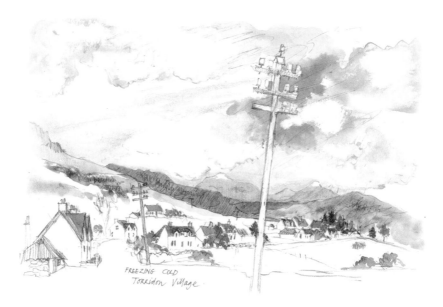

FREEZING COLD
Torridon Village.

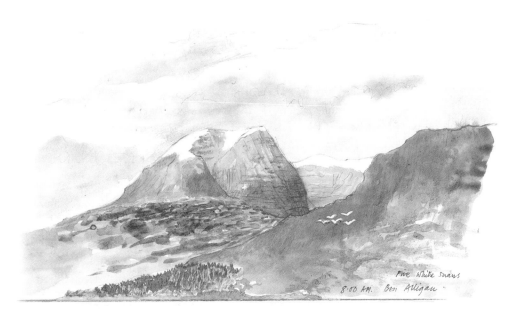

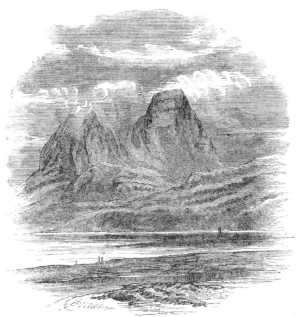

BEN ALLIGAN, LOCH TORRIDON.

The first sleety snows had capped Slioch and Ben Eighe. At Torridon my fingers froze as I attempted to sketch Ben Alligin. Gold-edged clouds sailed in a sea of cold blue sky, violently eclipsed by sleet-scudding showers slashing up Loch Torridon. The pictures are in my head should they never end up on paper.

139

By eleven o'clock I had eaten the Kinlochewe Hotel's packed lunch (in lieu of breakfast) and was bereft of all nourishment which I was greatly in need of. I stood for a long time in a telephone box just to keep out of the slicing rain. At times like that I could not care a toss for JTR and wondered why the hell I was in such a situation.

I walked back to Kinlochewe having missed the postbus. Not a car passed till nearly there. The NCC warden kindly gave me a lift in his Landrover. No, I did not raise the topics of the previous evening; some nurturing is better accepted without reservation.

At the shop it looked as if there would be no public transport to Gairloch until the next century. 'No lorries?' I queried. And as if on cue in rolled a Chalmers Mace supply van. The driver could take me all the way to Inverness if I wanted. Ullapool was where I was heading there being no boats from Gairloch to Stornoway as in JTR's day. 'Nae problem, I'll drop you off at Braemore junction.' A mere twelve miles from Ullapool. The last ferry to Stornoway was at 5.30 pm. 'Nae problem.'

A. B. Chalmers of Inverness started out like the shopkeepers in Inveraray with a delivery barrow, graduating to a pony and trap for outlying districts and in 1907 introducing the first steam lorry to the Highlands. Today the sixteen-and-a-half horse power Ford Cargo, one of a fleet of several serving the Highlands and Islands, is driven by Bill once a week to Gairloch, fortnightly to Kinlochewe and once a month to Applecross.

I asked him how he coped with the summer traffic on the twisting single-track roads. 'Ach, I've always got my newspaper for when they can't reverse. I just sit and have a good read until they are done. I've got all day and I'm being paid.'

Everything was 'nae problem' to Bill. I settled in for a relaxed, warm overview on the world high up in the comfy cab. Beinn Eighe still dominated the landscape as we headed for Gairloch. Streamers of snow blew from its sharp-toothed ridges. At each de-veiling of sleeting showers more snow whitened the tops and yet there were still leaves on the trees at the roadside. On Loch Maree the islands were dumpy, thick with Caledonian pines that would keep their blue black prickly leaves all winter. The hillsides would have been covered like this a few centuries ago – genuine deer forests. The names are still on the map – Flowerdale, Letterewe, Fisherfield.

In between the showers bright sun sparkled, the raindrops shivering on fence and electricity wires.

'Priority bulk items are beans, catfood and dogfood. And in that order,' Bill informed me. He was right. I carried in tray after tray of Whiskas to the Gairloch store. Storage seemed to be a problem. Lemsip, liquid fairy, firelighters and deodorants nestled in the steeply coombed attic. Cereals were stacked under the stairs, toilet paper above the door and 'thro' the back' was the repository for every shape and size of bottle.

Leaving Gairloch, the pinky red beach and recharged store, the panoramic journey continued up over the hill by Loch Tollaidh to Poolewe, past Osgood MacKenzie's Inverewe gardens and along the bleak coast to the next drop at Aultbea. There was a wild wind out to sea. A solid wall of hailstones came up Loch Ewe, ricochetting off the windscreen as it swept by, hell bent on lacerating Loch Maree and final immolation on the flanks of Slioch.

At Laide the council gritter was getting petrol at the shop. 'What's the forecast?' I asked, thinking of the boat journey to the Outer Hebrides. 'Frost tomorrow,' said the orange overalled driver.

'It's come quick, the winter.'

'And it better not go quick.'

'Why?'

'This is our jam.'

He smiled cheerily, dreaming of drifts and sheet-ice and overtime. Country and Western music blared from the cab.

Dundonnell Stores had not been in operation long. It seemed to be operating from the back room of a house. The steep track down to the gate gave the last trolley and Bill a stylish tango across the floor of the van.

The light was going as we headed inland from Little Loch Broom, An Teallach white-pinnacled to our right. On the desolate stretch over to Braemore junction we passed a young woman walking at the side of the road. She wore sensible walking gear but an air of not quite belonging. I distinctly remember Bill and I making no comment. He possibly through guilt at not stopping to give her a lift, though she hadn't asked. For myself, I just saw me out there in the gathering dark – and cringed. All those lonely main road trudges I had endured. Had others pitied me as they flashed past? Or worse, not even noticed me? Did I, did she, exist?

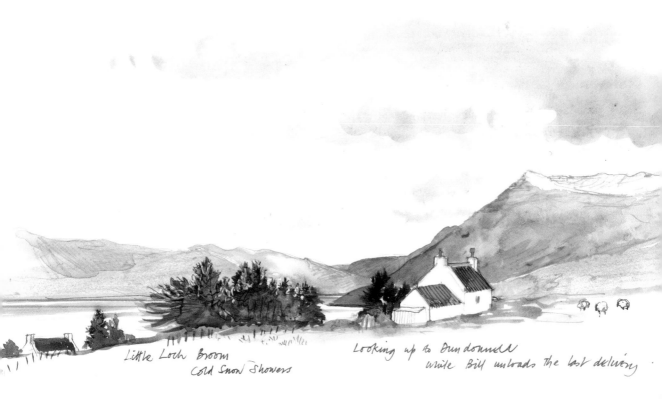

Little Loch Broom
Cold Snow Showers

Looking up to Dundonnell
while Bill unloads the last delivery

I was dreading the inevitable hitching to Ullapool. By then it was dark. 'You could come into Inverness and get the early bus back out to Ullapool in the morning … ' offered Bill as I climbed down from my position of elevation and security. No, that would be a false contrivance and anyway I still had a mad hope of catching that five-thirty ferry to Stornoway. Twelve miles in an hour?

The thumb was out as I resolutely walked along the road shielding my eyes from oncoming lights and wistfully following the tails lights of cars that sailed by. Not a house or steading light punctured the enveloping blackness in between. It was the first time that I had openly, assertively hitched. I wanted that boat.

As a car driver I have conflicting reactions to hitchers. If I am in the mood, fine. If not, it gets more complicated; guilt first at not being generous with my superior situation. But then I might have a passenger whose company I am enjoying and do not want the intrusion. If I give a hitcher a lift I expect social interaction and can't abide the ones that use me like a bus service, mute to the point of rudeness.

After the guilt comes the confusion and then the anger. Anger at being put in this situation. And who is the object of this anger? The poor hitcher, of course.

I now know that the anger is reciprocal.

What angered me most was the Gulag searchlight exposure of oncoming vehicles. I tried to compose my features into a combination of nonchalance and justification. From behind I could have been a man with my hood up. Women are more likely to get a lift? With the hood down my summer sun bleached hair might give the wrong message? Furious with myself for these creeping insidious thoughts I focussed on lengthening my stride and levitating the rucksack. The hood stayed down.

After six miles and double that number of overtaking vehicles, a car drew up, patiently waiting for my embarrassing clumsy backpacking lurch to catch up with it. A young couple, they had been out touring; she was driving and in charge. Once through the thankyous and the 'I *never* do this kind of thing, ordinarily,' I settled in the back, everything blissfully out of my control. There was an uneasy tension between the two of them. It turned out that she had gone for a hill walk on her own with an agreed pick-up point by him in the car. Somehow – it did not seem diplomatic to enquire too deeply just how – he had missed her at the arranged spot. 'I fell asleep,' he guffawed in a self deprecatory way. She was not laughing. She had walked many miles along the road before he had caught up with her.

Suddenly I recognised her. The woman on the road. I said nothing, diplomatic coward that I was, but wondered at her generosity in drawing up for me. Was she trying to tell her companion something?

I was very grateful to her, whatever the reasons.

I had missed the ferry by half an hour. A fisherman unloading boxes of fish, shimmering in the arc lights of the pier, told me the next one was not until midday the following day. No, there would not be any fishing boats going back out. It was Friday and all the boats tied up. It was at times like this that my physical and emotional stamina dangerously evaporated; nurturing was essential.

I treated myself to a night in the Ceilidh Place; I had not given up the habit of including the dangly earrings and the flowery trousers in the rucksack.

At dinner, the conservatory-like room was filled with couples in varying stages of partnership – lovers, outdoor companions, well-heeled oldies. Next to Paul Theroux and me were two lady companions. JTR had chickened out and was travelling south – 'we saw the first snows fall before we left … ' – to write up his chapter retrospectively on previous rambles in Skye, for some obscure reason. Maybe it was because of the snow or maybe he was getting fed up with me. Travelling companions do need a break now and then. We had been at it for three months now. I was glad of the break.

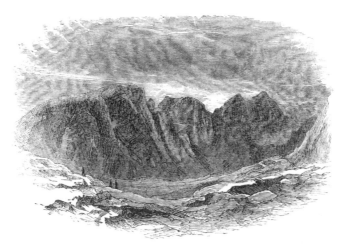

CORRIE, DUNDONALD.

Next morning I was a new woman, quite revitalised and waiting contritely for JTR who I had summoned back up from Edinburgh to get on with the Lewis Ramble.

'Do you mind if I join you?' It was one of the two gourmet ladies of the previous evening. I was sipping coffee in the coffee house of the hotel.

She and her companion had come up under full sail to my table.

'Are you a writer?' the other asked, once they had berthed. 'I was just saying to my friend, there she is scribbling again.'

They were genial enough and we exchanged pleasantries until the leading galleon said, 'Do you believe in destiny?' And before I could reply she rushed on, eyes moist with excitement. 'We came to meet someone who hasn't turned up. But now we have met you … !' And out it all came. They were canvassers for the Bahá'í Faith. JTR turn up quickly, please. It is you they want, not me.

Stalling for his arrival I asked about the religion. It originated in the East in Persia, made manifest in Bahá'u'lláh who was born in 1817 and 'spokesman for our age. John the

Baptist was his forerunner,' said the Galleon firmly, underlining his respectability. Bahá'ís do not disbelieve in any previous founders of world religions. Such leaders are all members of a spiritual relay race handing on the messianic baton it seems. Meetings are held every nineteen days, not necessarily Sundays, which must keep people on their toes. The world centre is in Haifa, Israel.

Seeing I was interested the ladies warmed to their subject – and victim. 'These are exciting times. Times of great change. That is when the current, the energy cannot be ignored. Our numbers are increasing.' They were doubly enthused when they heard about JTR – he had arrived, at last – and the evangelical parallels with the 1870s. I suggested that that economic disparity might be the link to all evangelical movements. They felt it was more to do with the wickedness of the world. 'But that is a form of wickedness, isn't it?' I persisted.

'What do they say in Iran about Bahá'u'lláh and the Bahá'ís?' I was getting bored and provocative. Did they realise? Maybe the Galleon did. 'What a perceptive question,' she commented, patronisingly. 'The Shah accepted them but not the Ayatollah; persecuted to annihilation.'

I wondered who the ladies were directly responsible to in the Organisation. I could tell that my questioning was slowly turning off the taps of their charm. I never did get an answer to that final one. I think they began to realise my destiny did not tie in with theirs.

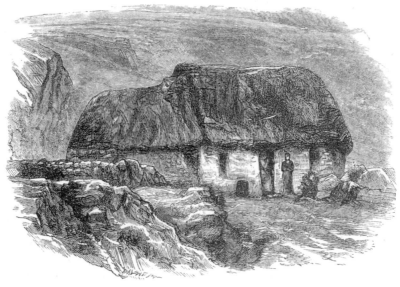

COTTAGE, LOCH TORRIDON.

Ramble Six

ISLE OF LEWIS
Stornoway · Gress · Garrynahine · Barvas Ness · Butt of Lewis

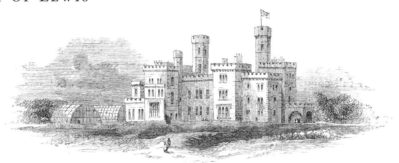

STORNOWAY CASTLE.

At Ullapool the midday early-November sun was low in the sky, white gold fanning down into the sea beyond Scoraig peninsula; An Teallach hid its snow caps, cut off by a cool indigo-grey cloud. The boat slurped and sloughed its way Lewisward through great troughs of waves blown from the north at forty-five degrees across our bows. The modern car ferry was like a nautical greenhouse with the sun streaming in the south-facing picture windows – passengers' heads wilting with heat and motion like so many tomato plants.

Ever moving currents of rain, with silver vertical folds of sun behind, touched the horizon line of the sea in dancing gold, silver and platinum. It is what I hope death will be; an everlasting ringseat show of stormy seas, sky and cloud, an island and headland or two silhouetted in the far distance. Those curtains are called 'precipitation' by meteorologists and are fast falling products of condensation in the atmosphere of rain, hail or snow. I love that word. Maybe I will die quickly, too.

This was a local's boat. Gaelic on both sides of the cafeteria counter. A few tourists were aboard; a couple with walking gear and their spaniel dog with one blind eye staring out of the low window, and a Canadian, rather loud, who had struck up conversation with a young Lewis woman who was coming back from visiting her husband working in Libya. She was obviously relieved to have got out and to be on the boat home. The Eastern problem and the emotions it had aroused were still with us. Saddam still held the world to ransom.

'Arabs! There are *no* words in the English language to describe them.' She was as loud as he.

The young Canadian took it upon himself in too domineering a fashion to explain about their religion, but she was having none of it. Would he just as keenly defend the strict Presbyterian religion of the island he was about to visit, I wondered.

I swear that dog was looking out to sea with his blind eye.

JTR At the pier [Gairloch] I waited the transport boats, seen in dim shadowy form coming from the steamboat that lay out in the bay, and listened to the plash of the oars. They had much goods for Gairloch, and not a little to take on board. Once on board, I took a look below, where many men folk were as comfortably spread on the saloon sofas as circumstances would permit, and finding a vacant space sufficiently large to stretch my full complement of feet and inches on, I tried to fall asleep before we got into rough water; but with the first movement of the screw, I was on my feet and on deck, having a view of the hills round Gairloch as they slept in the mist of night ere the faint streaks of dawn disturbed their repose.

As we receded from the mainland we ever sighted new mountain ranges: we saw them growing fainter and dipping out of our sight; to the southward the Skye hills lent a charm, and the Isle of Lewis loomed bigger and broader, till we steamed alongside of the pier and were landed 'mid the curing of a fine catch of herring taken during the night. The boats were sparkling with the glitter of the 'caller ou,' as our fishwives call them; and busily the men were throwing them out from among the nets into the creels, while the shore was lined by brawny-armed women clothed in waterproof aprons, who with marvellous rapidity were gutting the fish, and packing them in barrels with abundance of salt between each layer. As a whole the season had not brought a successful fishing, which, sad to relate, would condemn to bachelorhood for another year many Lewismen who waited a successful season to enable them to begin life in partnership with a fisher lass. Shortly thereafter I read in one of the local papers: 'The recent failure in the herring fishery has had a very depressing effect on the matrimonial market at nearly all the fishing stations. The decrease on the marriages in the three months ending 30th September is very considerable. In the island of Lewis, with upwards of 25,000 inhabitants, there were only two marriages.' An unsuccessful fishing is a most discouraging event to the dwellers in these remote western isles: hundreds leaving every year for the east coast; when fortunate, they will be able to bring home with them, after clearing all expenses for board, etc., more than enough to pay the rent of their crofts; but in a bad year they may come away in debt to the curer.

JTR's vivid description of Stornoway harbour and the 'caller ou' belongs very much to history. Those herring fishing days are gone. But not the drift to the mainland for work for the young men. The young woman back from Libya an example. Her man 'in the oil'. But Lewis has its own oil-based industry. Lewis Offshore has a fabricated yard for the oil industry at Arnish Point, a little south of the town. The week I was there the *Stornoway Gazette* had a page three article celebrating a fourth contract for the firm that would mean 120 jobs.

Nosing around the pier and harbour I learned that the fishing for '89 had been terrible, but not so bad for '90. It was impossible to ascertain how many of the boats moored in the harbour over the weekend were local. Since 1988 all fishing boats are registered in Cardiff. The majority of islanders who are fishermen are based in Ness to the very north of Lewis yet will tie up their boats in Stornoway and drive home. The young man in the Fishermans' Cooperative office was trying to be helpful. '£221,000 worth of business came through the Stornoway office this month.' That meant nothing to me. The harbour would never be the scene of activity described by JTR.

There was a late Saturday afternoon buzz in the streets of Stornoway. The inexorableness of the Sabbath was almost palpable, waiting just round the corner, to slap up grilles and padlock doors. Meanwhile the end of the world had not yet come. Life was for living – and buying. Third generation Pakistani youngsters, some Gaelic speaking, serve in family shops, the most north-westerly branch of their clans happily absorbed into the community. That dread word religion again, an ingredient of their successful assimilation. The Muslim faith has many similarities to that of the fundamentalist Free Presbyterian Church whose last stronghold is on the Isle of Lewis.

There are signs of cracks in the bonding however as bigger and better shops are being taken over by Pakistani families. But that is not religion threatening, that is money.

The number of stories about the power of religion in Lewis are legion. And there is no need to exaggerate for effect. The current story was about the innocent yet ignorant mistake the Scottish Chamber Orchestra had made in promoting their presentation of Stravinsky's 'The Soldier's Tale' which was to include professional dancers and actors and local schoolchildren who had been invited to participate. Manuscripts and scripts and advertising blurb were sent well in advance of performance date. Unfortunately, the SCO were not aware of the sin of incarnating the Devil and inviting everyone to a knees-up to 'shame the devil' after a 'devilish' evening's entertainment …

Several primary teachers from the staunch outlying districts would not let the children attend rehearsals let alone the performance in Stornoway. The children's loss but the fault lay more with the SCO's insensitivity to a cultural difference than to a lack of religious awareness.

The apparent bigotry, to an outsider's eye, of the Free Presbyterian Church has some good points. For one thing, I'm all in favour of workless Sundays though I draw a line at taking the cockerel out of the henhouse or padlocking the children's swings on a Saturday night. Imagine trafficless roads for one day of the week! We'd all start *walking*. For another, has the Scottish Tourist Board not cottoned on to the fact that this Sunday sailings issue is good copy. Ideally, of course, there should be the choice, especially for islanders having to work on the mainland who want to come home for the weekend.

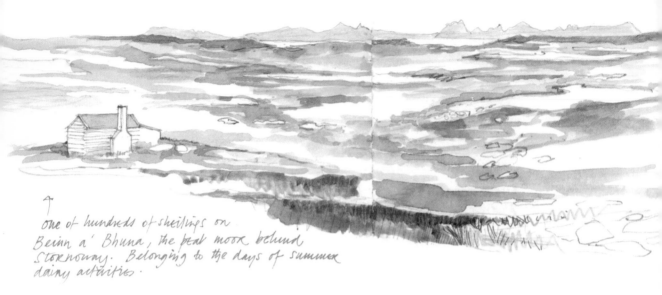

one of hundreds of sheilings on
Beinn a' Bhuna, the peat moor behind
Stornoway. Belonging to the days of summer
dairy activities.

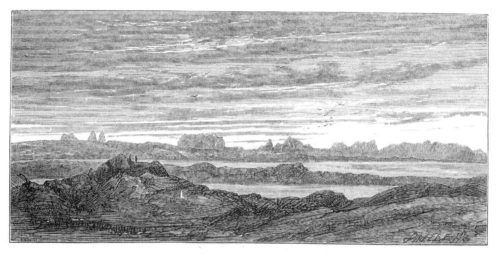

MAINLAND MOUNTAINS, FROM ISLE OF LEWIS.

Next day, Sunday, walking through the town, I was amused to see hired buses
(no scheduled services) and car loads of black clad churchgoers proving that some
compromises have been made. That's when I hit on the answer. Church service travel only
allowed on CalMac ferries on Sundays. What price an hour or two pewbound to get across
the Minch either way on God's day. Better still, services on the boats … Have them all –
Billy Graham, Moody and Sankey, Bahá'u'lláh, John, the Baptist. And JTR, of course.

JTR The most noteworthy feature about Stornoway is the castle and grounds of Sir James
Mathieson. It is a palatial residence, and occupies a worthy site, like the magnificent piles
of masonry built in our forefathers' days, to guard the people's home; this stronghold raises
its proud walls and towers, and commands alike the bay and every house that lines the
shores. There are no remarkable buildings in the town; there are banks, churches, very
many general merchants, and a few bakers, butchers, curing yards, ship-building yards and
suchlike, while in the harbour there is some shipping life.

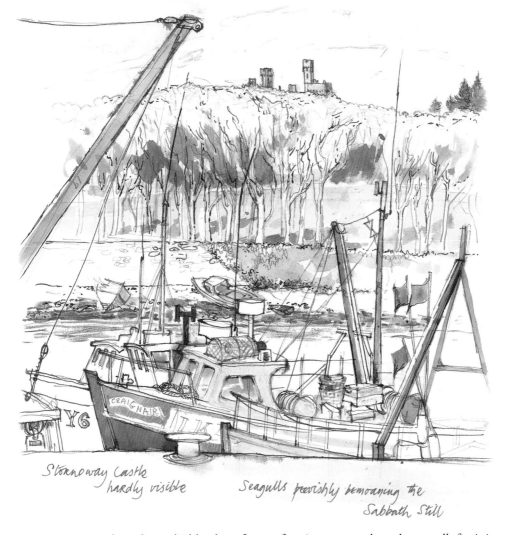

Stornoway Castle
hardly visible

Seagulls peevishly bemoaning the
Sabbath still

Stornoway Castle is almost hidden by a forest of ageing trees and maybe as well, for it is in a boarded-up state. Having been a College of Further Education for years, subsidence below the main tower has caused the building to be closed for reasons of safety. A modern complex out at the back is now the College. As luck would have it, I met a retired teacher walking through the grounds. He remembered getting grapes from the greenhouse in the '20s as a boy. Judging by the greenhouses in JTR's sketch there were grapes and more at the castle prior to the 1920s.

With glass and tender loving care it can be done. Those friends in Skye grow figs, grapes, peaches, nectarines and sweet cherries. It was their grape leaf wine that helped the Skye section of this book.

A Brother Brush friend of JTR's was staying in the Lewis Hotel. Its traditional upstairs windows are now uncurtained and uninhabited, two bars at street level its only function. Victim of bureaucratic and other forces it stands awaiting 'development', or heaven forfend and JTR's ghost, demolition.

JTR It is time to leave the capital and have a walk; let us rise betimes. My respected landladies, who are the double-distilled quintessence of considerateness and island hospitality, would think all good would leave their abodes if a dweller beneath their roof left fasting, so, in spite

149

of all my entreaties to the contrary, a cup of tea was prepared to forestall my start; and as I walked by the river-side and reached a road that skirts a number of very massive peat-stacks, and displays on the landward side an interminable host of peat-pits, the geniality of the sunshine was felt, and I would gladly have slackened my pace were it not that by so doing my good friends at Gress (some eight miles from Stornoway, where I was due at eight o'clock, if I remember rightly), might have waited breakfast for me. The road was very pleasant, and nice peeps were opened out along the shore, those scenes peculiar to this and neighbouring isles; long flat stretches of heath and sand, and lines of cliff … Many thatched cottages were built on the brow of a hill overlooking the sea; and a large potato-field, divided into elongated sections, gave ample scope for many Lewis families to prove that union is strength, for they were busily engaged lifting the crop: each family group was complete in itself; those who had the most children got most quickly over the ground: many hands make light work, and young backs bend easily. I was pleased to see so many hearty workers thus earnestly labouring early in the day. It was a golden day to them; for dry weather is the only safe weather for potato-lifting.

The pastoral scene described denied the back-breaking nature of the islanders' survival conditions. And it is a bit patronising, John, that bit about the 'hearty islanders … earnestly labouring so early in the day'. Typhoid and cholera and, most common, tuberculosis were rampant throughout the population.

That night in the B&B north of Stornoway the other guest was a visiting resident GP from Melbourne. She was taking a year out before specialising. I asked what the Lewis ailments were compared to those in Australia. 'Smoking and diet. Some hereditary problems, too.' Almost as an afterthought she added, 'There is a very high pain threshold here.' All those centuries of inherited stoicism?

JTR made merry at Gress, where breakfast was waiting and congenial company took him along the coastline to caves that, because of lack of stamina on my part, were never redrawn.

He was into his pastoral bit again with literary references for every pretty female encountered. He found 'a Shiella' and with her 'bounded over heath and rock, over hill and vale, barely conscious of the sloughs when marshy ground met us … '

His 'good friends' were most likely the MacKinlays who rented Gress Lodge from 1874 to 1876 from Sir James Mathieson, the island's proprietor. David MacKinlay was a Lewisach born and bred, educated at Stornoway, who made good in the outside world. He became the managing partner of a large mercantile firm in India, returning to Lewis for the fishing and shooting season.

Gress Lodge is now the private house of the widow of one of the island's doctors. 'He was a ship's surgeon. Came to Lewis forty years ago. We stayed put,' said seventy-three-year-old Jean Greig, showing me round the old house where JTR had fallen in love with sunny-hearted Shiella.

Leverhulme, subsequent proprietor to Mathieson, gave the lands of Gress to the Stornoway Trust, a crofter-managed organisation, the landless Lodge being sold to Dr Greig. His widow reminisced on the days of her children's upbringing. 'We hardly ever went to the mainland. It was a big expedition and very expensive.' I could almost smell the peat and oil from the lamps; the flour and the sugar in the big bins and sacks; and hear children's voices echoing through the rambling old house. How many dinner parties those walls must have entertained. There was a happy feeling; a sunny-hearted link with JTR.

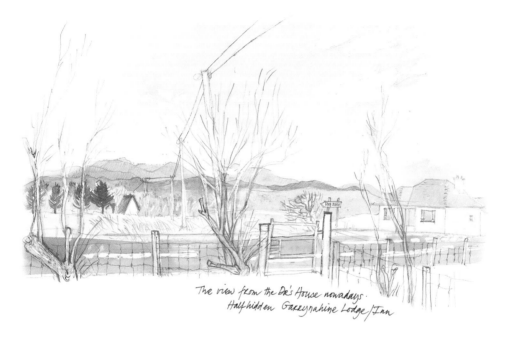

The view from the Dr's House nowadays.
Half hidden Garrynahine Lodge/Inn

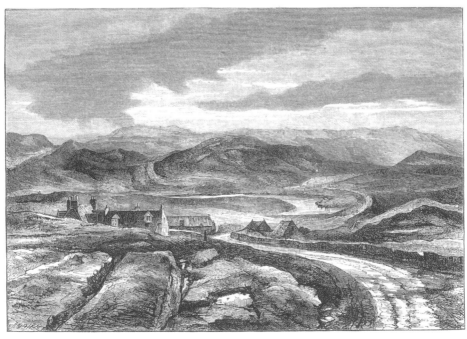

GARRYNAHINE, LEWIS.

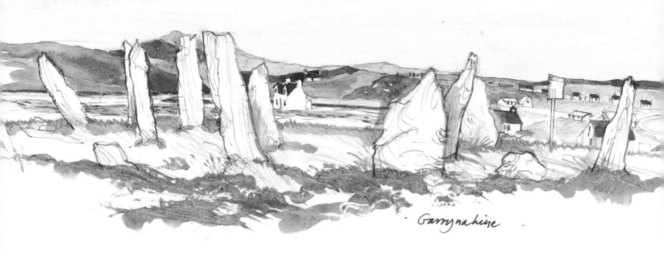

Garrynahine

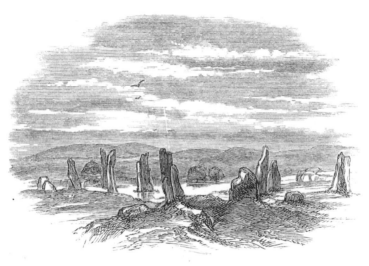

DRUID CIRCLE, NEAR GARRYNAHINE.

JTR I was glad to reach Garrynahine Inn, and after the fourteen miles of a walk was not unthankful to test the merits of a roasted wild duck for breakfast … I noticed a new house a short distance from the inn (it was being prepared for a doctor); was entrusted with the keys, and from one of the front windows looked out on the rainy scene depicted in the sketch of 'Garrynahine, Isle of Lewis.' It rained in downright earnest, and the noise of rain and wind on the roof, windows, and doors of the empty house gave the place an eerie feeling.

Garrynahine is the Lodge for a present day shooting estate – the reversals of time.
I did my sketch from that doctor's house. It is now called The Cottage, but Mrs Smith remembers that her father-in-law bought it in the early thirties and referred to it as

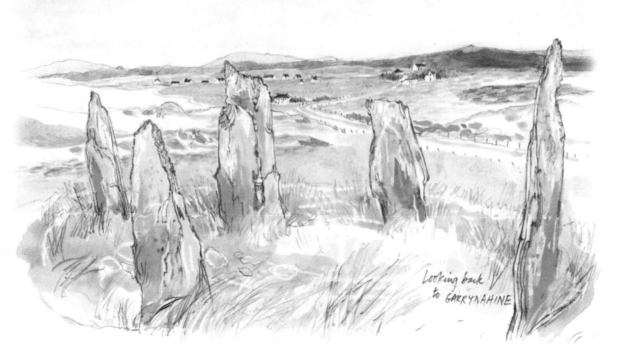

Looking back to GARRYNAHINE

'the Doctor's House'. She caretakes for the Lodge – 'a chew owns it' – and was amazed, as was I, by the tree growth that obscured the erstwhile Inn.

How bleak was so much of the landscape that JTR walked through. Thousands of imported sheep had left their devastating mark and the latest 'crop', the deer, finished off any saplings the sheep might have missed when they came down from the high tops in the winter. If the sheep subsidy is removed the latter part of our century might see another crop in the Highlands and Islands – naturalised trees. They have started to make an impact on the scenery already.

JTR I could not restrain myself from hastening to view one of those Druid circles, of which there are so many in the Isle of Lewis; that given in the small vignette is the first one I reached. It stood on a mossy hill, and was environed by an expanse of peat soil and many stacks of the dark-coloured fuel; and in reaching it, many most forbidding sloughs had to be rounded and jumped over. Other circles were within sight, the most notable being the famed Druid temple known as Callanish; and my imagination, I must own, was discovering Druid circles or single Druid stones wherever grey rocks were seen rising above or bedded in the dark moor.

I spent hours at one of those 'so many' stone circles near Garrynahine trying to get the same angle as JTR to no avail. Frustrated but secretly delighted that I had maybe caught him out with shoddy workmanship until an old fellow from Bernera stopped to give me a lift on the way past Carlaway and showed me the right ones, just before the main stones of Callanish. Here I apologised to JTR and learned that he must have been a very tall man. My five feet four and a half even on tiptoe could nowhere approximate his angle of vision.

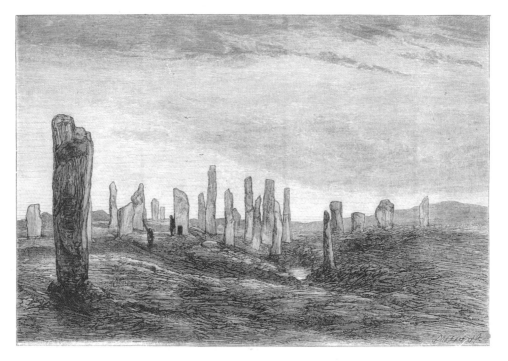

CALLANISH STONES, LEWIS.

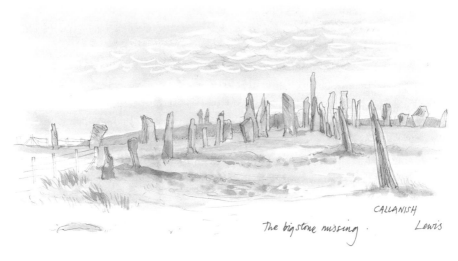

The big stone missing.   CALLANISH
                                Lewis

'Big shop day?' I asked the old man, his nose almost level with the steering wheel
of his equally elderly car. He had told me he was going all the way to Stornoway and
I could tell that it was quite an event.

'No, it is a matter of *business*,' he replied with beautiful but serious enunciation.
I thought it must be a visit to his lawyer or somesuch and politely asked no more.

154

But he volunteered the information. 'I'm reflooring my other bedroom floor' – emphasis was placed on the 'other' – 'and run out of wood nails. Fifty is all I need.' Serious business, indeed.

Everyone stops and gives you a lift in Lewis. After Callanish it was the local archaeological buff who was thrilled to see JTR's drawing of the famous stones. Crawford was the first person I came across in all the Rambles who immediately saw the historical value of JTR's records. Maybe it was obvious to most people but he gave me recharged confidence in the project. 'Definitely one stone missing since his time,' sharply observed Crawford. I implicitly trust your accuracy, JTR, I promise no more lapses of faith. As I hope others will see fit to so do with my own records …

At Barvas Lodge knickerbockered ladies with good stud pearl earrings invited me in for tea. Black labradors draped over chairs looked as 'buggered' as one of the ladies said they were after the four-hour walk in the wake of their shooting husbands that morning. They had all come back for lunch but the women had rebelled at going out in the afternoon. 'We are meant to be plucking the bloody snipe … '

Ann, the caretaker sitting on the arm of one of the chairs with her pale blue nylon tabard on, cosily sipped tea. She would do them. She was used to it. 'Fiddly little things. You need at least two per person.' Over the past four days five hundred had been shot. It was quite unbelievable. There can't be that number of snipe in the whole of Lewis let alone Barvas Estate, surely?

It seemed that the sad little snipe were the victims of a blood lust still carrying on from the heyday of Victorian game hunting. A slaughter for the fun of it, the challenge of it, certainly the skill of it, it would be argued. 'Lewis grouse good sport. Much smaller and stay very still,' I learned. But Ann would not be plucking five hundred snipe carcases surely? It would not be so disconcerting if they were all eaten, the poor wee souls.

I enjoyed my tea and glimpse into a way of life that would have been familiar to JTR. 'Call in anytime,' the hospitable ladies further invited as they rallied reluctant dogs and piled into the car to go and collect the men. Ann headed for the kitchen. I could not get that figure of five hundred out of my mind.

Barvas Lodge was a Temperance Hotel up until 1923. Possibly JTR had another wild duck for his breakfast when he stayed there. If so I hope he enjoyed it. There are not so many about these days.

JTR Next morning, after joining the family at worship, I turned my steps still farther north, having a desire to reach the most northerly part of the island. The landscapes differed from those of the last day's walk, and were seen in another mood; the rain-clouds floated high, the road lay over rocky ridges, the homesteads had an amplitude of stone wall fencing over these exposed seaboard cliffs; and they were built more compactly to withstand all assaults. These districts were not very fruitful in peat, and they would have to carry them from a distance of many miles; in some cases a pavement of large stones led from the main road to the door of the dwelling. This was, I think, because the soil all round was so softened and converted into cloggy mud by the habit of keeping the cattle within the gates in bad weather, when their high stone dykes served as a bield for the protection of the cattle. In the forenoon many groups of men and women passed me. I could not make out where they were going, and made several inquiries without getting any answers save in Gaelic; it might as well have been Hindostani. I thought they might be going to pay their rents, for I was told it was about the settling-time. At last some passed me with books; I stopped them, and found the books to be Bibles: it was all clear now, they were going to a week-day preaching, and shortly after, as the road wound down a glen over a burn, I met the Free Church minister on his way to the place of meeting. He was on horseback. There was a difficulty ahead; there is no inn or hotel at the Ness.

I have to include this extract if for no other reason but to draw attention to JTR's unconscious *dêja vu* language comparisons and the uncanny metaphor of 'the strongholds of a brotherhood in holy alliance with each other to withstand all assaults.' For Ness is the last bastion of Free Presbyterian fundamentalism and the miles of wall to wall crofthouses that line the single main road today have a pallisade quality. Who knows what goes on behind those net curtains. The inhabitants inside certainly know everything that goes on on the outside of their windowpanes, however.

Thinking to steal a march on watchful eyes I set off from the Cross Inn (not long established as the only hotel and bar) at 6.15 a.m. and headed for Port of Ness and the Butt of Lewis. I walked the neon-lit gauntlet of the road, houses on either side fading into pitch black. To the left the predawn roar of the Atlantic surge. A soft hint of spent peat from dying overnight fires. I remembered arriving in Cross the previous day on the school bus noticing the universal teatime re-fuelling of hundreds of fires and stores; fresh puffing chimneys as far as the eye could see. In the dimming day the skyscape was like a miniature Grangemouth but sweeter smelling.

The peatstacks loomed large to right and left in between each house. It is about four miles to the Port of Ness from Cross and I think I tiptoed the whole way. To the east a pale pearl skyline was appearing. The occasional house light, thick and orange behind curtains, crude by comparison.

The swathing sweep of the Butt of Lewis lighthouse faded the nearer I got to the Port. It was going to be another unusually wind free day when islanders take the opportunity to tie down any loose facings and fencings before the furies of winter. Frail souls and stronger can be dashed to the ground by gale force winds that blow for days on end.

How lucky I was. There was gentle warmth in the morning sun and flowering geraniums in a window by the harbour of the Port. It was 5th November. The zigzag of harbour walls and breakwaters below the cliff were deserted. Boats pulled up for the deceptive winter, the restless thud of the sea beyond the outer wall threatening to break into their sanctuary.

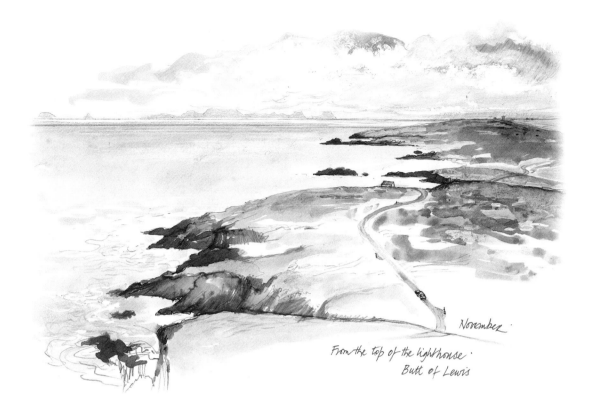

November.

From the top of the lighthouse.
Butt of Lewis

At the lighthouse, the keepers and contract workmen were taking the opportunity of the weather to carry out painting and maintenance work. No, the lighthouse was not open to the public and then the keeper relented. 'Take the key. We'll be up in five minutes.'

A whole lighthouse to myself. An eery echoing spiralling climb of 168 steps took me up to the light itself and 180 degree views stretching to hazy nothingness to the west and north; Harris hills to the south-west; the Cuillins of Skye to the south and the mainland mountains to the east.

The lighthouse was fourteen years old when JTR sketched it and by 1876 fish oil had been replaced by paraffin fuel. It was a hundred years later that electricity was first used. Erosion of the cliffs below have changed the profile of his view. The previous year to my visit a sizeable chunk had cracked off in a storm.

The day I was there was the still, silent kind of a winter day when the light clings to the skyline slowly moving round from east to south to west. The sky was grey pearl with immobile scuds of cloud above. The horizon line to the north would never lighten. It was a deep grey blue leading into the lands of sunless winter; the weak golden fingers to the south cannot stretch that far.

Standing on top of the world I felt the pull of the cool gold beyond Skye dragging me further and further south, warmer and warmer. A cheque book and an airline ticket – that is all it needed to bathe in that heat so far away.

Instead I warmed up retracing the predawn walk to Cross where I would collect the big rucksack and the last bus to Stornoway. I passed through townships kissed like the

Sleeping Beauty by the Prince. Not an appropriate analogy as fairy tales and pantomimes are the Devil's tools, I'm sure – Ness District deleted 'Devil's Dance' from the SCO posters – but all that had been asleep was now activated. Chattering starlings and continual dog barking backdropped carrying voices in the pelucid late afternoon air. Those puffing chimneys again and a strong peat reek now. Clacking of a loom in a shed.

Behind an impeccably pebble-dashed and bloomer-curtained house with Georgian teak panelled door, the old ways incongruously go on. A row of four oat 'huts' just like African beehive huts with pointy straw twisted tops preserved winter feed for the beasts.

And behind each house were the great moors and finally the sea on each side of the island. Viewing sunset and dawnrise skyscapes was secondary to viewing each other across the road. Who was that person walking by towards Cross? Coming from Port of

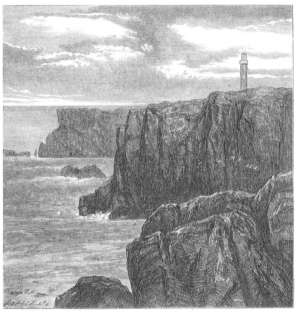

BUTT OF LEWIS LIGHTHOUSE.

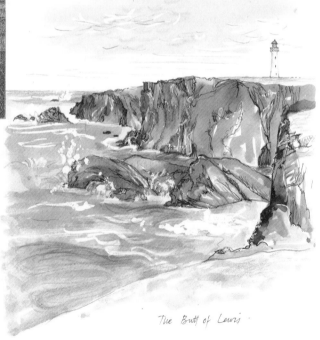

The Butt of Lewis.

Ness? Where had she spent the night? Cross? But why as she walking back towards it? Somebody had seen her mid-morning coming *from* the lighthouse … She couldn't have spent the night in Cross. Who *was* she anyway?

Passing Barvas Lodge in the bus I saw one of 'the men'. His shooting uniform of olive greens and tweeds as tribal as the black Sunday outfits of the Lewis churchgoers. Their isolation the same.

It was bonfire night and townships had long prepared stacks of driftwood and domestic combustibles. 'All that *kindling*!' An incomer friend – all of seventeen years but forever an incomer – in Ness had wailed. She had chosen to live and bring up her family with the old ways in mind and practice. A minority furrow to plough but plough it she literally did. 'Change comes slow when people have been repressed for so long. And is the Lewisach a farmer anyway? Like the Shetlander, he's a fisherman at heart.'

As the bus trundled on towards Stornoway I noticed a tup with a galvanised steel boat-cleat embedded through its horn. Why did I wince? It was no more painful than a ring through a punk's nose. In fact much less so in execution. And further evidence of Carola's theory of all Lewisachs being fishermen, not farmers.

Despite the diminishing fishing industry, material improvements are coming fast to Lewis. Once inside many of the houses, the door shut on the (some would say) bleak environment, the lifestyle and surroundings are no different from that on the mainland. 'It is only the water in-between that makes the difference,' one woman told me, proudly.

But the old ways and attitudes are still there behind the double glazing and the latest edition of *Neighbours*. All that celebratory burning of good kindling at the onset of the darkest and longest months of the year must assuage some deep primitive need. The very cavalier nature of such waste seems to cock a snook at the Presbyterianism that controls a large section of the community. This interweaving of pre-Christian, reformation and contemporary religions gives Lewis its unique flavour and an opportunity for a lot of us to take stock of all that is slowly being eroded in our own cultures.

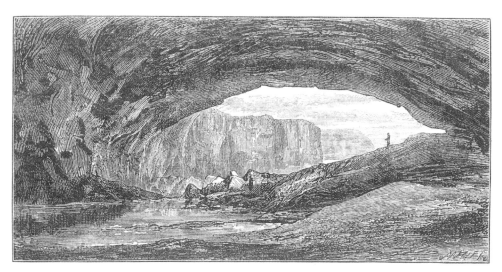

CAVE NEAR GRESS, LEWIS.

Ramble Seven

Wednesday, November 7 – Saturday, November 10

LEWIS · WICK (VIA DINGWALL) · THURSO

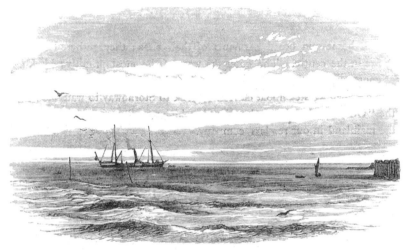

WICK BAY.

Lewis to Wick in one day via public transport? It can be done. Early morning boat ex Stornoway to Ullapool; bus to Dingwall, train to Thurso changing at Georgemas Junction for Wick. JTR took all day travelling, courtesy of the Highland Railway Company, from Inverness to Wick. He stopped off at Dingwall for a sketch or two and rejoined the train in Inverness.

JTR The train that leaves Inverness in the morning does not reach Wick till a late hour in the evening: the hotel folk know this, and are quite prepared to keep open house till after the arrival of the train. The last time I travelled from Wick to Dingwall was when the railway only reached as far north as Golspie; the other portion of the road was an overnight stage-coach journey; and to accommodate some ladies I took a seat on the top: it was a clear cold night, and the air was keen indeed. We may well endorse the saying regarding him who had so much to do with road-making in the Highlands and islands; 'if you had seen these roads before they were made you would have blessed brave General Wade,' and wish prosperity to the Highland Railway Company. I found my way to a temperance hotel advertised in the guide-book and found it a homely house.

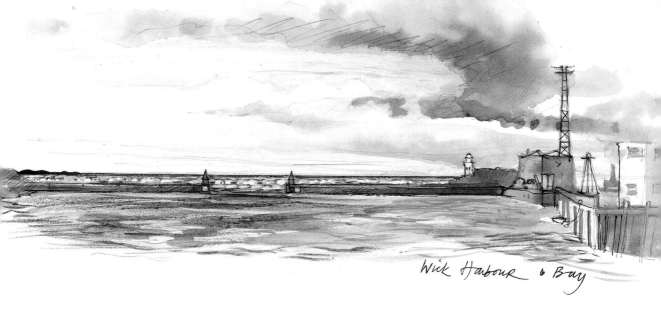

Wick Harbour & Bay

The renamed Temperance Hotel was dismissive of backpackers. The little B&B down by the harbour was far more in keeping with the thread of the sea that had kept with me the whole day's travel from west to east coast Scotland.

The woods, still leafy, and the mountains of Wester Ross were almost claustrophobic after the wide bleak expanse of North Lewis and the wastes of the Minch in between.

In Dingwall everyone spoke English!

Along the edge of the Cromarty Firth there were more seagulls in the fields than over the whole of Lewis. The land was so rolling and fertile and this was winter. Give a Lewisach a tiny corner of one of these great fields and he would be a cattle baron. Winter barley was coming through new green. Free-range pigs rootled around miniature nissen huts.

The day was faintly foggy; lights were on on the tall hazy meccano sculptures of oil rigs moored in the Firth. The deserted acres of the Invergordon smelter ghosted past with a corn stubbled field in tow, sixteen white swans standing on a rise. At Tain the ancient stones in the graveyard above the railway line looked in as I ate an apple bought in Ness in Lewis that had come from Spain. I found that quite amazing; something to do with the speed and continuity of the journey. After Tain the cold grey expanse of the North Sea and to the north the grey-blue hills of Sutherland. The tide was so high it gave the impression of the train being waterborne. Rafts and rafts of water birds floated in the flat sanded estuary. Coming inland a bit the land gets rougher. A little terrier dog ran parallel with the train, barking with joy. Fields get smaller and birch tree scrub predominates but it is all a Garden of Eden by Lewis standards.

Inland to Lairg, the birch woods give way to the heather moors of Sutherland. In 1875 the notorious Duchess of Sutherland, responsible for some of the most brutal Clearances, was in London with the Duke lionising Mr Moody. Every day she insisted on dragging her society friends, some very reluctant, to the Opera House in Haymarket where he was preaching. Moody was entertained at Dunrobin Castle near Golspie, and the Duke, who owned more acres than anyone in Europe, wrote to him, 'I shall never forget what I have heard from you. If you know what a life mine is, in ways I was not able to tell you the other day, and what a terrible story mine has been, you would pray for me much.' The Duke and Duchess were old by this time and salvation uppermost on the Duke's mind, it would seem.

At Rogart the hills were blanketed with autumn-coloured trees, the brown treeless moors beyond; in hollows of stubby hillocky straths little houses were dotted in isolation.

Extensive sheep pens at the side of the line at Rogart indicated that stock still travel by rail to the markets in the south. Here the guard changed over and the train headed back eastwards to the coast.

Lilting Orcadian voices chattered behind; this line goes to the furthest northern railhead of Britain. At Thurso the Orcadians then get the boat to Orkney. They had a long way to go.

Two ladies with identical spectacles and points of view sat with folded arms under the luggage rack packed with treats from Marks and Spencers in Inverness (most northerly outlet of that firm's empire). Some Orcadian cat was in for a good supper. Two of the labels on the 'cat gourmet triple pack' read 'Steak and Kidney Casserole' and 'Sea Food Flan'. The third choice was hidden by a pint of St Michael's milk. Imagine going all the way to Inverness for a pint of milk … Maybe that was for the cat, too.

At Brora the date 1895 was on the station building. It would have been a platformless stop for JTR, like the Wild West of America. The impersonal grey line of the North Sea kept us company to Helmsdale which nestles in the folds of heather hills close-cropped by winds that come relentlessly over that cruel water. The folds look as if they are pushing Helmsdale right into the sea; as though the river in spate had collected all the houses it could uproot inland and deposited them at the river mouth with just enough of a toehold to keep them there.

Once again the train loops inland through moors that make those of Lewis look like playparks. Silhouetted sticks of rotted snow barriers emphasise godforsaken desert stretching for endless miles. But no desert when it comes to wild life, for this is the Flow Country where David Bellamy brought to popular attention how deep he could sink as he cavorted from tuft to tuft of floating bog.

By Kinbrace the guard had given up advising what station we were coming to. Six or so houses, one with a satellite dish, and a little old graveyard on a lumpy knoll totalled the extent of the community. Lights were on in the primary school. It was 2.30 in the afternoon.

Numbers on the train were greatly reduced at Georgemas where those going to Wick had to dismount and wait for a connecting Sprinter. Here the land is flat and fertile like Ayrshire and as if on cue a herd of Ayrshire cows obliged by ambling by Loch Watten. Flotillas of birds sculled and flapped away from the train. A farmer was burning straw, the yellow billows of smoke spiralling lazily upward. Winter was coming in slowly to the North East of Scotland. Hundreds of greylag geese grazing in fields looked like some new

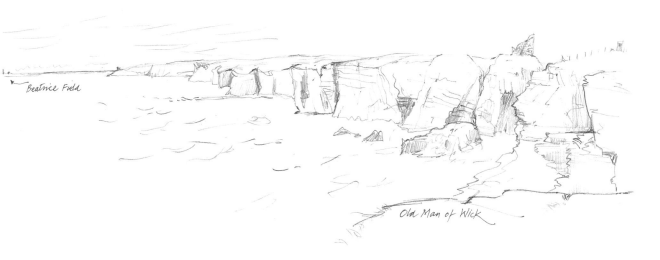

Beatrice Field

Old Man of Wick

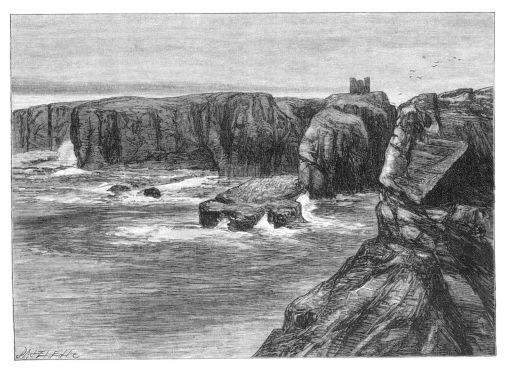

OLD MAN OF WICK.

cinerous winter crop until they flew thickly into the dim sky. We had disturbed their last feed of the day.

The street lights were very bright in Wick. It was 3.30 p.m.

The thread of the sea that had kept with me all day had not been literal. It was historical. Wick was where many of those impoverished Lewisachs, men and women, went to look for work that unsuccessful fishing season of 1874. They did not travel as I had, feet up, surveying the passing countryside with prawn and avocado sandwiches and a can of white wine. They would have come, some in their own boats, others by steerage in mail or cargo boats, round the wild coastline of Cape Wrath. A lot of the women, young girls for the most part, came overland as I had, packed in steamers and trains like the fish they were to gut.

On east coast boats in the 1870s, Lewis hands got a fixed wage of £7 to £10 for a six-week period with an additional 6d or 1/- for every cran (basket weight) fished.

The fisher girls were paid pennies for packing the barrels but this was still enough, if they were lucky in health and spirit, to buy bonnets and lace to take back to Lewis at the end of the season for dreamy bottom drawers.

Inevitably there was friction between the east and west coast men. The expansion of business and industry in all the main ports and towns of Scotland also brought with it an influx of work-hungry 'inlanders', as well as islanders, adding even more to the tensions. Drink the fuel for combatants and onlookers alike.

The harbour at Wick is fronted with Telford-designed buildings, beautifully proportioned, the little dormitory windows of the west coast herring lassies high above the larger windows of the managers' and traders' rooms, warehouses and storerooms below. Nowadays there is a sad, derelict air; a sweetie shop, a pub and a café at street level and nobody looking out of upstairs windows. It is as though Wick is still waiting for the fishing to come back, drink no longer a fuel, but a solace.

Wick's future lies in the balance. The other fishing stations of JTR's time on the west coast suffered the collapse of the herring industry earlier and have kept alive mostly through tourism (though Stornoway still tenuously has oil and fishing links).

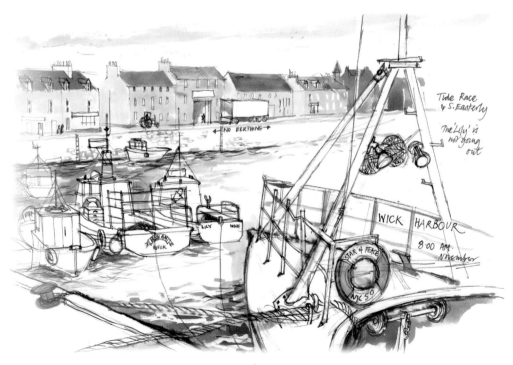

Wick waits, remembering the herring more recently; the lovely old buildings stare blankly over the vast harbour once a forest of masts. Now the masts total a small copse.

Wick, where the biggest shop is Woolworths and the young girls pass reeking of cigarette smoke, and CHRIST DIED FOR OUR SINS is writ large on the exterior of the Harbour Mission wall.

Leaving the harbour high on the Pultney side of the river I passed an old folks' home looking out over that cold North Sea; only the dawn in winter can show any warmth. An old man was out feeding the gulls in his carpet slippers. Thin bony shanks showed through his wind-fluttered trousers. 'We had to *throw* the herring away in the '20s. Now they'd be millionaires if they could have them.' He was referring to the British Government's 'bloody Tories' trade block against Russia whose revolution threatened European equilibrium. Over a million and a half barrels of herring a year had been exported to Russia prior to the embargo.

'The evilness of those in power who change the rules. There's always those that suffer.' His old eyes behind smudged spectacles talked to the seagulls and the North Sea as much as to me. 'The Messiah's Second Coming is the only thing that will change man's wicked ways. We get chance after chance to make it right and what do we do? Fight.' His mounting anger was making his speech more and more incomprehensible through his stroke-stiffened mouth. 'Look! Look! There's another *war* brewing … '

I shook his hand to calm him as much as to show respect. 'May the Lord bless you and keep you … ' and he reeled off the whole benediction, still clinging to my hand. Then he tottered to the home, polybag empty of crusts. The seagulls wheeled off and up over the harbour.

It wasn't the wind that brought tears to my eyes as I turned to walk along the cliff path.

JTR It was too late to witness the fishing life, which is the leading interest attaching to Wick, but when on the Orkney passage, I have sailed through the fleet of herring-boats, and it is a fine sight. The Aberdeen and Shetland mail steamers call at Wick Bay, *weather permitting*; this clause has a deep meaning in it, as many can witness who have seen how the waves break on that shore at times. After sketching the steamboat, as she lay in the bay unlading her cargo, from the bridge over the water that divides Pultneytown from the old town of Wick, I got into one of the boats leaving the pier, and was landed on board the 'St. Nicholas,' thinking it would be more pleasant to visit Thurso by sailing round the coast than to go by rail.

I was to be at the harbour at 8 a.m. At 7.45, with a knot of sickness already tightening in my stomach, there was not a soul about. It was bitterly cold but dry. I had arranged to go out in a crab boat to get JTR's coastal sketches. Trawling the harbour the previous afternoon for a lift was not easy – not many boats to choose from and a distinct wariness on the part of the seamen. But a pirate with a paunch said 'OK – eight on the dot.'

Behind me a boat yard opened up. Men in blue overalls with newspapers sticking out of back pockets wandered in. Children in warm anoraks passed on the way to school. 9.15. The local dog staked out his territory, cocking a leg.

Pirate arrived with a screech of rusty Ford brakes without any acknowledgement of my huddled form sheltering by his fishboxes on the quay. I could tell he had forgotten the arrangement. Or had chosen to. His boat was small and open with a minute wheelhouse that would dangerously wedge his bulk. There was a young lad with him. No doubt as to where I would be standing for the eight-hour day, two miles out to sea. At the stern. I watched the dog lifting his leg again and wondered if my idea was sensible. I was not even going to get a lift to Thurso out of it.

'Six spoonfuls of strawberry jam before you go out the harbour. Sweet going down, sweet coming back up,' the man in the boat yard had said the previous night. Beyond the breakwater the waves were getting bigger as the Pirate effed and cee-ed, bent over the uncovered inboard engine. Something was wrong with the pump. Men, obviously out of work, had gathered by me and the pile of fishboxes. Advice started to volley back and forth. Only the Pirate knew why I was there and was not letting on. The atmosphere became excruciating. There is nothing like a band of men in their working environment to make a single female feel like a page-three Martian.

The timing to walk away from such a situation is crucial; unless you are in the mood to parry age old male posturings and sexual innuendo. Just then I felt that my unspoken liberation, symbolised by the backpack, was a criticism of their trapped unemployed state.

The sketchbook is a great aid at times like this. There was something terribly interesting to sketch further along the quayside. And I just kept going. Tired and cold and full of anticlimax. And needing a pee.

The café was warm and smelling of fish scales. Three young men with loop and stud earrings in one ear (the lad on the Caledonian Canal fishing boat was not as individual as I had thought) had three beefburgers and a pie each and then a chocolate KitKat with their tea. Rows of sweetie jars lined the shelves. I bought some Liquorice Perfections after my pie, beans and chips and sucked them on the bus to Thurso.

Rivalry exists between Thurso and Wick but in reverse to when JTR visited. Wick was the big prosperous town and Thurso a little village just being developed by the wealthy for residences 'whose whereabouts a Wick man can scarcely discover on the map'.

> Tea in a bowla/Floor sconags/Soor sellags/Dirty Thirsa
> (Tea in a handless cup/Flour scones/Sour fish/Dirty Thurso)

So went the old rhyme. But the last line goes 'Dirty Weeckers' nowadays. Thurso has got a swimming pool and a wine bar. And Dounreay, which for the moment is the major employer of highly trained and specialised employees; wage packets are accordingly high.

Yet Wick is the Royal Burgh despite its current depression. Thurso could not afford the £300 needed for the charter in 1876 when, hard on the heels of the Prince and Princess of Wales' visit to 'The Exhibition', the Town Council proposed applying for the honour.

JTR Thurso my readers will have heard much about, at the time when his Royal Highness visited it to open the Exhibition there in the autumn of 1876. I saw that Exhibition, and did find it a great treat to see so far north some of the choice gems of painting from South Kensington. Many other contributions were of interest! but it was strange to look on this picture and on that – to see on the same walls so many poor efforts at painting alongside of *chef-d'oeuvres* of artistic power.

Concerts were being held in the building. The fruit of the little enlivening the quaint old northern town has got through the Exhibition may be seen by-and-bye. It was certainly unique, such an Exhibition, so near the northern shore and the Pentland waves. We will leave the waves to sing a plaintive closing requiem over the Exhibition that was held, and hope Thurso may enjoy much true prosperity.

Exhibitions were all the rage at that time, and not just for the artistic élite of the big cities to the south, much to JTR's misgivings, obviously. John T. Reid, not only are you a religious groupie, a thwarted poet of the Romantic School, a fitness freak, a possible paedophile, you are an artistic snob as well ...

At 'The Caithness and Sutherland Industrial and Art Exhibition' to give it its full title, a labourer was charged with having done damage to the extent of £8 by falling upon a glass case and breaking a valuable jug the property of one John Fitsgibbon, china merchant. A fine of fifteen shillings was imposed. Maybe JTR helped pick up the pieces, or did he watch the poor man's agony from afar?

The *John O' Groats Journal* and the *Caithness Courier* were full of the details of the exhibits. The Duke of Sutherland (had Moody saved his soul yet?) sent deer heads, geological specimens and paintings. The MP Sir Tollemache Sinclair (who desperately wanted Thurso to become a Royal Burgh) sent the largest collection of items including oleographs, prize-winning inlaid walnut cabinet and ships' models. The Flagstone Quarrying Co. exhibited an immense flagstone. 'A navvie sent a beautiful polished piece of stone from Spittal quarry.' Maybe he was the one that broke the glass case ...

Caithness fields are fenced with these stone flags. Like gravestones they lead to Dounreay. The Des. Res. on the clifftop that joins Thurso to Scrabster are not interested in the loads of driftwood washed up below. Oil tanks hide behind pampas grasses and dried-up clematis.

An oyster catcher piped aboard a peach orange sunset all of three o'clock in the afternoon.

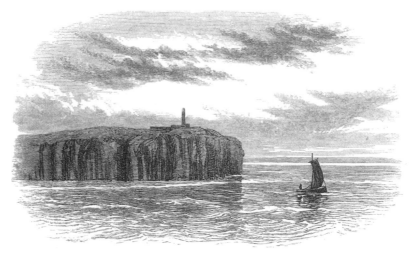

NOSS HEAD.

Ramble Eight

ABERDEEN · BRIDGE OF DON · BALLATER · BALMORAL · BRAEMAR · DEVIL'S ELBOW · SPITTAL OF GLENSHEE

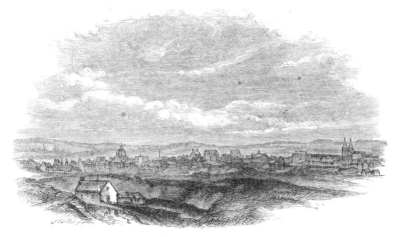

OLD ABERDEEN.

JTR Aberdeen Station was a welcome sight to me after fifteen hours in a railway carriage, and welcome too was the face of a genial friend, who was waiting my arrival to convey me to his bachelor's quarter, where we had a royal time.

The markets held in Aberdeen are on an extensive scale, and are dissimilar to any I have seen in other parts of the country. There is one held in Castle Street, one in the Market House, and a third at the back thereof, having an old well as a centre: this last is called the Green Market, and is the subject of the sketch; that under cover is for dairy produce, and it was a very great treat to go through this market, and see the women sitting in long rows, comfortably dressed, and having a copious display of spotless white in caps and shawls, and the butter and eggs and fowls all so well – so temptingly laid out. Here also flowers were on sale, and many shops have permanent stances, and sell *souvenirs, &c.*; here also, and in the gallery above, the butchers have their benches; while underneath are the fish-shops, – among them one kept by 'the Bonny Fishwife.' I had a look at her face, and while owning the justice of her appellation, I know in her younger days she must have been very much bonnier (more lovely).

The market with the old cross in Castle Street for a centre has various attractions. 'What is not here to be purchased?' is the question you incline to ask. Many of the

169

merchants, you would judge, have all their stock carried thither, and the country people, instead of treading the hard pavements of the streets for hours, can get all they desire at this weekly fair in a short space of time. Here you find the confectioner and the fruiterer, the new and old shoe-stall, displays of new clothes, screens hung with left-off garments; here is the grocer, the cheesemonger, the vendor of small wares, picture sellers, tool merchants, coopers and tinkers, also dealers in furniture, and now and again noisy men selling universal medicines and other wonders, and also the Birmingham salesman, with his caravan of goods to be given away by Dutch auction at nominal prices.

JTR had come up from Edinburgh after another of his city breaks. The days were getting so short I kept going from Wick via Inverness to Aberdeen.

It was Armistice Day. The Police Pipe Band was in full swing down Union Street though the pavements were all but deserted. Maybe they were just setting out on their triumphal march. I did not follow them to their conclusion where dignitaries, a minister or two and lots of scouts and guides, cold-kneed cubs and brownies would sustain the myth that giving one's life for God and Country was the highest honour given to man. Or woman? The newspapers still carried pieces about 'Our Lads' out East. I suppose leaders like 'OUR GIRLS GO IN' do not quite have the same stirring ring to them. But they were out there too. And how many red poppies would be for them and their male compatriots the next Armistice Day? Are there ever any wreaths for the thousands, as in

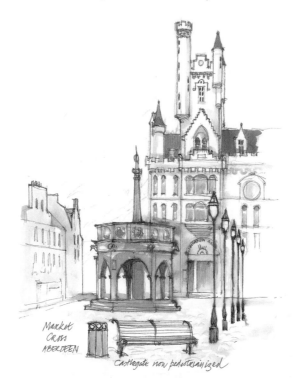

Market
Cross
ABERDEEN

Castlegate now pedestrianized

170

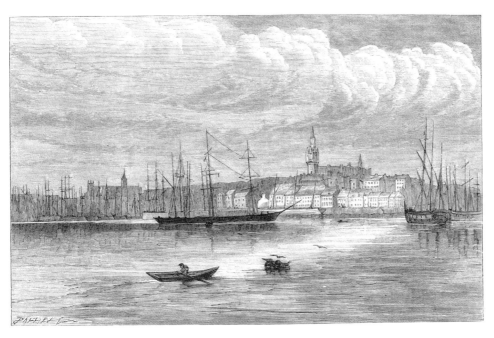

ABERDEEN HARBOUR.

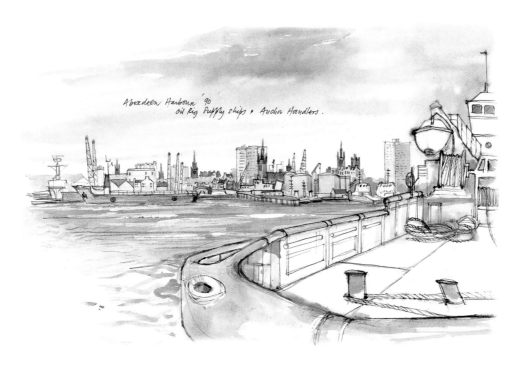

this 'war', of civilians that had no say in the 'crisis' in the first place? Just one. Made with black edged petals. To remember them.

If Armistice Day could be one of total mourning without the panoply of glorification I might go.

The editorial in the *John O' Groats Journal* (Nov 2, 1876): 'Prof Levi has made an estimate that this country had to pay for war during a period of a century and a quarter the monstrous sum of £11,040,000,000 sterling. The magnitude of this sum staggers conception. The following are a few of the items. Seven Years War £88,000,000, the American colonial war £98,000,000, the wars with France £1,000,000, Kaffir Wars £2,000,000, the Chinese Opium War £8,800,000, Russian War £69,000,000, Persian Expedition £900,000, New Zealand War £800,000, Abysinnian War £8,000,000. We do not notice in these sums the Indian Mutiny, the earlier Burmese 'war', nor any of those contentions on the Gold Coast. Yet the total will surely cover all that. These statistics, at the present time, show what vast resources have been sunk by this country in holding her own and other people's possessions.'

Our own papers were doing the exact same exercise in estimating the long drawn out Kuwaiti costs, several more noughts going on to the 1876 figures.

The 1876 Editorial went on: 'The position in the east is believed to be slightly easier,' no doubt hoping that there would be a few less noughts on the end of that military bill. Our own eastern position was getting more complicated by being dragged out in a war of nerves in which Saddam Insane was cleverly squeezing out time and the last laugh which I am sure he still believes is his.

As I write this Alistair Cooke, my favourite analyst of the world's madness, tells me that there have been more than two hundred and forty wars in the past forty years.

The taxi driver waiting hopefully in the rank by the shopping centre, breast heavy with war medals, pointed me in the direction of the site of Market House and Green Market down below Union Street near the station.

The area is in a sad state of dereliction. 'Row going on about knocking down the remaining old houses,' the taxi driver had said. 'Funny how some buildings get no support for preservation and bloody awful things can't get pulled down.'

The Market House was pulled down many years ago and Aberdeen Market, a shopping centre, built in its place. Its back curves concretely into the derelict cobbled square like the goal post end of a covered stadium. A large Black Bottle Whisky advertisement on a hoarding had the illusion of the rear view of a man toasting the repeated image of himself in a mirror. It seemed appropriate. The clack of pigeons' wings was the only sound in the deserted square. Crumbling buildings showed warm irregular round-edged stones so much more pleasing to the eye than the sharp edge masoned granite of modern Aberdeen which looks like unrendered breeze block to me.

The Green Market Cross was removed to Castle Street which is ominous for the future of the old square. Castle Street is pleasantly pedestrianised, its impressive medieval market cross overlooked by the tall Victorian Gothic Salvation Army Headquarters. General Eva Burrows smiled out of the Public Relations window. Coming down the entrance stairs was a chattering flurry of those ever so attractive and complimenting bonnets. They bobbed and bustled around the male Major. Everyone was having a very jolly Armistice Day.

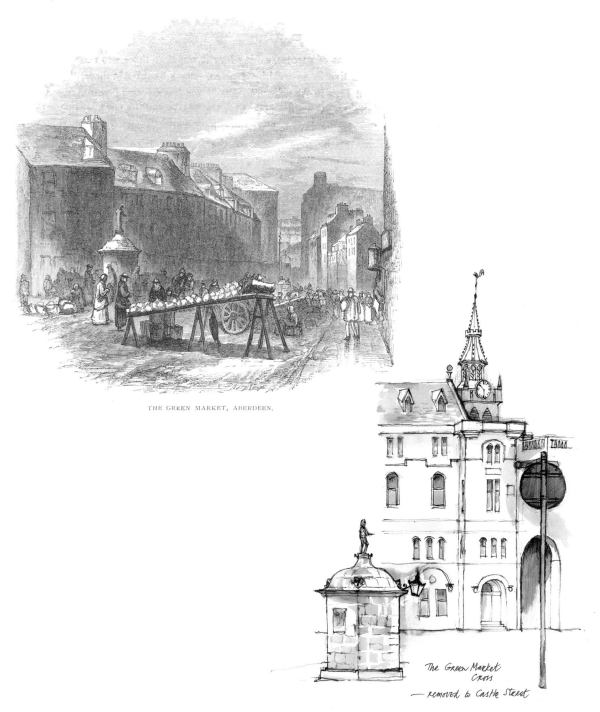

THE GREEN MARKET, ABERDEEN.

The Green Market
Cross
— removed to Castle Street

JTR I was curious to have a peep at the shows that come to Aberdeen to provide amusement for the people. Down near the harbour is a corner where there is a stance allowed them. I was well pleased with the tone: I do not think I heard one word or saw aught that might not with perfect propriety be enacted in any drawing-room of the kingdom. I am, happily, ignorant, so far as being an eye-witness, of the low music halls, of which such dark pictures are given to us; and it is a joy to me to bear record that, even among what we are accustomed to look upon as the lower stratum of society, there is an appreciation of exhibitions of what the gentleman who performed called 'natural science' and 'magical feats,' apart altogether from that pandering to baser tastes, which is too often done in theatrical exhibitions. Another pleasant incident is the confidence with which the little boy or girl is sent round with the hat after performing, and the general chinking of coppers that are cordially dropped therein. In this case, Puss, the performing cat, a regular giant of the feline race, was rather indisposed – had caught a heavy cold, and was excused from exhibiting his skill; but we had fire-eating, magical multiplication of articles out of a hat, mesmerism, and the like.

Oh John, I am almost too ashamed to include this extract in our book. How can you think and say these things? We are nearly at the end of all our journeyings and I am having to try very hard to keep friends. We have got that long walk south through Glen Shee still to do.

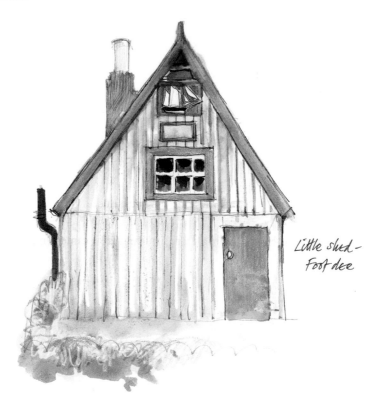

Little shed –
Foot dee

Mesmerism? And you so involved in the Church ... Will I ever get the measure of you?

There is something of the worst of the missionary in you, I suspect. Definitely, a voyeur. And if you think this in your own country what would you be like abroad? Will I ever know?

Codona's Amusement Park, larger by far than 'a stance', is along the Esplanade from the harbour at Footdee. No one there would dare indulge in such superior voyeurism these days.

People walked their dogs on the great stretch of beach. The day was mild and sunny. In summer the residents in Footdee must be fed up with tourists peeping in the windows of their prettily preserved fishermen's cottages. Even in November there was a busyness about the Square. Washing on poles, tiny gardens and a colourful assortment of little sheds opposite each cottage. Water spiggots with clown lion mouths were individually painted and in the middle stood the Footdee Mission Hall, the focus of the fishing community a century ago.

JTR A walk by the shore is also of interest, for the waves come with great force, and wrecks are frequent. I give a sketch of one I saw when there ... The wrecked schooner 'Dunchattan' was on her way for Inverness; stress of weather caused the master to make for Aberdeen Harbour; he mistook the lights, and finding his ship abreast of the north pier, there was only left to him the option of running against the pier or on the beach; he chose the safer alternative, and ran ashore opposite the lifeboat-house. After striking three or four times heavily, she grounded about one hundred and fifty yards from the beach. The tide was almost full. Speedily the fishermen of Footdee manned the lifeboat and rowed through the breakers to the rescue. Of the crew of four, three were taken safely on board; the fourth fell between the lifeboat and the ship, a wave having carried the boat from under him at the moment when he made the leap: through his having taken a rope with him, he got into the vessel again till the lifeboat got alongside and rescued him. Barely ten minutes elapsed from the striking of the vessel till the time when the crew were landed.

Skimming through the Aberdeen Journals for Autumn 1876 I came across the report of the wrecking of the *Dunchattan*. Suddenly I was near to JTR again and forgot the less pleasing aspects of his personality. We were hand in hand once more.

The wreck happened at seven in the evening and pitch dark it would have been the date being Wednesday November 8th. The seventy-six ton *Dunchattan* had left Sunderland the previous Friday with coals for a Mr Baillie of Inverness. The gas-fuelled breakwater beacon could not be lit on account of seas washing over and that was where James Johnson, Master, made his mistake. They were all 'comfortably quartered' in Footdee after the ordeal. The mate came from Nairn on the coast near to Inverness. If it

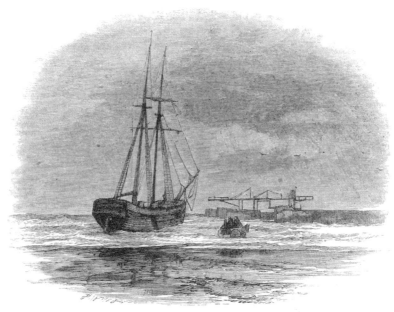

WRECK OF THE "DUNCHATTAN," ABERDEEN BAY.

was he who slipped into the water he might well have wondered if his own corpse was going to end washed up below his own house further along the coast.

The report goes on to say that the schooner belonged to the Master 'who we understand had no insurance.' It does not relate what happened to Mr Baillie's coal.

Of course, I yearned to find a piece of ancient driftwood as I walked along the shore. Or even a lump of coal. The only boats in sight were far out beyond the breakwater, front heavy supply ships for the oil rigs moored in the bay.

JTR Old Aberdeen, unlike Old Edinburgh, is a distance away from New. The drawing of it engraved shows it in a November day, as the snows were coating here and there the fields and hills beyond. It is interesting to walk to it, and be shown through the old cathedral of St. Machar, also to walk by the Brig of Don or Balgownie. Byron had seen it when a boy, and retained a vivid impression of it: he thus refers to it. 'The Brig of Don, near the auld town of Aberdeen, with its one arch and its deep black salmon stream below, is in my memory as yesterday. I still remember, though perhaps I may misquote, the awful proverb which made me cross to read it, and yet lean over it with childish delight, being an only son, at least by the mother's side. The saying, as recollected by me, was this, but I have never heard nor seen it since I was nine years of age:

> "Brig of Balgownie, black's your wa',
> Wi' a wife's ae son, and a mare's ae foal,
> Doon ye shall fa'!" '

176

I can add to JTR's literary reference: Byron attended Aberdeen Grammar School from 1794 to 1798 and he would no doubt be pleased to know that the Brig o' Don or Balgownie Brig still stands. No longer accessible to vehicular traffic it is beautifully preserved and showing more buttressing than in JTR's sketch. Its future maintenance seems assured. £20,000 of the Trust Fund set up by a local landowner, Sir Alec Hay, is still in the bank.

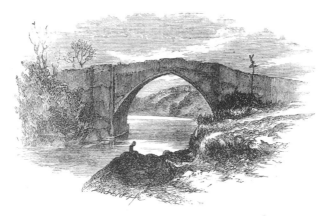

BALGOWNIE BRIG, NEAR ABERDEEN.

The Abrahams had recently bought the old salmon netting station house and ice store at the foot of the bridge. It had lain empty and derelict for years, its title in dispute. As in crofting inheritance, the ancient salmon netting rights and ownership of the building had been passed down through families so often that individual ownership 'was now a third of a sixteenth or somesuch.' The new owners were thrilled to be part of such history and had great plans. Light was dimming as we looked down-river. A seal popped its head up out of the pool in the foreground. A good sign, maybe not for the salmon, but of a pollution-free River Don on the edge of Scotland's third largest city.

Heather and Graham had cleared out four hundred glue cans from the vandalised property. As though in apprehension of further desecration they acquired a Bull Terrier from a dog home in the south. She had been stolen by dog fighting thugs and dumped, her owner never traced. She was old and grey muzzled and looked as though she would never say 'Bowf' to a goose, let alone a glue sniffer. But you can never tell …

It was dark walking towards Old Aberdeen. The floodlit twin towers of St Machar guided me on. Students from the university passed by on end-of-weekend errands of socialising or even study. There was a service in the cathedral in an hour's time at six o'clock. I decided to stay, apologising to the beadle for my heavy walking boots and woolly jumper. I do not know why I had decided to slow down. I had intended to get to Ballater on the bus that night, fresh for the start of the big walk next day down Royal Deeside. By going to the church service I would have to spend another night in

Aberdeen. Maybe I wanted a time of peace with JTR before we had our final few days together doing what we both liked best. Being in the wild places.

I asked the beadle where the nearest telephone box was. I wanted to phone the previous night's B&B, still a good walk into town, and book a bed. 'Just use this one', and I was led into the minister's empty inner sanctum. I found that gesture one of the most touching of the whole trip. Off he bustled preparing hymn sheets and lighting. I could have been phoning Australia.

By six o'clock about twenty people, mostly young couples, had turned up and we were asked to sit in the choir stalls, the numbers being so small. I was disappointed. I knew there was going to be massed choirs, the altar candles quivering in the resonance, the 16th century oak ceiling glowing with emotion. St Machar had been a companion to St Columba, the two of them setting off from Ireland to preach to the Picts and save their souls. The original chapel or cell of St Machar was built in the second half of the sixth century. The vibrations should have been strong.

The minister had a hard time getting anyone to sing, his own tentative tenor a solo performance for the most part. The cathedral is very 'high' Church of Scotland. I did not recognise any of the hymns so could not help him out.

The sermon was delivered by a young female minister, her subject Abraham and beautiful Sarah, his wife. They were travelling in Egypt and Abraham told her to say that she was his sister. Pharoah would kill him to have Sarah if he knew that she was his wife. As custom had it, Sarah being his 'sister', Pharoah gave Abraham many gifts on account of her beauty. But 'God made it known' to Pharoah that Abraham had tricked him. 'Here,' said Pharoah, 'take your wife and go. You have deceived me.'

Lucky man to get off with his life. The young minister then updated the moral of the story by explaining that Abraham had behaved in the way of the *world* and not the way of *God*. I could not quite see the connection myself. He was only trying to save his wife from a lecherous old Pharoah.

If we observe God's will, we were told, all will be well. She alluded to the Middle East crisis in the middle of all this. *Our* God's way the only way … The proprietorialness of some Gods. At least the Bahá'ís share him around.

The incumbent man of the cloth spent the whole sermon with a finger to his side temple, looking at the floor. The last hymn was announced. 'Now at St Machar's we stand immediately at the announcement of the hymn and give it all we've got,' he almost shouted. Another tenor solo wafted up to the mediaeval ceiling. The final prayer was penitential. We were sinful.

I remembered the tea and biscuits in the little Linlithgow church all those months before and the friendly occasion it had been.

It was time to go. The majority of the congregation, the young couples, stayed behind. They were preparing for First Communion. Marriages were obviously in the offing and hoops had to be gone through if that white dress was to float down the aisle of

St Machar's. Would the young men palm their wives off as sisters if a Pharoah ever turned up?

JTR The time in Aberdeen was spent so pleasantly, it flew fast, and only the call of work tore me away from the Granite City and my friend's bachelor hall. The route I chose for the home-coming was *viâ* Balmoral. The journey is by rail as far as Ballater; the line for a great part of the way keeps within hail of the River Dee, and leads through a considerable variety of wild Highland moor and wood and mountain-land, by village and many castellated mansions embowered amid trees, now almost leafless, for we were now fully launched into the middle of bleak November. Snow-showers were frequent; there had been one mantling in snowy garb of mountain and valley, one blocking of the line of rail; we were able to trace the places where the drift had been gathered to the greatest depth.

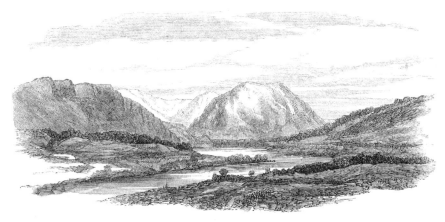

ON THE DEE, FROM BALLATER.

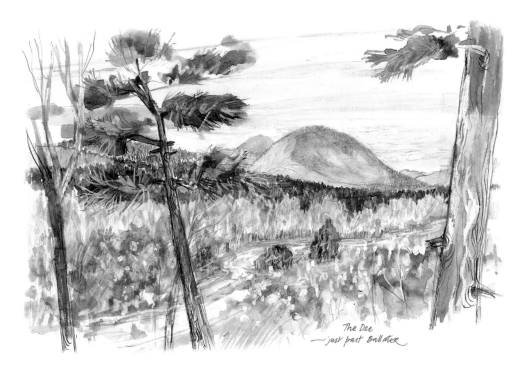

The Dee
— just past Ballater

'At the end of the year,' reported the *Aberdeen Journal*'s Record of Events, 'a great storm raged on the East coast extending over 7 days during which railways were snowed up and from 50 to 60 vessels with 270 lives were lost.' JTR was witnessing the preamble.

Thanks to global warming the bus to Ballater meandered through dank, hazy farmland, new green film of sprouting winter crops; the creamy backs and black heads of sheep wading and grazing through dark green kale.

By Echt we had moved into soft hills, forestry cloaked. Beech woods were still thick and bronze with leaves. Strong stolid farmhouses with large bow dormer windows as distinctively north east as the smaller two up two down windows of the West Coast crofthouses. Cattle boorached around a big silage bale and, heavens, two sets of twin lambs huddled by a gate. In November?

The bus went ambling on 'the scenic route' to Ballater, picking up and dropping off neat and tidy old ladies in pale olive green berets and gaberdine coats. The driver gave everyone a cheery 'cheerio'. At Torphins mums waited at the school gate for lunchtime children with one dad, very bearded and jeaned.

By Lumphanan rain was smirring the windscreen. A low mist wreathed in amongst the pines on the hillsides that folded into the lovely straths and valleys past Tilly Lodge. A newly repaired snow fence at a bend in the road warned that snow might come. Hundreds of ravens jounced like marionnettes in one stubble field; five cock pheasants held a conference in the middle of another.

Coming down the hill into Tarland the windscreen wipers were at maximum speed. The first real heavy rain for weeks and I had lost my umbrella somewhere in between Wick and Aberdeen after five months' companionship, albeit rolled up in the ice axe loop of the rucksack but invaluable when needed.

JTR Ballater, on the afternoon of Monday, 13th November, looked dreary enough. The hotels were deserted, the lodging-houses forsaken, the windows cased in brown paper till another spring, the river inky in colour, the dark brow of Craig-en-Darroch (the Rock of Oaks) reigned a very grim rock, with weather-worn features, but who in summer-time sends down on the village he protects floods of genial heat which his height enables him to catch as he looks on the sun; and I saw little token of the great healing powers of the Wells of Pannanich, for nobody was traceable in the grounds.

On Tuesday 13th November 1990 Ballater was pleasantly quiet, little sign of brown-papered windows. Pansies smiled in flower beds and the gift shops were still open but none had collapsible umbrellas. The smell of damp soot hung heavy in the air. The Alexandra Hotel had been completely gutted by fire a few days previously. Workmen were carrying out a smoke-blackened refrigerator from the kitchens.

A surprisingly brisk fire blazed in the old Station Waiting Room Tea Room, the Victorian panelling and door handles intact. The railway reached Ballater by 1866 and rails were laid to Balgairn Water with the intention of going on to Braemar. Queen Victoria blew the whistle on the enterprise, preferring her Highland retreat of Balmoral to retain its privacy. The rails were used as a tramway to extract timber, however.

JTR spent the night in the Temperance Hotel. It is now called the Green Inn, its menu and decor enticing. But try as I might the new owners were 'not open' being involved in extensive alterations. It was always a great disappointment finding the actual building that JTR had slept in and then finding for whatever reason I could not. It was as if I was being denied as opportunity for osmosis. Walls can tell, sometimes.

On his walk to the Wells of Pannanich he would not have trod over the present bridge that spans the Dee. It was built in 1885 replacing the timber bridge that had served from 1834 after the collapse of the Telford Bridge whose arches were blocked by floating timber during great floods in 1829. And I saw nobody at the Wells of Pannanich either.

The Pannanich Wells Hotel was established in 1760. A woman was cured of scrofula by taking the waters from the Well. There is little evidence of any healing promotion nowadays. The hotel was quite shut up, a deep freeze supplier's catalogue rolled up in the handle of the door. Its elevated position looks down on the valley. Ballater, early lights on, was drawing in an evening of fog around itself. Walking back down the hill the side of the road was a ginger padded path of fallen birch leaves. A pheasant coughed. The Dee chortled under the bridge, the only thing moving with purpose in the landscape. A listless chill numbed all activity save that of the river heading for Balgownie Brig and the sea.

Shops in Royal Deeside covet 'By Appointment' plaques above their doors. These prestigious decorations have to be applied for and only after three years' regular patronage by the Royals and a specified amount of money spent can the process of application be considered. George Smith in Ballater is now retired from the family shop, long honoured. His house adjoining is a cornucopia for Victoriana and in the midst his grandfather's framed certificate and seal of appointment. Mrs Smith apologised for the clutter. The Ballater Victoriana Exhibition had just finished and their contributions returned. I should think their items constituted the bulk of the affair. A pretty little curled up stuffed vixen, her nose in her tail and cleverly crafted into a footstool, eyed me with a yellow glass eye. Only a Victorian could rest his feet on her. How she must have longed to bite all their toes.

George insisted on lending me a precious old book on the area, the library being shut, and the evening long ahead. I suggested that things had not changed that much since Queen Victoria's time what with the present day Royals down the road during the season and the fishing and the shooting and the art galleries still exhibiting and selling the romanticised wilderness images. He dared to say what many people dependent in the area on tourism refused to comment on – the scarcity of salmon in the river Dee. 'Being netted at sea by Danes and Germans. The Victorians were the last to enjoy the wealth of the wilderness without any inhibition of conservation.'

The old footpath to Braemar goes alongside the river through a great oak wood. Once again trees obscured JTR's clear view of over a hundred years ago. There is a little wooden bridge over a small chasm on the track. This was the Postie's Leap before improvements or possibly the ageing of the postman.

Reluctantly I had to accept the ending of the path at a junction to the main road. But it was dry and mild. A silvery sun fleeted on and off over a silvery Dee. And only a few oldies touring in cars at respectable speeds. Workmen mending the snow fence at the pass of Ballater said it would take an hour to walk to Balmoral.

JTR After a night in the temperance hotel, a walk the following morning in the rain brought me in sight of the Scottish home of our much and justly-esteemed Queen. Her Majesty was still in her Highland retreat, and our hearts beat in fullest sympathy with her who loves so devotedly her mountain girded-palace; nor is it hard to unravel the taste that prefers communing with a few select friends, and sacred never-to-be-forgotten memories, to the ceaseless routine of official life. The whole district, despite the bleakness of November days, was replete with pictures I may not endeavour to convey in words. My reader who loves such scenes has hundreds of them in his own mind: they live there intensely real, and yet if you try to put them on paper, the charm seems gone. How can we communicate the thrill of joy that goes direct to the heart at the sight of a shadow passing over a hill-side and sailing over a sullen stream, or that which comes to us as glints are playing sportively into distance and foreground, or breathe to another the exhilirating influence of mountain air?

Well, dear John, you have been trying to do that very thing for the past 150 pages of your book. Sometimes to great effect but sometimes your combination of words beats even my irregular unions. How can you 'unravel' taste?

And your verbose excuse at not being able to capture pictures was surely to do with visibility. To be totally honest, Balmoral and its environs must have looked quite dreich, Lochnagar blanketed in cloud. That was why your sketchbook was not filled to overflowing with very commercial subjects. The Royal Scottish Gallery and South Kensington drawing rooms were denied such treasure trove. How mad you must have been at the weather.

JTR A thorough wetting gave increased thankfulness for the comforts of the 'Invercauld Arms,' the little inn within two miles of Balmoral; and towards evening of the next day, after the rain ceased, I thought it wise to be on the move, and walked to Braemar. It was all under a very mysterious influence – the woods, the hills, the river, and the mountains beyond, and so also was the village. On the way the royal party passed, and I saw Her Majesty, as if in a pensive semi-slumber reclining in the open carriage, going homeward.

What matter no great sketches! You saw Queen Victoria! What a scoop for a book …

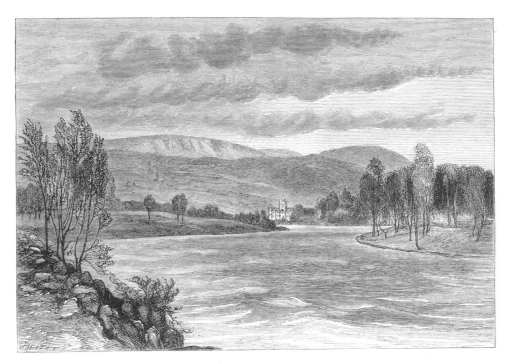

BALMORAL.

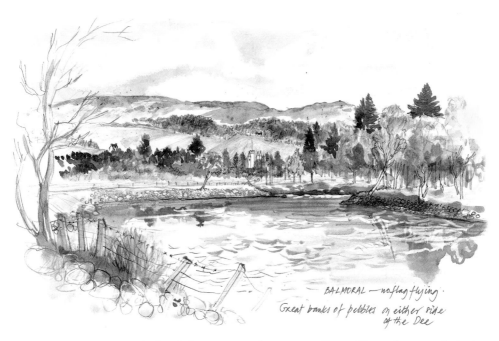

BALMORAL — no flag flying.
Great banks of pebbles on either side
of the Dee

Unbelievably you make light of the event. Did you wave? Bow? Throw her your jacket? She must have been freezing. The *Aberdeen Journal* recorded four inches of snow in Aberdeenshire that week. You were witnessing hypothermia – a body slumped in an open carriage, mid-November, Scottish Highlands. We have undoubtedly gone soft. For the likes of JTR cold baths started the day and 'air-baths' were very fashionable; JTR recommended them literally after describing, somewhat sensuously, a clothed version, albeit in the summer.

183

JTR It is truly delicious in a midsummer morning to be on board a yacht, cruising among our western or northern isles. The air searches through your tweeds, and seems, as it showers over you the truest elixir of health, to say 'A glad good morning!' to every pore of your body. Dr. Benjamin Franklin had great faith in air as a tonic, and prescribes an *air-bath* he believes himself to have received benefit from it. I know of a talented minister of the Established Church, lately located in Scotland, who believed in open-air baths; he roamed at large in his birthday costume on the grassy tops of the cliffs that girded his parish, to the great bewilderment of his new parishioners.'

Queen Victoria was in her fifty-seventh year and fifteenth year of widowhood when she passed by Brother Brush. She lived for another twenty-five years after the momentous occasion. Of which she was quite unaware, of course, which proves that JTR must have had on all his tweeds that day.

I had my own contact, somewhat diluted, with royalty. Unsought, I hasten to add. The area had an uncomfortable air to it; I had a great fear of meeting a savage corgi. Instead I was offered a lift by a charming lady. 'Just going home up the road but my husband is waiting for the car and he is going on further.' Home was the manse and husband was the Revd Angus of Crathies Church. Comfortable and chatty in his tweed fishing hat – were there flies in it? I could not look too close, him having blessed Royals. He told me he had been there for eleven years. This will be your quiet time, I ventured, the royal season well past. 'Oh, no. Busy right up to Christmas. February is quiet.' Of course, the man has other parishioners …

Dying to ask if they sucked Imperial Mints or ever yawned, yet too proud to, I asked where he had been before. Gourock. My childhood home and strict introduction to the faith that I turned my back on the day I left home. And then I remembered the white dress several years later that had walked down the aisle. But I had earned that rite of passage. And how. Still, ministers always make me feel a little bit guilty. Corgis yapped at my heels as I walked the final bit into Braemar.

The population of Braemar is four hundred. It is four thousand in the summer and 24,000 come to the Highland Games in August. Figures are creeping up in the winter too. Cheap rate November oldies filled The Fife Arms on the Mar Estate side of the village. Braemar is split in half by two estates – Invercauld to the north. And so there are two villages halls, two large traditional hotels. Invercauld Arms is very elegant and I was losing my confidence these winter months to brazen the double stares in places such as these. I had long since removed the lightweight flowery trousers from the rucksack, space needed for extra woollies and the fancy earrings would have looked very suspect with a climbing jumper.

JTR mentions the Invercauld Arms or Inn three times as hostelries in the area. Invercauld Estate stretched for miles and such stopover places would have been owned

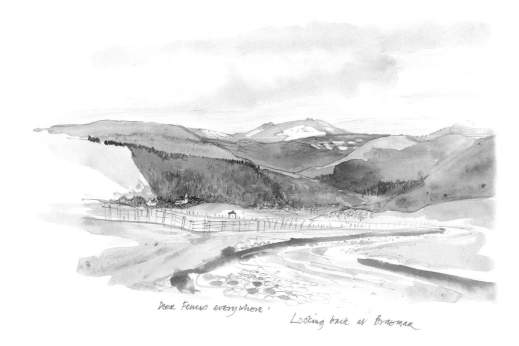

Deer Fences everywhere.

Looking back at Braemar

by the estate. With time and private ownership, confusion has gone. In Ballater the name is now Monaltrie House; in Braemar, Invercauld Arms remains, and next port of call, Glen Shee, it is the Spittal of Glen Shee Hotel.

I opted for the anonymity of the Fife Arms despite the loud oldies, instead of the intimacy of a B&B. Another long night lay ahead. I wandered through the dark village window-shopping like an orphan, nose pressed against windows: tweeds and leather, crystal and Royal Doulton, sheep horned walking sticks and deer antler corkscrews. And tins and tins of shortbread with the Queen Mother atop. The Village newsagent shop was just closing. I commented on how neat and tidy Braemar was. 'Need planning permission for a flower box,' said the retiring shopkeeper.

Gardens were immaculate, shadowy with the street lights. A pretty village hall, indistinguishable from the equally pretty cottages on either side of it, genteely beat out Highland dance music. It was the children's dancing class. I could hear winter coughs as they waited their turn for instruction.

Walking out to the velvet dark outskirts of the village I could hear wilder sounds. Stags were roaring in the hills. There seemed to be two herds, many miles apart. The day had been dry and light winded. The wind had completely dropped by nightfall. The moon was in between last and new quarters but there was enough glow in the sky to make out the silhouetted forms of one set of Monarchs of the Glen.

'Barravouraching' is the phoneticised Gaelic word for the roaring of the stags. It is an eerie sound. Primeval. Exciting. The territorial barracking dwindled away to a foggy cough or two as one herd moved further into the hills. It was the turn of the nearer lot to raid the immaculate gardens later on in the night once the oldies and me were sound asleep in bed. I would certainly be there before any of them. Ladies in décolleté dresses showing vulnerable rounding spines sat in cocktail bars with men with slightly shiny trousers in groups of foursomes.

'Ee it was loovly meal.'

'Station 'Otel, Peurth was good too.'

'Absolutely beautiful.'

'Ee loovley.'

This paean was interspersed with family talk.

'He's every right to do with his money what he wants. Look at what he spends on the children. Of course they're only where they are because of what we've given them …'

'Ah like the curtains.'

'Absolutely beautiful.'

'Ee loovley.'

'There'd be no jobs for these locals if it wasn't for people like us. We're paying for all their heating and lighting.'

The bell for bingo mercifully broke up the cocktail hour.

I sneaked off for one of those soaky baths down a long corridor and was fast asleep before the first stags louped fences or the last oldies climbed the stairs.

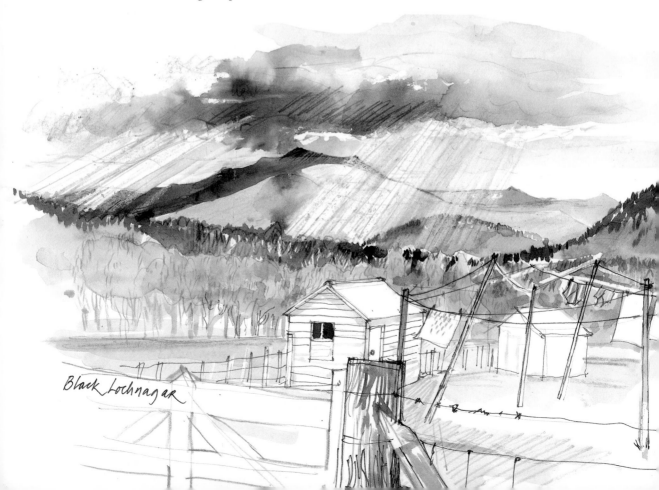

Black Lochnagar

JTR The walk from Braemar village through the Braes of Mar to Glen Shee, was one of surpassing interest. The whole vale was filled with clouds of mist, whose risings and fallings and transparent veilings gave a weird atmosphere to the whole. For hours the clouds were manœuvring, and the uninitiated traveller could easily be led to linger till nightfall among their revellings; not so the dwellers within some miles of this hill road. These clouds were about to give the mountain leagues a copious benefit, and I had a good share before the 'Invercauld Arms' at Glen Shee provided a welcome shelter. How much we have in these days to be thankful for when travelling, if we compare our circumstances with those of tourists a quarter of half a century ago!

! I must add my own exclamation mark. If the weather had been like that for me I would have had the most miserable last day in the hills with JTR. It was a sparkly sunny morning. Coachloads of 'tarraas' headed north for Balmoral. I started the long fifteen-mile road plod for Glen Shee, at least having the old road for a few miles up the west side of Glen Clunie. In a cottage by the golf course an old man was getting in coal. One ginger and white and five black and white cats wove around his legs.

'Braes of Mar?' I was trying to find JTR's titled sketch.

'Any of the hills around here are the Braes of Mar.' Was he referring to their topography or their ownership … ?

The low early morning winter sun shone through the yellow golf course flags stretching the length of the valley bottom. Like battle flags of a great Liliputian army awaiting the call to charge Braemar. A grouse chortled in the heather up to my right. On the main road over the left side of the glen a lone campervan laboured up the straight incline to the old bridge over the Clunie Water where I would be forced to join in. Meanwhile I had the compensation of an incline with twists and turns.

Sheep were in their Garden of Eden – a field of kale. Like hairy earthbound locusts they had stripped half of the crop. More grouse took up matins. What *do* they do? Rattle, quackle, whirrawhirrarr? A stag, possibly full of Brussels sprouts, roared in a high corrie.

At the bridge the uphill slog got serious. The hills ahead shifted and changed with veils of cloud, just as JTR said. I kept waiting to be enveloped but the wreaths kept to their mountain fastness. A few cars passed, a coach called Wilfreda, all heading for the Queen Mum on a shortbread tin in Braemar.

Sheep were being gathered in from the high hills. From a distance they wriggled down the slopes looking like maggots. They needed no coaxing through the gate into the grass field. Sun patches scudded overhead, gilding everything they touched. Deer high on the skyline were silhouetted like little trees above a crown of scree. Save for the road surface, the snow poles and occasional traffic, I was in JTR's landscape minus the downpour.

And then labouring my way up the Cairnwell Pass and looking skyward to the slopes of the foothills below the Munro of Glas Maol there was a different kind of silhouette – ski tows, like abstract totem poles, ill at ease in the snowless landscape.

So were Tommie and Maggie sitting at the top of the Pass waiting for the winter snows. A couple of November oldies, they were having an air-bath sitting on a bench. Maggie, legs crossed over, her hand shading one eye from the sun, stared endlessly to the tops of the mountains; Tommie, his hands clasped over his belly, looked benignly down the Glen to Braemar. They were tough, like Queen Victoria, not an anorak or pair of fleece-lined boots between them. In fact Tommie still had his slippers on. They dangled from his fibre glass legs suspended in air. Last winter's snow and ice had eroded away the earth from his feet.

The Scottish Sculpture Trust tells us Tommie and Maggie are part of the 'only exhibition of its kind in the World where sculptures can be seen in truly winter conditions – available freely to the public – and in harmony with these ancient Scottish hills.' The other sculptures are further from the road and are abstract; one like a giant damaged kirby grip made of stainless steel, white against the brown and peat of the scarred slopes.

There was a seedy feel to 'the exhibition' (opened in 1975) in the snowless skiers' playground. Tommie desperately needs to get his feet on the ground again before blizzards give him false security.

The skiing season at Glen Shee is best in January and February. I was the only customer in the large occasionally ripped leatherette bench-seated restaurant. Fruit machines pestered for attention, repeating their irritating electronic whinge as I supped the most delicious home-made mushroom soup I have ever tasted.

Out of the big picture windows I could see Tommie and Maggie still staring at their respective views, half turned away from each other. A couple of men tinkered at a snow plough. Time enough yet.

The old military road on which the A93 is built breaks free for a couple of miles close into the side of the Cairnwell leaving the A93 to its own steep zigzag descent via the Devil's Elbow.

It soon reverted to rough boggy ground. Me and the big rucksack were being a little foolish at over two thousand feet. Down below, three timber lorries edged their way round the Devil's Elbow, getting into lower and lower gears.

From now on it was all downhill. I raised a white hare. Snow must be coming soon. And then two roe deer, their bums brilliant white, bounded over the dead headed heather. More grouse startling the living daylights out of me and themselves as they clacked and whirred up from my feet. The Donald Ducks of the high moors. I had got their sound at last.

To the right Carn Mor and Creagan Bheithe, lightly touched with smirr, curved down to Ben Gulabin four miles south as the crow flies. To the left, half hidden with cloud Creag Leachach and the descending cairns of Ait, Aig Mhata, Chomh-Stri and an Daimh, ran parallel to the opposite sweeps of hill both ending in a V in the far distance where the tiny hamlet of the Spittal of Glen Shee nestled. The A93 snaked its way along the valley thousands of feet below. The cloud would stay high enough. I would keep the road in sight … As usual not a soul in the whole wide world knew where I was. Not even Tommie or Maggie.

It would be alright.

I wanted to wander for a bit without the rucksack and celebrate just me and the mountains. I was right in the middle of the eastern land mass of Scotland; Creag Leachach, shrouded to my left, was on the south west edge of the sprawling Mounth plateau that boasts not a mountain under 2,500 feet and eighteen of them Munros – or Muriels, if you are into that kind of thing. I contoured a little round the Cairnwell, looking down the perfect valley to the Spittal and the beginning of the Eastern Lowlands and where I would be sleeping the night. It seemed very far away. I was loath to start the descent.

What spirit had guided me here to this open hillside to find such a vantage point, the last and highest of the Rambles?

There just below and beyond the scampering roe deer was a simple white cross made of concrete and almost half hidden in the tall heather. It said 11.1.85 DAVID R. NICHOLAS L/B POLICE. It was a shocking, disturbing moment, initially, in the midst of such splendid isolation … and then I thanked him for showing me and sharing with me his very private place.

He must have known that I would like to have the same one day – but nearer the sea.

I descended slowly even though the light would be fading soon and there was still the long valley to travel. As I reached the road I left far behind me, hovering high, a buzzard, peeinging guard.

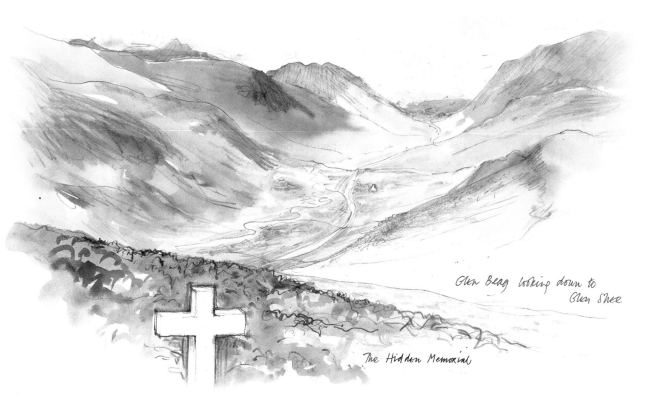

Glen Beag looking down to
Glen Shee

The Hidden Memorial

The bedroom window of the Spittal of Glenshee Hotel (ex Invercauld Arms) looked straight back up the valley. Again another quiet still night, stags occasionally barking and just enough light to make out the peak of Cairnwell and the soul up there with part of mine. And many others of us, all weaving and drifting free to go anywhere really but liking our own private place to rest awhile. I had a terrible yearning to go west and reach the sea and the islands.

JTR And now just one sentence to describe my journey from Glen Shee to Edinburgh. A rainy morning and a very rainy day enabled me to get a good wetting, to see many gorgeous bits of colouring, to sketch Bridge of Cally when the river was in full spate, and to sympathise with a poor drooket packman, who was bound for the inner reaches of the glen, to sell small wares and national songs; and it hastened me home, spending a night in the fair city of Perth, and a couple of days in bonnie Dundee – both of which places I must leave meantime, and hasten across the Tay, by rail through Fife, and over the Firth in the ferry-boat, and say good night till we meet on a summer morning in my study in the classic city of Edina.

No, I was finished with John T. Reid. I had left him somewhere up in the hills. I could not bear to return to Edinburgh, its rich, its poor, its cultural mafia, its city slickness and snobberies, its *traffic* …

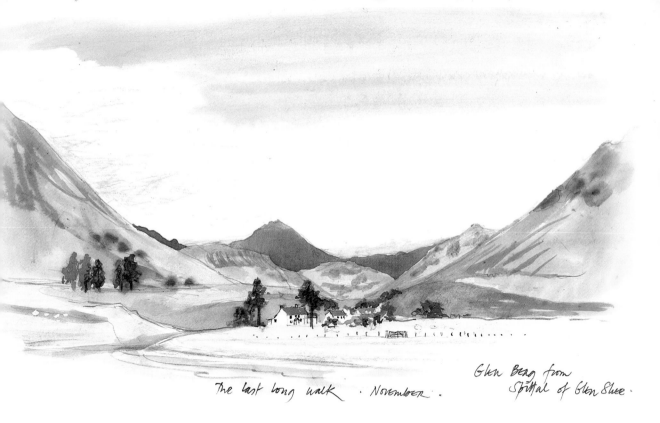

The last long walk . November .

Glen Beag from
Spittal of Glen Shee.

Spittal of Glen Shee Hotel
November 1990

Dear John, my Brother Brush,

Thank you very much for your kind invitation to meet you in Edinburgh next summer.
I would love to visit your 'snug study in the artist quarter' of the city. We would have plenty
to talk about; we shared many experiences the past five months and I am dying to see your
originals.

I want to tell you how much you have taught me about myself and my times, as well as
the landscape we both love so passionately. To share that with someone so intimately is very
special and not all that common. But – please do not be upset or take this personally – I think
I have finally got my adulatory obsession with you and your generation out of my system.
My love affair with the past is over. Thanks to you.

I need a long space to think about it all and decide where I am heading next.

I apologise for the ambivalence of my relationship – nay, anger at times. After all, I had
invited myself along, hadn't I? It was no way to behave. They were – are – your Rambles.

Please excuse me for not joining you in the journey back to Edinburgh from Glen Shee.
A track goes over the hills westward from here and I know of a place on an island out there
where I'll get it all sorted out. I don't think I'll be travelling for a while.

I am sorry we could not have enjoyed a dram together. Maybe if I had met you earlier?
Love and Thanks

Mairi

your Sister Brush.

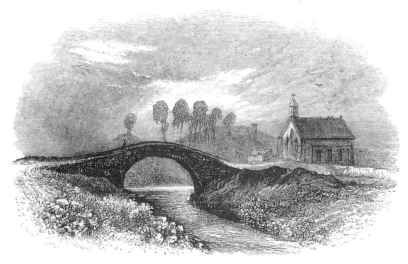

GLEN SHEE.

In 1887 John T. Reid responded to the 'Call for a Hundred Missionaries for China'. He married one of his co-respondents. Three daughters were born of the union who subsequently married into the China Inland Mission.

REID, John Thomas, sometime Artist, Edinburgh, afterwards residing at Gaul House, Murthly, Perthshire, thereafter of The China Inland Mission, Takutang, Kiukiang, China, died 6 May 1917, at Iyang, Province of Kiangsi, China, intestate. Confirmation granted at Edinburgh, 4 January, to Isabella Cameron Reid or Ritchie, wife of William Walter Peel Ritchie, Postal Commissioner of Shanghai, China, Euphemia Paton Reid or Cunningham, wife of Robert Cunningham, Missionary at Kiukiang aforesaid, and Margaret McLeod Reid or Taylor, presently residing in Edinburgh (usually resident in China), wife of Alexander John Reid Taylor, presently Capt., R.A.M.C., his daughters, Executrices dative *qua* next of kin. Value of Estate, £377. 17s. 11d.

from the Calendar of Confirmations and Inventories 1918
Central Region Archives, Stirling

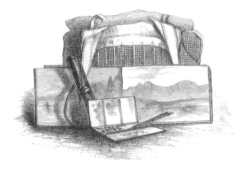